GENDER
POLITICS

ZAREH GHAZARIAN is a Senior Lecturer in Politics and International Relations in the School of Social Sciences at Monash University. His research and teaching interests include public policy, civics and citizenship education, and political parties and leadership. Zareh is a leading commentator on national politics and his latest book is *The Making of a Party System: Minor Parties in the Australian Senate* (Monash University Publishing, 2015).

KATRINA LEE-KOO is an Associate Professor of Politics and International Relations in the School of Social Sciences at Monash University. Her research interests include women's leadership in politics, and the leadership and participation of women, youth and children in global peace and security. She is the co-editor of *Young Women and Leadership* (Routledge, 2020) and co-author of *Children and Global Conflict* (Cambridge University Press, 2015) and *Ethics and Global Security* (Routledge, 2014).

GENDER POLITICS

Navigating Political Leadership in Australia

EDITED BY ZAREH GHAZARIAN & KATRINA LEE-KOO

UNSW PRESS

A NewSouth book

Published by
NewSouth Publishing
University of New South Wales Press Ltd
University of New South Wales
Sydney NSW 2052
AUSTRALIA
newsouthpublishing.com

© Zareh Ghazarian and Katrina Lee-Koo
First published 2021

10 9 8 7 6 5 4 3 2 1

A catalogue record for this
book is available from the
National Library of Australia

ISBN   9781742236933 (paperback)
        9781742245218 (ebook)
        9781742249773 (ePDF)

Design Josephine Pajor-Markus
Cover design Lisa White
Cover image Liberal MP Julie Bishop addresses the media during a press
conference at Parliament House in Canberra on Tuesday 28 August 2018.
Photo by Alex Ellinghausen. *Fairfax*

All reasonable efforts were taken to obtain permission to use copyright
material reproduced in this book, but in some cases copyright could not
be traced. The editors welcome information in this regard.

CONTENTS

FOREWORD: 'WHY THIS, WHY NOW?'

This is a timely and important book. Each chapter considers the role gender plays in shaping our Australian governing institutions – who participates, the norms, behaviour, organisation, processes, language and leadership.

If our society's aim is to achieve a more equitable, inclusive and sustainable society, we need to identify what role gender bias plays in the persistent under-representation of women in our parliaments, political leadership and diplomacy. This book should help us understand why the most powerful and best-rewarded positions are mostly held by men, and if it matters. For example, do gender considerations affect the issues brought forward or help shape the solutions? Are there societal understandings (reinforced by the media) that ascribe different personal qualities and performance measures for leaders according to their gender? Do those understandings boost or hinder the leadership prospects for individuals, or the achievement of a more equitable, inclusive and sustainable society?

During the 20 years that I was a Federal Member in the Australian Parliament, I often observed the media gleefully report their assessments of a minister's mastery or competency according to the volume and originality of insults they hurled during Question Time. Did Question Time's rude and raucous behaviour impress the schoolgirl watching in the galleries, or did it chill her nascent political aspirations? What would happen if Question Time was no longer televised and the chamber's layout rearranged? What if the media, now accommodated immediately behind the Speaker and facing the politicians, was instead assigned to the schoolgirls' seats in the gallery, behind soundproof glass and behind the politicians? Would the muscular, aggressive shouting deemed commanding behaviour in a powerful male become more modulated without the cameras, the grins exchanged with journalists and the live texting? Would a calmer and more collegiate parliament become more gender-inclusive and influence the public's perceptions of the legitimacy and authority of its parliamentary democracy?

These and other such gendered complexities are examined in this book.

I was a Federal Member of Parliament from 1996 to 2016, and then Australia's Global Ambassador for Women and Girls until 2020. When I consider if my gender was a barrier to my election, advancement and contribution to the greater good, I find myself in agreement with Julia Gillard's observations. I think that being a woman in the Australian Parliament surrounded by the overwhelmingly white, Christian, English-as-a-first-language, RM Williams–booted men commanding the heights explains some but not all of my experiences.

As the Global Ambassador for Women and Girls, I had to regularly dispel the expectation that I would only need to meet with other women, even though men's engagement was essential in tackling gender-based violence, as well as women's economic and political disempowerment.

Recently, the Global Institute for Women's Leadership reviewed the impacts of women's political participation and reported the consistent findings that when women exercise political leadership, there are gains for the whole of society.[1] The research showed that women work harder than men in their constituencies, they are more likely to tackle corruption and improve the public service, their states are less likely to go to war, and they create more collaborative and inclusive political environments.

In this book, writers identify the great paradox for a woman aspiring to political leadership. The feminine cultural norms anticipate that women will be caring and kind and responsive to the needs of her electorate. However, a leader aspirant is also expected to embody the authentic expressions of the traditional hetero male, including aggressiveness, assertion, confidence and loyalty to 'the mates'.

Clearly, a woman who aspires to political leadership must be deft, retaining some non-threatening feminine attributes for some purposes, while demonstrating male virtues in the party room and on the chamber floor. She should not shed tears, except at a time of extreme (and therefore rare) national or personal tragedy. She should give as good as she gets when abused in parliamentary debate, as former prime minister Julia Gillard understood. She should convincingly perform her domination of her party colleagues and demonstrate her ability to humiliate the opposition in the media every day.

No matter what her command of the facts, it is trouncing the enemy that earns the greatest accolades, drawing her into the orbit of political powerbrokers. She knows the costs of calling out misogynist behaviour, inequitable work-life balance and time wasted on dysfunctional parliamentary processes. She is aware that embracing victimhood is disempowering and inviting contempt. She is regularly reminded in the party room that 'disunity is death', and playing in the team is all.

In Australia, the requirements for party allegiance and an adversarial attitude to all but your colleagues are so strongly enforced and rewarded that it diminishes the prospect of any gendered alliance. Ours is one of the few democracies without a cross-party women's caucus. By working as a bloc on their policy priorities, a women's caucus could perhaps achieve a gender quota, a more family-friendly parliament, more collegiate and respectful debate, as well as some measures to enhance greater government transparency and accountability.

The only example of Australian women politicians leading a campaign across party lines was in 2006 when the health minister planned to maintain a veto power to stop access to the medical abortion pill. Women successfully obtained a conscience vote, allowing party members to cross the floor without the usual career-limiting consequences of party defiance.

There has always been a gender difference between how women

and men vote in Australia. The first woman candidate for a Federal seat stood in 1903, yet the first woman elected to Federal Parliament was in 1943. The influence of the candidate's gender on the voting behaviours of women and men is under-researched. What is regularly polled and analysed, however, is the woman's preferred prime minister, invariably a choice between two men, each performing their masculinity according to what they think will have the greatest voter appeal.

Writers in this book identify the range of masculinities employed by past leaders. These have included protector, good provider, grandfather, tough and strong, sporty and competitive, nerdy but earnest, strongly corporate and hypermasculine. Further value may be added through the performance of being a devoted husband and father, which is repeatedly acted out on television in letterboxing or via your hand-held device.

The same range of characteristics that are praised as benign and authentic in men are often considered incompatible and less than desirable in a woman seeking office. The disjunction is between women's traditional gender identity as caring, kind, collegiate and nurturing, and the tough and decisive performances required for successful political participation and leadership.

How can she really be a good woman (a caring mother and loving wife) if she wants to absent herself for half the year in that adversarial and misogynist place? Preselection candidates are familiar with the questions. Who'll mind the children? Do you think the dad will do it all? So you don't have a family?

Beliefs that there are unhappy consequences for women who step beyond traditional gender roles are reinforced every time a woman retires from parliament or defers promotion, citing her reasons as the loss of family connection. It reads like an admission that she has neglected her responsibilities; she has failed.

Parliamentarians work within their electorates every day, and parliament sits some 12 hours a day for 20 weeks a year, meaning MPs are away from home for extended periods. Commutes to work on Sundays, limited leave options, and no workplace flexibility create barriers to participation for women who carry the additional burden of feminine expectations to maintain home duties.

On the other hand, these conditions advantage, and are perpetuated by, the men who are not expected to be the carers, and who have a supportive partner dedicated to the home and family duties. This is a zero-sum game that advantages the majority who command the heights.

Some writers in this collection analyse the significance of language, signs and symbols in gendering impact. When I was sworn in as Parliamentary Secretary for Finance, the Governor-General quipped: 'I guess if you run a household budget this will help your portfolio.'[2] Gender stereotypes trumped my PhD in Economics and Business.

When challenging a decision made by my party's cabinet, which significantly impacted my electorate's economy, one of the cartoons depicted me waiting for the prime minister under gallows, the noose made from his blue tie while I stood armed with a rolling pin tapping my nails. The cartoonist probably would not have chosen kitchen equipment and nail tapping for a depiction of male anger and agency.

The first female premier of Victoria, Joan Kirner (1990–1992), did not own a big sack-like spotted dress, but it became the derisive cartoon image used repeatedly to infer she was a middle-aged frumpish woman, out of place in a man's world of state leadership. As authors in this collection note, sexual objectification reduces a woman to physical attributes, denying her competence and moral and emotional capacity.

In 2009, *The Australian* reported that a group inside the Liberal Party, known as the 'big swinging dicks', was plotting to remove Julie Bishop from her deputy leader role.[3] This group, basking in the macho name with references to dominance and hypermasculinity, engineered a challenge against the party's leading woman, anticipating personal advancement and a majority of their colleagues' approval.

Perhaps not surprisingly, no women belonged to this group. The crude references and machismo signalled that this was a man's place.

As the authors in this collection reveal, it is hard for a woman to be seen and heard, but it is even harder when they are outside the room. When women are absent or ignored, the hegemony and hierarchy of the prevailing order is less likely to be disturbed.

The writers in this volume consider gender as a powerful force that shapes political leadership. Does it matter? The Australian Leadership Index 2019 reported the nation's sentiment from their survey: 'Against a backdrop of unethical conduct, irresponsible leadership and distrust of authorities and institutions, there is a pervasive sense that we are not well served by our leaders.'[4] The Federal Government was ranked lowest in respondents' estimates of leadership not delivering for the greater good.

This book shows that gender can be a transformative force in a nation's governing, and that who leads does matter.

Hon Dr Sharman Stone
Professor of Practice, Gender, Peace and Security, Monash University

INTRODUCTION:
THE GENDERED POLITICS OF LEADERS, STRUCTURES AND CULTURES IN AUSTRALIA

Katrina Lee-Koo and Zareh Ghazarian

In 2010, Julia Gillard became the first female prime minister in Australian history when her party supported her challenge to incumbent Kevin Rudd. Less than three years later, her colleagues voted to replace her with the man she had toppled, and Rudd returned to the prime ministership.

The rise and fall of Australia's first female prime minister has had a lasting impact on federal politics, especially as it shines a spotlight on gender issues in the national legislature. Often, this spotlight focuses on the numbers: political analysts in academia and the media highlight the number of women in parliament, cabinet and contesting elections. Some have used this data to reignite debates about quotas, candidacy selection procedures and the value of diversity in leadership. Others have explored the role that gender and gender politics plays in the representations, experiences and fate of senior political leaders, like Julie Bishop's failed bid for Liberal Party leadership in 2018, or Scott Morrison's unexpected 2019 federal election victory. This begs questions on how gender shapes the cultures, institutions, practices and fortunes of leadership in Australian politics.

In considering these interconnected debates, it is worth remembering Julia Gillard's reflections on gender and politics as she left office: 'It doesn't explain everything, it doesn't explain nothing. It explains some things and it is for the nation to think in a sophisticated way about those shades of grey.' This collection seeks to be part of that critical conversation on the ways that gender shapes political leadership in this country. These chapters all draw from scholarly research by political scientists, historians, journalists, media and gender studies scholars and policy experts.

We argue that gender can be – and often is – a powerful force that shapes Australia's political leadership. Sometimes this is clearly visible. At the time of writing, only 26 per cent of government ministers are women. The continued dominance of men in the senior echelons of Australia's political leadership is clear. At other times, gender bias is subtle: it plays out in how journalists frame and choose photographs, how headlines are written, how leadership decisions (and decisions about leaders) are made, how the structures and cultures of parliament and government create barriers to participation, or the tone and content of political discourse. Sometimes the gendered nature of politics is undeniable; other times we find ourselves in heated arguments regarding the role that gender plays in political leadership. Our aim is to explore these debates and the overt and subtle ways in which gender politics affects Australia's political leaders and its leadership culture.

'Gender' and 'gender politics' are highly contested. We think about gender as a series of socially determined ideas that are associated with gender identities, relationships and roles in society. Political leadership is often associated with what are traditionally considered to be masculine values. These include rationality, independence, confidence, assertiveness and sometimes even aggression. For many, these are the values that strong leaders possess, but they are also the values that strong men supposedly possess. For example, in 2003, former US President George W Bush congratulated Australian prime minister John Howard for being a 'man of steel', while in 2019, Donald Trump lauded Scott Morrison as 'a man of titanium' because of the masculine strength of his leadership.

Creating these often-unspoken associations between strong leadership and certain types of masculine values excludes most women and many men. Thinking about how our society constructs gender identity is important because it shapes what is seen as the legitimate roles of people in our society. It is no coincidence that when women in Australia began to challenge senior political leadership roles in federal politics, it was in service provision portfolios such as social/human services, education and health. The first woman to hold a ministerial position at the national level was Margaret Guilfoyle, who was appointed Minister of Education and Minister of Social Security in 1975 under the Fraser government. Guilfoyle was known as the 'Iron Butterfly' for her ability to mix femininity with political discipline. She set the standard for navigating the gender double bind that women in leadership roles would need to follow.

More recently, female leaders have been appointed to traditionally masculine portfolios such as foreign affairs and defence, but this has not been without gender-based commentary. In September 2015, Liberal Senator Marise Payne was appointed the first female Minister for Defence. While some commentators were openly sceptical about her appointment (*The Australian* described her as a 'novice' with 'no serious knowledge of the portfolio')[1], others used more subtle gender coding to seemingly question her capacity to be effective in the role. Following her appointment, one ABC report noted that she would need 'time to devote to what is actually a complex portfolio',[2] while another noted that 'it's arguably the most daunting and complicated job in the ministry'.[3] Such statements are not explicitly about her gender, but gender politics are present. Having spent 12 years on the Joint Standing Committee for Foreign Affairs, Defence and Trade, she was arguably more qualified than her two predecessors, and yet, as the first female in the role, her credentials were consistently called into question.

It can be difficult getting to the heart of how gender politics operates in Australia's political leadership culture, and what its impact might be. Raising issues of gender disadvantage can attract accusations of 'playing the gender card' (a tactic only women are accused of), which is presented as untoward and manipulative. To understand the controversy that such gender contestations ignite, we need to explore a number of factors. First of all, gender is not simply something that 'is' in our society. It exists with other aspects of identity (like race and class), and often in a hierarchical structure. Gender relations are power relations, and they play a role in shaping political privilege and bias. When we talk about Australia's political leadership culture, certain types of masculinity trump femininity in terms of establishing legitimacy, authenticity, authority and instilling confidence. Sometimes, the only way to see this is to ask the hypothetical question: 'Would this happen to a woman/man?'

Second, gender is not just something that we 'have'. It is – to borrow from prominent theorist Judith Butler – something that we perform. Julie Bishop's red shoes and Tony Abbott's blue ties are a performance of their particular gender identities. Bob Hawke's larrikinism, Malcolm Turnbull's corporatism and Scott Morrison's 'everyman' persona are all, to some extent, political performances of their gender that are designed to cultivate political legitimacy. If we look carefully, we may also see it in the way political leaders perform and what they say to promote certain policies and issues. For example, on the eve of the 2019 federal election, Small Business Minister Senator Michaelia Cash scoffed at the opposition's policy on electric cars. Instead, she made a promise to tradespeople: 'We are going to stand by our tradies. And we are going to save their utes.' Such appeals to utes and tradies promote a type of masculinity that is authentically Australian, while the subtext is that electric cars are weak and the antithesis of masculinity. In 2014, Australia's Finance Minister Mathias Cormann borrowed a phrase from former Californian governor Arnold Schwarzenegger to describe the then-opposition leader as an 'economic girlie man' to attack him as being weak on economic policy. We could also argue that former prime minister Tony Abbott's promise to 'shirt front' Russian President Vladimir Putin in 2014 over the MH17 flight disaster, and policy platforms such as 'Stop the Boats', find some of their legitimacy in their appeal to masculine values that invoke sovereignty, independence, strength and militarised control.

Third, it's important to remember that gender identities and gender politics are not fixed or isolated. This makes gender politics hard to lock down, but it is nonetheless an integral piece of the political puzzle. In the first instance, gender identities and power relations change across time and across society. For example, the 2017 national postal survey on same-sex marriage showed that social attitudes towards homosexuality have shifted significantly in recent decades. However, while we may claim marriage equality, this does not mean that heteronormative biases in our society have evaporated. Instead, changes in power relations often come in waves, with moves towards equality later forced back by backlash. Some have described the continually referenced, but unimplemented, national legislation on religious freedoms as a 'payback' for marriage equality. Similarly, the rise of so-called men's rights advocates like Bettina Arndt, who was awarded a 2019 Order of Australia medal, may be seen as a backlash to the #MeToo movement or campaigns to highlight family violence. While we can take snapshots of moments when gender-based inequality is called out, it's never a linear progression towards positive change.

Furthermore, gender politics is interweaved in the fabric of politics, making it hard to separate from other issues. When Julie Bishop launched a bid to lead the Liberal Party in August 2018, few questioned her experience, popularity or ability. So, why did she fail? For some, it had nothing to do with her gender. In fact, media commentators and members of her own party argued that factional politics and the strategic direction of the party stopped her from becoming Australia's second female prime minister. For others, gender politics played a crucial role – perhaps in the form of an unconscious bias – in her colleagues' attitudes towards her capacity to navigate factions and promote cohesion. Some may have been concerned about the electorate's response to a woman prevailing in a leadership spill, given the negative responses to Julia Gillard less than a decade earlier. Still, others argued that it was not only attitudes towards Bishop as an individual woman, but rather a broader cultural problem within the

Liberal Party and the parliament. Such issues were aired by Liberal MP Julia Banks, who identified 'cultural and gender bias, bullying and intimidation' of women in politics prior to the 2019 election.[4] This was echoed by other MPs at the time, claiming that this culture was deeply entrenched.

Even when discriminatory gender politics are called out, there remain challenges in measuring its impact on political leadership. Analytically, it requires us to carefully map the cultures, language, policies, practices and structures that dominate political leadership, as well as the career trajectories of individual leaders. This helps us to understand why some gender identities remain dominant, others are under-represented and some are completely absent. While this book focuses upon cisgender men and women at the federal level of political leadership, it is important to note that the Australian national parliament is generally not reflective of the broader community, especially in terms of ethnic background, gender and education.[5] Introspectively, this requires us to think about what needs to change in order to strengthen the inclusivity of political leadership in this country.

This collection addresses four core areas of concerns. The first section examines the careers of *individual leaders* to understand how they absorb and respond to gender politics in their political careers. Gender politics disciplines and impacts on the behaviour of political leaders, both men and women. The chapters in this section profile a number of senior political figures in Australia's recent history to understand how they performed their gendered identities and responded to gender-based commentary and representations of themselves.

The second section seeks to understand how the *political structures* of leadership are gendered. These structures may be a product of historical, cultural or social practices, but they can result in the inclusion and exclusion of men and women from leadership roles. The authors in this section look at the Australian Constitution, parliament, political parties, ministers' offices, and foreign affairs agencies to identify how gender operates in these core governance areas.

The third section of this book explores the ways in which *political cultures* of leadership are gendered. The chapters in this section argue that there is a cultural alignment between political leadership and certain forms of masculinity. It operates to position and legitimate dominant men, their experiences, and masculine values as the standard of political leadership, but in doing so it can create barriers to women's participation. This can be seen through the ongoing social expectation that women – whether as political leaders or partners to political leaders – continue to take on the unpaid labour of caring for families. It can also be seen in the girls and young women who watch the treatment of female politicians and turn away from political leadership as a viable option for them.

The final section considers the role that the *media* plays in shaping Australia's political leadership culture. This includes discussions of how men and women leaders were represented differently by the media, the gender issues associated with journalism and reporting as an industry, and the gendered nature of Australia's political leadership discourse. The chapters in this section demonstrate the significant role that the media plays in generating and perpetuating the types of gender biases and power relationships that are identified and analysed throughout the collection.

In short, we seek to provoke the reader and offer an invitation to consider how gender bias might operate in Australian politics. The chapters are designed to encourage an open conversation about the malignant manifestations that gender politics and unequal gender relations have on our society, and how they might be addressed to create leadership opportunities that are more equal and inclusive.

LEADERS

THE GENDERED IDENTITIES OF AUSTRALIAN POLITICAL LEADERS: FROM HAWKIE TO SCOMO

Carol Johnson

How political leaders perform their gender is an important part of their image and one that is frequently used to engage with, and sell their policies to, the electorate. Australian politics has tended to favour strong leaders who promise that they will offer economic benefits to the Australian people and protect them from harm. Not surprisingly, this process has been deeply gendered. After all, in traditional gender roles, it was the heterosexual male head of the household who both protected and provided for his family.

Male political leaders have drawn on this traditional (heterosexual) male role model in their own political images, reassuring concerned citizens that their leader has the masculine traits necessary to safeguard them from both internal and external threats while providing a secure economic future. Male political leaders have also used this traditional model to belittle the masculinity of their political opponents. Meanwhile, Australia's only female prime minister had to negotiate the difficulties involved in political leadership that was traditionally coded as male. This chapter will provide some key historical examples of the gendered identity of Australian political leaders before giving a more detailed analysis of the gendered identity of Australia's current prime minister, Scott Morrison.

Father figures, mates and alpha males

There are many images of masculine leadership in Australian history. As one might expect, it was particularly important for wartime leaders. Labor prime ministers John Curtin (1941–1945) and Ben Chifley (1945–1949) were not warrior-like themselves, but they were reassuring and protective father figures who pledged to defend Australia from Japanese invasion. They also pledged a brave new postwar economy that would offer jobs and prosperity when soldiers returned from the war. Their Liberal successor, Robert Menzies (1949–1966), may have failed as a wartime leader, but he was a very successful peacetime one, pledging to build a prosperous postwar Australia and protect citizens from both Labor Party socialism and international communism.

We do not need to go back to the 1940s and 1950s to find examples of masculine images at work. They have been very much evident in male prime ministers over the last 40 years.

Prime Minister Bob Hawke (1983–1991) cultivated the image of being an ordinary, sports-loving Australian bloke. 'Hawkie' was also a bit of an Australian-style larrikin who loved a drink, albeit a bit too much, so he generously pledged to give it up for the duration of his prime ministership. While projecting the image of being a man's man, Hawke was also prepared to show a soft side. He would cry over his daughter's drug addiction issues and the massacre at Tiananmen Square. Indeed, Hawke forged a real emotional rapport with the Australian people. His image as a caring bloke reinforced the belief that he would protect citizens. Hawke was the people's mate who would overcome the claimed divisiveness of the Fraser government years that threatened 'to poison … the true, decent, Australian way of life'.[1] He promised to bring all Australians together, including both business and labour, to build a prosperous country that would benefit everyone. That included women. Indeed, Bob appreciated women so much that he advocated affirmative action policies, arguing that greater gender equality was not only a social justice issue, but that working women would be good for the economy too.

His treasurer and successor as prime minister, Paul Keat-ing (1991–1996), may not have had 'Hawkie's' easy rapport with ordinary Australians, yet he still projected a particular kind of masculinity. Despite (or perhaps in order to compensate for) being from a working-class background and having left school before he turned 15, Keating projected suave, cosmopolitan, masculine sophis-tication. He was a collector of antique clocks, he dressed impeccably in Italian-designed suits, he loved opera and classical music. Keating even had the temerity to suggest that some popular images of Aus-tralian masculine identity, such as 'yobs' who put 'shrimps on the barbecue', needed to be replaced with more sophisticated images that would help Australia succeed in the global economy and become an international tourist destination.[2]

At the same time, Keating's alpha maleness was asserted through his mastery of economic discourse (albeit a free market version that hadn't previously been in Labor's lexicon) and his ability to emasculate his political opponents. For example, Keating denounced Opposition leader John Hewson for giving a speech that 'was the limpest performance I have ever seen … It was like being flogged with a warm lettuce. It was like being mauled by a dead sheep'.[3] At the same time, Keating could give masterful and charismatic expla-nations of the economic reforms he argued were required. Cultural commentator Meaghan Morris claimed that Keating had succeeded in 'eroticizing economics'.[4] Tough decisions needed to be made, and Keating positioned himself as the real man who could make them. He promised to protect Australia from being an 'economic museum' and a 'banana republic'.[5]

In his younger days as a politician, Keating deplored the fact that women were going to work to increase the family income. Later in office, he suggested, like Hawke, that women's equality was benefi-cial given that women would be contributing their skills (albeit often in part-time work) to grow the economy. Keating had transformed from a socially conservative male head of household providing for his own family, to chief economic provider for the nation, promising us a brave new future in Asia and on the information superhighway. In the process, Australians would throw off their old colonial British identity, and the monarchy along with it, reconcile with Indigenous Australians and take our place as a proud independent nation. Keating was not just projecting his own identity, he was projecting a new national identity, with new forms of inclusive and cosmopolitan masculine identity implicated in it.

Compared to Hawke and Keating, John Howard (1996–2007) projected a very different kind of masculinity. Howard's masculinity was socially conservative and grandfatherly, but it was still a protective one. Howard promised to protect us from the so-called political correctness and divisive special interests (from feminists to Aboriginal activists) of the Keating years. He did not have the suave, cosmopolitan masculinity of Keating. Rather, Howard turned Keating's image against him, arguing that Keating had alienated 'mainstream' Australians in his support for 'elite' progressive views on social issues. By contrast, Howard championed Anglo-Celtic identity and traditional families, arguing that Labor policies had penalised stay-at-home mums. He denounced overly negative views of Australia's colonial history. He promised that, under his strong and steady leadership, 'mainstream' Australians could be 'comfortable and relaxed' about the present, future and past.[6] They wouldn't need to embrace social and cultural change. Economic change would occur, but Howard would steer Australia to a bright economic future through policies that were even more free market than Keating's (while lacking Labor's social and industrial safety net). He would provide a better economic future for us all.

Howard's protectiveness was also displayed in other ways. After 35 people were shot in the Port Arthur massacre, Howard introduced tougher gun controls despite objections from some conservatives. Howard was in Washington during the 9/11 terrorist attacks and was proclaimed a 'man of steel' by US President George W Bush.[7] Howard pledged to protect Australia from international terrorism and also from a flood of asylum seekers, which the government claimed might also be concealing terrorists, via his border protection policies. Howard's masculine strength was contrasted with that of 'flip-flop' Kim Beazley, the Labor opposition leader, whom Howard accused of lacking 'ticker'.[8] In other words, the Coalition attempted to emasculate Beazley just as Paul Keating had tried to emasculate John Hewson.

However, Howard's image of protective masculinity was to be seriously damaged by industrial relations issues. Emboldened by the government gaining control in the Senate, Howard passed his Work-Choices legislation, claiming that it would give Australian workers, including women workers, greater flexibility and choice. Yet, in the electorate's view, Howard was removing essential workplace protections. A forceful ACTU television campaign highlighted the impact that WorkChoices would have on families. One advertisement graphically depicted the distress of a mother who was given the impossible choice of suddenly being required to go into work due to capricious roster changes, despite having no childcare arranged, or losing her job.[9] The campaign seriously undermined Howard's fatherly and grandfatherly credentials and contributed to his government losing the 2007 election.

Howard lost to a Labor opponent with a very different form of masculinity. During the 2007 election campaign, Kevin Rudd (2007–2010, 2013) depicted himself as still being a safe pair of hands when it came to looking after the economy. However, he also depicted himself as more caring, and less market-oriented than Howard when it came to looking after peoples' industrial and social wellbeing. Rudd promised to protect Australians against the neoliberalism of 'Howard's Brutopia'.[10] He would also be a protective fatherly figure who would apologise to the stolen generations of Aboriginal children when Howard would not. Rudd projected an image of being nerdy but earnest (and therefore unthreatening), but more able to negotiate the contemporary world than Howard. Rudd spoke Mandarin and depicted himself as having a better understanding of the rising Asian economies than Howard. Unlike Howard, Rudd also had a highly successful, wealthy, working wife. He positioned himself as a new age man.

Rudd's nerdiness was to prove a potential liability when Tony Abbott seized the opposition leadership. Abbott mobilised his hypermasculinity, first against Rudd (2007–2010), then against prime minister Julia Gillard (2010–2013), and then against Rudd (2013) again. Abbott projected the image of a super-fit action man who got things done, while emasculating Rudd for being 'all talk and no action'.[11] Abbott depicted himself as a strong leader who, like Howard, would stand up against what he identified as politically correct nonsense. However, he also demonstrated a protective side, as evidenced by his work as a volunteer lifesaver and firefighter. At a Liberal Party campaign launch, Abbott's daughter Frances stated: 'My dad looks out for everyone and I know he will look out for you'.[12] His protective masculinity, drawing on his fatherly role, was used as a political weapon, suggesting that he was a strong leader who would look after, and understood, ordinary Australians. Abbott also used it against Julia Gillard when she became prime minister. He highlighted that he and his wife Margie understood the everyday economic concerns of Australian families because they knew what it was like to handle mortgages and kids, thereby drawing attention to the fact that Gillard was unmarried, albeit in a de facto relationship, and had never had children. Abbott talked of Gillard's need to make 'an honest woman of herself' and suggested that Gillard's carbon price was the 'mother of all taxes', thereby implying that Gillard had grotesquely given birth to a tax rather than to a child.[13]

Coalition members of parliament suggested that Gillard had betrayed her femininity by ousting Kevin Rudd as prime minister. They likened Gillard to the evil Shakespearean character Lady Macbeth (who had expressed a wish to be unsexed from her womanhood so she could better perform her nefarious deeds). They also likened Gillard to Madame Defarge (a fictional Dickensian French Revolution character who advocated guillotining opponents and, like Gillard, enjoyed knitting). In short, they repeatedly suggested that Gillard was a cruel, evil and conniving woman who would sooner knife you than protect you.[14] They implied that Gillard was unfeminine while simultaneously playing to those men who felt unhappy at their own treatment by a woman.

Such attacks illustrate the widely acknowledged gender issues that Gillard encountered as prime minister. Gillard had additional problems in depicting herself as a strong and tough leader who would protect ordinary Australians. While it enhances a man's masculinity to be seen as strong and tough, it can bring a woman's femininity into question and make her seem less likeable. Gillard tried to demonstrate that she was a warm and engaged prime minister whose government would address the 'stress, anxiety and confusion' associated with the current age, and who cared about issues such as children's education, disability, inequality and victims of child sexual abuse.[15] However, it was hard to convince some sections of the Australian public that she was anything other than the untrustworthy, ambitious woman who had knifed Kevin Rudd and allegedly lied about introducing a carbon tax. While her famous speech against Tony Abbott's misogyny won plaudits from many supporters, it also potentially transgressed the traditional role that women are meant to play. After all, women are meant to make men feel good about themselves, not hold them to account! Perversely, Gillard was accused of playing the gender card – a card that had long been played by men against her as well as against male opponents whose masculinity had been questioned.

As Gillard's unpopularity grew, she was briefly replaced as prime minister by Rudd in a desperate attempt to at least save the deck chairs on the *Titanic* in the face of imminent defeat. During the 2013 election campaign, Rudd attempted to undermine Abbott's masculine image by invoking his own. He suggested that Abbott was scared of debating with him: 'It's time we have a properly moderated debate … Mr Abbott, I think it's time you demonstrated to the country you had a bit of ticker on this. I mean, he's the boxing blue; I'm the glasses-wearing kid in the library.'[16]

While Abbott succeeded in defeating Rudd, he was not able to withstand a palace coup. Abbott was replaced by Malcolm Turnbull (2015–2018). Turnbull exhibited a suave, sophisticated and cosmopolitan form of masculinity, although without Paul Keating's scathing powers of evisceration. Turnbull's alpha maleness derived from his success in business and personal wealth rather than Abbott's physical prowess. Unlike Abbott, Turnbull was seen as a socially progressive, moderate Liberal (although he had to temper his positions to assuage conservatives in his party). Like Rudd, he also projected an image of being a new age man. Turnbull highlighted his relationship with his very capable and successful wife Lucy, and was more supportive of gender equality than Abbott or Howard.

Nonetheless, opposition leader Bill Shorten questioned Turnbull's masculinity, depicting him as 'a weak man beholden to the right wing of his party' because of his failure to stand up to conservatives on social issues, including same-sex marriage.[17] Labor depicted Turnbull as a member of the wealthy elite who was out of touch with, and therefore would not look after, ordinary Australians. Consequently, Turnbull's protective masculinity was undermined. According to Liberal leaks, internal party polling suggested that his entrepreneurial rhetoric, in which he said that Australians were living in 'exciting times', scared many voters who were worried about their jobs.[18] At least one Liberal politician suggested that voters would have preferred Howard's promise of being relaxed and comfortable. The prospect of getting excited about developments in the economy just scared them.

It is clear from this analysis that issues of gender and leadership have played at least some role in Australian politics over the last few decades, even if they are just one factor among many others. However, what does this mean for more current Australian politics? The following section explores issues of masculinity, and protective masculinity in particular, and how it explains some of the issues that Scott Morrison has faced as prime minister since he replaced Malcolm Turnbull before the 2019 election.

Scott Morrison's first masculinity fail

Scott Morrison forged a particular masculine image that served him well during the 2019 election campaign. Morrison was 'ScoMo', the likeable daggy dad from the suburbs, who loved the footy and a beer down the pub. It was an image that was carefully crafted to undermine Labor's election messages. Labor's campaign was based on mobilising ordinary Australians against the 'top end of town'. It had worked well against Turnbull, given he was an incredibly wealthy former banker. However, Labor's campaign was to prove much less effective against a prime minister who cultivated an anti-elitist image of being one of us. Morrison's suburban family man image also made him seem dependable at a time when Labor leader Bill Shorten was being depicted as untrustworthy and shifty.

Morrison specifically targeted Shorten's masculinity in the lead-up to the election. He suggested that Shorten wanted to 'end the weekend', given that the electric cars Shorten advocated for wouldn't have sufficient grunt to pull the family boat or trailer.[19] The implication was that real men, who provide for their families, don't drive electric cars. Morrison also depicted himself as supporting male blue-collar jobs in the coal mining industry, while suggesting that Shorten was prepared to abandon miners in order to follow the Greens' climate change agenda.

Morrison's masculine image subsequently came unstuck in the face of the 2019/20 summer bushfire crisis. While many daggy dads were evacuating their families from Australian beachside holidays or filling up buckets with water to defend their own homes, Morrison was holidaying with his family in Hawaii. Although Morrison protested (from Hawaii) that Australians understood he'd promised his family a break and 'I don't hold a hose, mate', some courageous daggy dads were leaving their families to be volunteer firefighters.[20]

Scott Morrison's 'fail' was not just a failure of strong leadership, it was also a failure of his version of protective masculinity. Morrison had promised to protect Australian voters from the economic consequences of a big taxing and big spending Labor government. However, Morrison was patently failing to play the role of masculine protector when it came to the bushfires. The Coalition's reservations over climate change science and policy meant that he didn't take the threat of climate change seriously enough. Not only had Morrison taken an overseas holiday at a predictably bad time, he had also failed to meet with former fire chiefs to discuss the looming threat. Furthermore, despite calls to do so, the federal government had failed to order more water bombers before the fire season began.

There were also many courageous female volunteer fire fighters as well as ordinary women who joined in efforts to defend their family properties. Female political leaders such as NSW Liberal premier Gladys Berejiklian displayed real leadership during the fire crisis. Conversely, Scott Morrison's masculine image had been found wanting compared with the heroic and iconic forms of protective masculinity displayed by male firefighters. Scott Morrison did not need to hold a hose himself. However, he needed to display the type of strong and empathetic leadership that predecessors such as John Howard showed in crises (in Howard's case, this includes the 2003 Canberra bushfires).

Morrison's masculinity fail was made particularly clear by a viral video incident. Volunteer bushfire fighter Paul Parker was enraged both by the Prime Minister's absence and by a Morrison statement implying that volunteer firefighters didn't require financial subsidies because they enjoyed fighting fires. Parker stopped a news crew to yell out of a fire truck cabin: 'Tell the Prime Minister to go and get fucked.' Explaining his position later, Parker added that Morrison has 'got no understanding of what real people in Australia go through. And he doesn't care anyway. Any real man would never have left the country while his country was in turmoil'. In a subsequent interview, Parker elaborated upon his comments, not only repeating that a 'real man would not have left his country when it was in turmoil', but adding that 'Bob Hawke wouldn't have left... and John Howard wouldn't have left, either'.[21] Morrison had fallen short, not only of popular expectations, but of the standards of protective masculinity set by his predecessors.

The marketing savvy that helped create the image of 'ScoMo' deserted Morrison in this case. He has since tried to shore up his leadership credentials (and his protective masculinity) by mobilising the Australian Defence Force to assist in fire-ravaged regions and establishing a bushfires royal commission.

Morrison also asserted himself as a strong, protective leader early in the COVID-19 pandemic. He moved swiftly to close Australia's borders to prevent foreigners bringing the virus in. He sacrificed the Liberal ideological commitment to budget surpluses when his government brought in financial measures to support Australian businesses and workers impacted by the COVID-19 lockdown. A raft of temporary measures was introduced, including substantially increasing unemployment benefits (JobSeeker allowance), subsidising the wages of many workers who would otherwise be unemployed (JobKeeper allowance) and temporarily introducing free childcare. Morrison depicted himself as someone who would make the hard decisions to protect Australians from disease while also being prepared to open up the Australian economy once the appropriate time came. In other words, he pledged to protect both Australians' health and their economic wellbeing.

Morrison appeared as a strict but fair headmaster-type figure, firmly instructing hoarders to stop, but also offering the public an 'early mark' (a colloquial NSW expression for being allowed out of school early) after Australia's success at social distancing enabled the easing of lockdown restrictions to be brought forward.[22] His tough masculine image was reinforced by his argument that Australians should not be wimps when it came to opening up the economy again. He stated that 'it is important that we all hold our nerve'. While we could 'stay under the doona' and 'never face any danger', he urged us to 'get out from under the doona at some time. And if not now, then when?'[23] He also depicted himself as standing up to China over Australian demands for an investigation into the origins of the virus. Indeed, Morrison did this at a time of heightened international tensions.

Morrison's softer, good-bloke persona has also been evident at times, and not only in the financial support given to Australians facing major economic impacts from the virus. His father had died a few months earlier, and he explained that what 'really tears me up … is how many people have had to deal with loved ones who passed away and to go through funerals with so few people. That is … just horrible'.[24] His softer, more amenable side was also evident in his initial co-operation with Labor premiers in national cabinet meetings, and his expressed desire to facilitate agreement between unions and employers on reforms to the industrial relations system. In this instance, Morrison put aside his previous aggressive measures against unions and almost channelled Labor's Bob Hawke.

In short, Morrison has attempted to invoke both a strong and a caring form of fatherly, protective masculinity. It is an image that portrays less dagginess and more of a statesmanlike determination to do whatever it takes to see us through unprecedented hard times. In moving fast to shield Australians from the pandemic, Morrison transformed a massive masculinity fail during the bushfire crisis into a resounding success just a few months later. The metamorphosis arguably influenced his increased approval ratings, with a nearly 30 per cent rise in Morrison's satisfaction rating (from 37 per cent to 66 per cent), as measured by Newspoll between January and June 2020.

However, maintaining such high approval ratings is difficult in normal circumstances, and particularly difficult in an unprecedented health crisis. The federal government initially avoided significant blame for failures in quarantine. Nonetheless, by late July 2020, the spread of COVID-19 into aged care homes in Victoria had already exposed deficiencies in the federal government's management of the aged care sector. There were also complaints that the federal government should have introduced paid pandemic leave early in the crisis to prevent sick employees in financially vulnerable situations from going to work. Meanwhile, both healthcare and aged care workers had long complained of being unable to obtain sufficient protective equipment (including basics such as N95 and P2 masks) from the national PPE (personal protective equipment) stockpile. Given the subsequent Victorian outbreak, Morrison was lucky that key premiers retained state border controls at a time when he was urging leaders of states with no community transmission to wind back their border restrictions. But the federal government faced criticism for withdrawing too late from mining magnate Clive Palmer's High Court case against Western Australia's strong border restrictions. The federal government also faced criticism over the adequacy of its economic support packages for business, workers (particularly women workers) and those on unemployment benefits. As such examples demonstrate, despite his initial success, the health crisis and its economic consequences will pose challenges to Morrison's image of protective masculinity for as long as the pandemic continues.

Both leadership and election outcomes are usually decided by multiple factors. This chapter has suggested that the performance of gendered leadership can be one of them, with forms of protective masculinity and images of the masculine provider playing particularly significant roles. The prevalence of masculine models of leadership only added to the issues faced by Julia Gillard when she became Australia's first female prime minister. Consequently, the gendered nature of political leadership remains a potent factor in Australian politics for both men and women.

GOOD BLOKES?
GENDER AND POLITICAL LEADERSHIP
IN THE AUSTRALIAN LABOR PARTY

Frank Bongiorno

In 1982 the historian Humphrey McQueen published a short story, 'Stiletto Inheritance', in which his narrator, the biographer of the Victorian politician Jack Murray, accidentally stumbles on a well-kept secret: that Alfred Deakin was murdered. But this is not all. He discovers that Deakin was also a 'transvestite' (transgender person) who had been killed to prevent him from revealing that an organisation of such people had been running Australia since federation: 'All Australia's prime ministers have been transvestites. From Barton to Fraser. All of them.' Deakin had apparently endangered the secret when, during his mental decline, he began referring to himself as 'Alice'. If this seems unlikely, a recent Australian prime minister turns up to confirm this story: 'Unmistakable even in a tweed skirt, blouse, sensible shoes, make-up and wig', Gough Whitlam removes his clothes to reveal a woman's body:

> Did you expect a man? How old-fashioned you gays really are. We have kept up with the times. Our group has contained women since 1904 but we were never considered eligible for the prime ministership. Fraser and I put an end to that prejudice. And, I might say, encouraged us all to be a little daring. For as long as the PMs were men they'd confined their dressing-up

to private gatherings. Once the sisterhood secured control we demanded the right to appear in public. That's why Fraser goes to Fancy Dress Balls in dinner suits. People think he's being dull or cautious whereas she's laughing up her tailored sleeve.[1]

McQueen's playful story – more a reflection on the nature of conspiracy than about gender – prompts the question: Would our understanding of Australian political history be different if it turned out that all prime ministers since federation had, indeed, been transgender?

This chapter will explore a few performances of manhood within the Australian Labor Party since the 1960s. It is intended to evoke a current direction of scholarship on gender and political leadership as well as some possibilities for future research. I end the chapter with a brief discussion of the performances of manhood by two Australian Labor leaders – one a highly successful prime minister, the other a failed opposition leader – in the context of a specifically masculine leadership performance. The leaders concerned are Bob Hawke (prime minister, 1983–1991) and Mark Latham (opposition leader, 2003–2004). Both sought to embody and perform a larrikin masculinity. Only one of them succeeded. The reasons for these differences do not lie wholly in personality, capacity and context. I argue that Hawke was much more successful in the liminal nature of his performance of manhood, and in his capacity to balance different ways of being a man in the public sphere.

Gender, sexuality and political leadership

Political history and political biography have often taken for granted the masculinity of the political subject. The congruence between a male gender identity and a public sphere understood as male space has, at least until the 1980s, pre-empted the consideration of male political subjects as specifically gendered actors involved in embodied practices and rituals that assumed male dominance. It was arguably the growing presence of women in political life, especially in the wake of second-wave feminism in the early 1970s, that unsettled these assumptions. Women entered a political space assumed to be masculine. and have, ever since, had to negotiate what it has meant to be a woman in that adversarial environment. Those who have risen to high ministerial office, party leadership or, in the case of Julia Gillard, the prime ministership, have experienced these dilemmas in their most acute forms.

That space is also heterosexual, and the particular kinds of masculine and, now, feminine performance that it validates have also been shaped by heteronormativity. Male political leaders whose interests run to culture rather than sport have become the subject of often absurd rumours that they were gay. In the case of Liberal prime minister Billy McMahon, the 'liking for fashion, the regular proclamations that he had been a "balletomane", his light step, and his long-running bachelorhood' led to persistent but seemingly unfounded rumours of homosexuality. He also enjoyed the company of women – invariably a source of confusion and anxiety in a country where the homosocial cult of mateship is the gold standard for heterosexual male behaviour. McMahon's perceived failure to measure up as an Australian man in his private life and public performance was the source of considerable gossip.[2] In the case of South Australian Labor premier Don Dunstan, gossip had more solid foundations, since Dunstan was indeed bisexual. Angela Woollacott's recent biography of Dunstan, however, traces the wider patterns of this new style of masculinity for an Australian political leader, as well as their connection to his vision for his state and his policy achievements: the 'elegant clothes, jewellery, coiffed hair, educated speech, rich voice, theatrical performances, successful cookbook and air of cosmopolitanism'.[3]

All the parties that compete for government at the federal level in Australia have in recent years been subjected to criticism on the grounds that they were male-dominated spaces that provide an unfriendly environment for women, one in which toxic male behaviour is tolerated and double standards remain acceptable. In 2018

Julia Banks, a federal Liberal parliamentarian, left the party complaining that the parliament was 'years behind' the corporate sector in its treatment of women.[4] Emma Hussar, a federal Labor MP, attributed the destruction of her political career to 'vicious slut-shaming'.[5] Nonetheless, it is the Coalition's gender problem that has generally received more sustained public attention and critique, fuelled by a sexist campaign mounted by some Liberals inside, and outside, the parliament and their supporters in some media outlets against Australia's first female prime minister, Julia Gillard. Gillard's eventual response in her 'Misogyny Speech', which received global attention, reinforced the idea that Australia's conservative parties had an especially acute 'woman problem', an impression that seemed to receive confirmation when the Abbott Government found just one place for a woman, Julie Bishop, in its cabinet after winning the election in 2013.

The Labor Party is often seen to have resolved these matters through its use of quotas and it has undoubtedly improved the representation of women in parliament and on its front bench. After the 2019 election, women comprised 47 per cent of federal members of the two houses of parliament; the figure for the Coalition was just 23 per cent.[6] A few generations back, this would have seemed an unlikely scenario. When the Labor Party, led by Gough Whitlam, won office in December 1972, there were no women in caucus. And while the Liberal Party was no beacon in such matters, its record was a little better. Half a dozen Liberal women had served as senators between 1947 and 1972, and a couple in the house – notably Dame Enid Lyons. The Liberal Party's organisational structures had been more open to women's involvement and influence than a Labor Party whose structure and culture were permeated by a male-dominated union movement. The Country Party, predecessor to today's National Party, had until recently a particularly poor record in relation to women's representation. 'The Nationals women have always punched above their weight', the party's website proudly declares.[7] More realistically, as a historian of the Victorian branch of the party has recently shown, the party has not generally been a haven for advanced feminism.[8]

There is a substantial body of historical and biographical research on women in the Australian Labor Party, but historical work on gender and gendered leadership in the broader sense – including the performance of masculinity – has been much thinner on the ground. The effects of the culture and ethos of the Labor Party itself are poorly studied. It is as if the modernisation of the Labor Party from the 1960s, including the well-known phenomenon of middle-classing,[9] and the more stringent measures taken from the 1990s to increase the number of female parliamentarians, have meant that commentators lacked a vocabulary for seeking to understand how gender works in relation to modern Labor.

One of the best biographical studies we have concerns Hawke, although it covers the period before his prime ministership. Blanche d'Alpuget's 1982 study of Hawke, influenced by both feminism and psychobiography, is among other things a remarkable reflection on Hawke as a man, and as embodying a certain style of masculinity rooted in the Freudian family romance, Hawke's upbringing and development.[10] The work of Carol Johnson on Australian political leadership has also been sensitive to the performances of masculine identity that have underpinned policy continuity and change in the ALP.[11] More recently, a doctoral project by Bethany Phillips-Peddlesden has led to the publication of some ground-breaking research on the embodied masculine political performance of Australian prime ministers from federation through to 1975, and the relationship between gender, authority and political legitimacy.[12] Yet, the manner in which gender was elevated as a prism through which to comprehend political leadership during the Gillard prime ministership did not produce much in the way of wider historical reflection on gender and the Labor Party itself. Gillard's misogynist tormentors were largely seen to have operated in the opposition, the Twittersphere, or right-wing media; the ABC's role in persecuting her via a tasteless satirical series (*At Home With Julia*) seems to have largely disappeared from collective memory of that time.

The Labor Party and gender

It is stating the obvious to point out that the Labor Party has not only been a party dominated by men, but an organisation that elevated certain codes of male behaviour while tolerating others. Phillips-Peddlesden remarks that early Labor prime minister, Andrew Fisher, a former miner, was seen as a 'stronger man ... and a more virile character' than his predecessor Chris Watson and, as a result, was thought 'better equipped to lead'.[13] Of all the federal Labor leaders of the twentieth century, the figure who is arguably best seen to embody the party's traditional working-class ethos was a physically large manual worker who, before entering politics, engaged in the very manly business of driving a train. Manual workers have been far from dominant as federal Labor leaders, so the manner in which Ben Chifley became the archetypal Labor leader speaks eloquently of the models of gendered leadership that have been most attractive within the party.

What was this masculinist ethos like? In the case of Fisher and Chifley, it was a respectable masculinity that was being celebrated; the working-class man capable of a comportment that would pass in the male middle-class world of parliamentary politics. But there was also a 'rough' version of working-class masculinity that is perhaps most evident in the homosocial tribal struggle of internal party affairs.[14] Here is Arthur Calwell, that fine Catholic gentleman, giving South Australian Labor Party boss and federal parliamentarian Clyde Cameron a piece of his mind after he heard a rumour that Cameron had been agitating for Calwell to resign his seat in favour of Jim Cairns: 'You sneaky little cunt. You've always been a sneaky little cunt, haven't you? A man ought to piss on you. At least that would make you smell like a man!'[15] Cameron, an ex-shearer who had seen and heard a thing or two in his time, thought it funny rather than insulting. Similarly, in *The Latham Diaries*, the former Labor leader tells a story, which he attributed to Whitlam, of an early 1970s ALP National Executive meeting in which 'the conversation ... inevitably turned to dick sizes' as this all-male gathering waited for somebody to show up.[16] We are here in the presence of a bawdy masculine sub-culture with deep roots in Australian masculinity, and from which women were absolutely excluded.

What kind of leadership has Labor's masculinism produced? The political psychologist Graham Little's typology of leadership styles remains useful. He distinguished between Strong Leaders, Group Leaders and Inspiring Leaders. Strong Leaders tend to be preferred in parties of the right, and they emphasise structure, order and discipline. Group Leaders – Bob Hawke is an example – are seen by strong Leaders as 'weak' and tend to stress 'neighbourliness, translating the experience of life in smaller groups, like the family, into the nation as a whole'.[17] In Hawke's case, the nation was arguably an enlarged version of the male-dominated spaces of the sporting club, the trade union and the public bar. Inspiring Leaders – think John F Kennedy, Pierre Trudeau or Gough Whitlam – value 'cosmopolitanism, innovativeness, a creative society that is diverse and changing'.[18] Little's was not a gender analysis as such, but he was alive to the issue. Strong leadership, he argued, tended to be associated with the masculine. Soft proposals – for compassion, for co-operation – were associated with the weak and the feminine. As he puts it, 'distinction or differentiation is masculine, while the feminine implies loss of self from being too close to others or thinking too much like them'.[19]

Bob Hawke

Bob Hawke came to his parliamentary career with a well-earned reputation for womanising and drunkenness, as well as a notably aggressive public style. D'Alpuget reports that his mother, who already had a boy, wanted a girl, and Hawke was conscious of not being the desired 'Elizabeth'. The biographer speculates that his 'defiant masculinity' and 'swashbuckling virility' might have owed something to the struggle between 'his biological maleness' and this 'phantom Elizabeth'.

She also traces his unusually close relationship to his clergyman father as the origin of Hawke's 'capacity to feel, and without embarrassment, to express love for his own sex'.[20]

Despite his university education, middle-class upbringing, and lack of background in strong, masculine labour, Hawke was seen to epitomise certain traditional Australian male traits and behaviours, as embodied in the larrikin and the sporting hero. Yet, when he came to his parliamentary career, he had promised to leave the more dissolute pleasures behind. As Labor prime minister, the reformed masculine self became symbolic of the reformed economy and nation. His message was 'consensus', the very style of leadership – group leadership – that Little suggests can be associated with 'weakness' and 'femininity'. Yet his consensus – at least as represented by the national economic summit of 1983 – was a consensus of men: one critic called it a 'suited recovery'. Hawke was also conspicuous in his identification with sporting success, such as the America's Cup yachting victory of September 1983, another characteristic seen as representative of Australian masculinity. He quickly came to identify closely with thrusting entrepreneurs of the era, all men, and his favourites were those such as Kerry Packer and Alan Bond, who most obviously embodied aggressive, sporty and masculine assertiveness as distinct from the more ambiguous and 'cultured' images of corporate masculinity associated with Robert Holmes à Court and Christopher Skase.[21]

In 1984 Hawke shed tears over the drug addiction of one of his daughters. The history of weeping has been a recent subject among cultural historians, with Thomas Dixon providing a major account over several centuries in his *Weeping Britannia: Portrait of a Nation in Tears*, and demonstrating that extravagant displays of male emotion have quite often been a feature of politics in Britain.[22] My own account of both Hawke and Australian cricket captain Kim Hughes – conspicuous weepers of 1984 – in a wider study of Australia in the 1980s suggested that this moment represented a watershed in the history of the public emotions in Australia. There was no Australian political leader of the twentieth century before Hawke who was so willing to display such emotions in public. Yet, as with his embrace of consensus, Hawke managed to weep without presenting as a weak leader, one lacking masculine self-command. He had his critics – the Liberals' John Howard accused him of having 'a fragile glass jaw' and Wilson Tuckey of lacking 'moral fibre' – but he received many sympathetic letters and much positive media coverage for being willing to display his emotions over a family tragedy.[23] The New South Wales premier Neville Wran, later famous for declaring that Balmain boys (such as himself) don't cry, nonetheless opined that 'it's not an indication of weakness to show you love your children'.[24] But after Hawke broke down again in a radio interview the following day, a commentator in the *Weekend Australian* thought the second bout of tears 'gave credence to those less kind, boots-and-all types who reckon that public tears signify character weakness'.[25] Performing masculinity in politics is a delicate balancing act.

When Hawke died in 2019, an incident in his prime-ministerial career that attracted considerable attention was his emotional and compassionate response to the Tiananmen Square massacre of 1989. That was another time of public weeping, as well as a promise that Chinese students in Australia would not be sent home.[26] This aspect of Hawke's leadership performance lives on in public memory as surely as his exuberance at the America's Cup victory of 1983. There are, by way of contrast, few images of Hawke in the adversarial atmosphere of parliament that have endured in the collective memory of the era – in contrast with his treasurer and successor as prime minister, Paul Keating. Such images are overshadowed by Hawke's more ambiguous and sometimes emotional public performances of masculinity, displays that in the context of another man's career might have been put down to weakness.[27] Hawke's was a fundamentally successful performance of a certain liminal style of masculinity.

Mark Latham

What might we make of the gender performance of one of the Labor Party's greatest leadership fails, Mark Latham?[28] Unlike Hawke, Latham was working class in background and he relished a self-image of rough masculinity, one that he took into the parliament with him after his election in 1994. He crafted a political persona as the authentic, sometimes crude, but 'plain-speaking anti-elitist' man from western Sydney and, by implication, the voice of the working-class suburban outsider everywhere.[29]

Latham became notorious for crude language, but whereas Hawke successfully made the case that he had reformed his character – that in the interests of party and country, he had become a different kind of man, and a better one – Latham's undertaking that there would be no more crudity when he became leader did not dissolve the suspicion that he was unfitted for leadership. His efforts, moreover, to present himself as an authentic suburban dad never quite managed to allay fears that there was something elemental, unruly and dangerous about his masculinity.

Those Latham sought to elevate – the outsiders who lived in the suburbs – were seen to have well-defined gender identities in which men were men, women were women, and real people were implicitly heterosexual and fertile. The inner-city elites that he despised were, by way of contrast, characterised by gender and sexual ambiguity and, therefore, a lack of authenticity.[30] A couple of years later, when he no longer needed to worry over alienating voters, they would become 'metrosexual knobs'.[31]

Where Hawke's complicated private life did not seem to pursue him into his political career, Latham was dogged by incidents allegedly involving violence: such as a late-night altercation with a taxi driver that resulted in the latter having his arm broken, and a supposed 'king-hit' on a man at a Labor Party function.[32] The media left Hawke's famous womanising alone; he even managed to quietly resume an affair with d'Alpuget in 1988.[33] But in the case of Latham, they located an aggrieved former wife and published details of his relations with women, even while he was a single man.[34] Polling indicated that Latham was unpopular with many women voters. But he was seen reading to children in schools, and made much of the need for male role models by supporting efforts to encourage men to take up teaching.

In contrast with Hawke's more ambiguous performances of masculinity, Latham played up differences between men and women while enjoining men to act responsibly for the sake of their children, and especially their boys. As in the case of Hawke, the implication was that his own masculinity – once working-class, rough and unruly – had been tamed. But voters seem to have sensed that it was all a thin veneer with Latham. Malcolm Turnbull, campaigning to enter parliament via a safe eastern suburban Sydney seat, thought that 'Latham had an air of simmering anger about him, as though he was about to explode'. It was, Turnbull recalled, 'women who woke up to him first. A typical comment was, "I just don't like him; he reminds me of a boyfriend my sister had," followed by a grimace'.[35]

Voters seemed more impressed by the restrained strength exuded by John Howard, his opponent: the male sturdiness of the plain suburban man who might not always be right but knows what he thinks and is prepared to do and not just talk. Where Latham had sought to portray Howard and the Coalition as sycophantic and weak in their dealings with the United States, President George W Bush had referred to Howard as a 'man of steel'. While that might not have impressed voters in itself, the idea of Howard as a man of strength and conviction was entrenched after his handling of the asylum-seeker issue at the 2001 election and the elevation of national security issues that came with the war on terror. A widely circulated image of Howard and Latham shaking hands on the eve of the 2004 election, with Latham clumsily trying to dominate Howard physically, confirmed the impression of a man unable to control aggressive male instincts.

In the end, Latham's was a politically unsuccessful performance of gendered leadership – and one that, 15 years later, has seen him join a party committed, among other things, to the cause of men's rights. He has criticised gays, lesbians and transgender people. While he was not doing that in 2003–2004, he had already expressed hostility to identity politics back then, and there is a fairly straight line between his gendered Labor leadership performance and his latter-day right-wing populism as a parliamentarian in New South Wales representing Pauline Hanson's One Nation.

The focus here has been on Labor leadership, but there is a great deal in the prime-ministerial performance of Liberal Scott Morrison to remind us of the mesmeric effect of Hawke's prime ministership almost three decades after his retirement. Morrison does not obviously model his leadership on the most successful Liberal prime minister of the recent past, John Howard. His approach is not primarily that of the 'strong leader' in Little's typology, even if he does seek to incorporate aspects of that model. He is more of a conservative 'group leader' who wishes to translate the neighbourliness of the suburb, the pub, the sporting club and the church to the nation as a whole – the latter conceived as a collection of families who are respectable, hard-working, mainly Christian and heterosexual. They are led by successful men like him, each with his own version of 'Jen and the girls' – a reference to his own family. And he increasingly presents himself as a consensus leader in the style of Hawke, even down to proposing to bring business, unions and government together to reform industrial relations, as Hawke did.[36] Whether these remain persistent strands for Morrison it is impossible to say, for he is also a former marketing man seeking a successful political formula and may well move on to something new before we have had time fully to assess the old. But what cannot be missed is that, as with some of the Labor performances examined in this chapter, manhood is at the heart of his political leadership.[37]

'SHADES OF GREY': A PERSONAL AND POLITICAL REFLECTION ON JULIA GILLARD'S PRIME MINISTERSHIP

Paul Strangio

A decade has elapsed since Julia Gillard toppled Kevin Rudd to become Labor leader and the first woman prime minister of Australia in June 2010. It ushered in a tumultuous incumbency that concluded with her ousting by Rudd three years later. In her parting speech to the media in June 2013, Gillard briefly addressed the effect of gender on her prime ministership. 'It doesn't explain everything,' she declared, 'it explains some things. And it is for the nation to think in a sophisticated way about those shades of grey.'[1] In a further reflection shortly after her deposition, Gillard ruefully observed that 'smashing through a glass ceiling is a dangerous pursuit. It is hard not to get lacerated on the way through'.[2] Yet in her political memoir published in 2014, she admitted that it remained difficult for her to define the influence gender had on her time in office: 'But of all the experiences I had as prime minister, gender is the hardest to explain, to catch, to quantify'.[3]

Stripped of the febrile atmosphere that surrounded her prime ministership – and with the perspective gained by watching the struggles of her successors – are we now better placed to assess Gillard's legacy? Are we closer to thinking about her prime ministership in the 'shades of grey' she spoke about in her farewell address? With greater distance, has it become easier to 'quantify' the gender effect on her incumbency? And, several years on, how much confidence can we have in Gillard's defiant prediction in her final prime-ministerial statement that as a result of her pioneering office-holding 'it will be easier for the next woman and the woman after that and the woman after that'?[4]

This chapter is both a personal and political reflection on Gillard's prime ministership. I haven't disclosed this before when writing about Gillard's leadership, but I know – or more accurately I knew – Julia and very much liked her as a person. I first encountered her in the mid-1990s when she was appointed chief of staff to the then Victorian state Labor opposition leader, John Brumby. My wife was a media adviser on Brumby's staff. They were unforgiving times for state Labor in Victoria, hopelessly outnumbered as they were by a Coalition government headed by the seemingly unstoppable Premier Jeff Kennett. The lopsided nature of the political contest encouraged a backs-against-the-wall camaraderie among Brumby's staffers. Long days of political trench warfare merged into evening socialising. Once in a while I joined in and so became initiated to Julia's mischievous, good-humoured ribbing of her colleagues and infectious laugh.

Knowing that I was a chronically underemployed, recently graduated doctoral student when she was elected to the House of Representatives in 1998, Julia approached me to write a book about an intrepid grassroots community campaign in her western Melbourne electorate of Lalor. Against the odds, the campaign had frustrated a determined effort by the Kennett government and the multinational company CSR to establish a major toxic waste facility in Werribee. That invitation became the basis for a two-year part-time project, which Julia financially supported. Consequently, we were in regular contact throughout that period, which culminated in the book's publication in 2001. Around the same time, we attended Julia's fortieth birthday celebration at Werribee Mansion. During the speeches, the newly installed Labor opposition leader, Simon Crean, spoke fondly about Julia, which says something about the fragility of friendship in politics in light of his later perverse performance in turning against her leadership in early 2013.

As Julia's star rose in Canberra (she was promoted to the shadow cabinet when Crean became leader in November 2001), I saw less of her. There was still, however, occasional contact. When Jim Cairns, the former Whitlam government deputy prime minister and postwar giant of the Labor left (and one of her predecessors as the Member for Lalor), passed away in October 2003, Julia reached out to me for information for her condolence speech because I had recently written a biography of Cairns. I reminded her what Cairns had replied when asked who he wanted to replace him in Lalor when he retired in 1977. Cairns said that he hoped the seat would pass to a woman: 'Women are less dangerous ... A woman feels the value of life'.[5] I was delighted when Julia concluded her condolence speech for Cairns in the House of Representatives by citing that quote.[6] Later, when she became prime minister, I was similarly chuffed when a newspaper photograph of her office showed a copy of my biography of Cairns sitting on her bookshelf.

Given this history, I was naturally pleased and admiring as I observed Julia's rapid political advance in the early 2000s: emerging as a prominent shadow minister in the federal Labor opposition, first under Crean and then Mark Latham; elected deputy Labor leader to Kevin Rudd at the end of 2006 (they were dubbed the 'dream team' by the media); and a popular and highly competent deputy prime minister and multiple portfolio holder after Rudd led Labor into power in November 2007. Like the public at large, I was shocked, and not without misgivings, when Gillard deposed Rudd in June 2010. Still, I felt a kind of vicarious pride at her pioneering status and recall being optimistic about her leadership. In turn, I became dismayed and felt a hurt protectiveness towards her at the awfulness that engulfed her over the next three years. At that stage, I was periodically contributing op-ed articles to the Melbourne-based *The Age* newspaper and, in a piece published in late 2011, I endeavoured to account for the campaign of calumny being waged against her. I proffered various reasons: the means by which she had obtained office, the Australian public's unfamiliarity with minority government, the intractability of some of the policy challenges she was grappling with and, unremark-ably, I also suggested that part of the explanation was 'her gender and status as an unmarried woman'.[7]

In early June 2013, with her prime ministership all but terminal and some scribes and opponents cavalierly damning her as Australia's worst ever national leader,[8] in an essay for the Fairfax press I specu-lated about Gillard's longer-term prime-ministerial reputation. The background to that essay was a volume I had recently co-edited on prime-ministerial performance in which I had written about the results of a survey initiated out of Monash University in September 2010. In the survey, historians and political scientists from across the country were asked to rank Australia's former prime ministers from Edmund Barton to the recently deposed Kevin Rudd. The results of that poll had suggested that while electoral success (longevity in office) was one key determinant of prime-ministerial prestige, still more decisive was the scale of the policy footprint left by an incumbent.[9]

In the Fairfax essay, I extrapolated from that key finding and ventured that 'posterity will treat Gillard with more sympathy than her legion of contemporary detractors'. In doing so, I pointed to the Gillard government's achievements, such as the first major response to climate change, the National Disability Insurance Scheme (NDIS) and a new school funding system, which seemed to have the makings of a substantial policy legacy that had been 'eked out in the unfamiliar and inhospitable conditions of minority government'. In addition, there was, of course, the fact that Gillard was the nation's first woman leader: 'a distinction forever hers'.[10] The reaction to what I considered a largely unremarkable prediction of how history would view Gillard was swift and severe: correspondents filled my inbox with hate mail. They told me they 'despised' Gillard and that they loathed me for not accepting that she had visited disaster on Australia and was the embodiment of political evil. Nothing I have written before or since has come within cooee of inciting such visceral antagonism.

Has my 2013 judgment been vindicated? Partly to answer that question, I organised another prime-ministerial rankings survey in

2020. Because these leadership ratings exercises (which have a long history in the United States and are now catching on in parliamentary systems) are typically confined to rating former office holders – those whose leadership project is complete – the 2010 poll ended with Rudd. Ten years on, however, I was able to include Gillard, Tony Abbott and Malcolm Turnbull. I was intrigued to discover how Gillard would rank beside Rudd, Abbott and Turnbull. In other words, that beleaguered group of office holders since the era of John Howard, all of whom have struggled in the context of a transforming party and media landscape, and who have governed in a period of political volatility and policy flux.

Sixty-six historians and political scientists participated in the 2020 survey.[11] On the question of overall performance, which asked respondents to grade prime ministers in one of five categories (outstanding, good, average, below average and failure), Gillard was rated well ahead of Rudd, Abbott and Turnbull. In fact, she finished in the middle of the pack of former Australian prime ministers, whereas her three contemporaries languished at the rear. A second set of questions asked respondents to rate the leadership of each prime minister in nine performance areas. The results here afforded insight into why Gillard outranked Rudd, Abbott and Turnbull. She scored far more strongly on management of cabinet and party and on personal integrity and policy legacy. On the other hand, she trailed the other three on communication performance and was rated behind Rudd and Turnbull on relationship with the electorate.

The 2020 prime-ministerial rankings reinforce my confidence that it is not sustainable to maintain the argument made by Gillard's most rabid critics while she was in office that she was a national leadership dunce: the poorest prime minister Australia has ever had. One thing that is likely to have softened the negativity towards her over the past decade is the graceful way she has comported herself since leaving office. Dedicating herself to noble causes, both globally and in Australia, she has eschewed the rancorous point scoring indulged in by many other departed national leaders. According to one writer, who is not normally disposed to praising Labor politicians, Gillard has been 'a model of dignity and class' and 'set an especially high bar for former prime ministers, forging a meaningful life away from politics'.[12]

On the more substantive matter of policy legacy, if we again confine the comparison to post-Howard prime ministers, Gillard does have a strong claim to having left the most significant footprint. While metrics about legislative productivity (the number of Bills enacted per time in office) ought to be treated with caution, Gillard left each of her contemporaries in the shade when measured by that benchmark. Indeed, she tops the performance of any other Australian prime minister on that criterion.[13] And there were major yields from that legislation: for instance, the Clean Energy Future package that priced carbon to deliver a decline in Australia's greenhouse emissions;[14] the NDIS, which enjoys bipartisan recognition as the most significant social reform since the advent of the universal health care scheme in the 1970s; a needs-based funding system for schools; a plan for managing the water resources of the Murray–Darling Basin; an internationally pioneering measure to enforce plain packaging of tobacco products; and the landmark Royal Commission into Institutional Responses to Child Sexual Abuse.[15] As an aside, Gillard's former chief of staff, Ben Hubbard, has remarked to me that, in retrospect, he has come to regard the royal commission into child sexual abuse as possibly the most significant initiative of her government. He said that the consequences of the commission, namely the radical improvement in child safety, the holding to account of powerful institutions for their failures, and the support of survivors, were all difficult to foresee at the time. Hubbard added that the former prime minister was regularly stopped and thanked by survivors and their families, as well as by members of the public horrified by the abuses.[16]

There are caveats to this catalogue of achievement. Some of the measures closed on initiatives commenced by Rudd (e.g. the Murray–Darling Basin scheme); others did not long survive the fall of Gillard's government (e.g. the carbon price was repealed by the

Abbott Coalition government in 2014); and others were rushed and have been subsequently marred in their implementation. Moreover, the policy accomplishments of Gillard's prime ministership were offset by some notable fiascos: one example is the erratic handling of the vexed issue of asylum seekers where the government came to resemble the proverbial rabbit caught in headlights. Notwithstanding these imperfections, however, Gillard's policy legacy was substantive, especially for what was effectively a single-term minority government.

Though Gillard may earn reputational kudos for the policy impact of her government, as the 2020 rankings suggest, her prime-ministerial standing is weighed down by a record of failure to win favour with voters. Her sole electoral test of August 2010 resulted in Labor losing its majority and, while poor leadership polling has become something of a default setting in Australian politics during the past decade, she was deeply unpopular for most of her prime ministership. Since the inception of Newspoll, only Paul Keating has registered a lower rating than Gillard endured by 2012.[17]

There were several bedevilling factors at work here. The first was the original sin of how she became prime minister: it poisoned the legitimacy of her leadership from the start. The act of precipitously felling Rudd fuelled a cycle of revenge and internal destabilisation that constantly ate away at her authority. Secondly, while Gillard's trans-actional style of leadership proved remarkably well suited to minority government, this had a downside in that the public was easily per-suaded to equate the necessary deal-making and compromise with expediency. Lastly, there was her gender, which complicated and nega-tively coloured the media and public response to her as a leader.

At the same time, there is no denying that Gillard, a person who has a reputation among those who know her as warm and unfailingly good-humoured, and who inspires great affection within her inner circle, struggled to strike the right emotional register to communicate with voters.[18] She frequently presented as scripted, wooden and stub-bornly undemonstrative on the public stage. Her insistence on being judged on administrative competence and a functioning, productive parliament, and her impatience towards expectations that she emote or indulge in image-making fripperies, were admirable. But compared to some of her contemporaries (especially the politician-cum-celebrity Kevin '07 Rudd), it was a disadvantage in an age of personalised politics in which there is an intensified onus on leaders to develop a 'virtual relationship' with voters: to be an 'intimate stranger'.[19]

Some writers have persuasively attributed Gillard's stoical leadership style and battle to establish an affinity with the public to gender. For instance, in an insightful essay published towards the end of Gillard's tenure, writer Anna Goldsworthy noted that her habit was 'to deflect any speculation about who she was'. Goldsworthy continued:

> Despite having more to explain than the average prime minister – besides her gender, there is her professed atheism; her childlessness; her de facto living arrangements – she has not provided any reassuring narrative of herself ... Instead, she just keeps on *doing* stuff, resilient as a Duracell bunny: forging alliances, making deals, retracting promises, passing legislation ... *Getting on with it* speaks to a recognisable truth of female pragmatism.[20]

On the other hand, my intuition tells me that there is at least one other non-gender factor that compounded Gillard's communication and other limitations as a leader. From the time she joined the Labor Party as a student at the University of Adelaide, Gillard trod an undeviating path towards a career in politics: as an officer of the Australian Union of Students, as a lawyer with the Labor-aligned firm Slater and Gordon, as a chief of staff to the Victorian state Labor opposition leader, and as an aspiring parliamentarian. The latter goal was thrice checked by male party powerbrokers before she won preselection for Lalor, but the pattern is clear. Like many of her contemporaries, male and female alike, Gillard fits the mould of the 'career' politician in a professionalised party machine. And this species of politician has frequently proved lacking in rhetorical (and visionary) range.[21]

What about Gillard's legacy and the issue of gender in politics? One by-product of her prime ministership was a small avalanche of literature analysing her term of office through a gender lens. Previously there had been a relative dearth of scholarship on female leadership in Australia, despite the fact that by the time Gillard entered office in 2010 the country had had a total of seven women leaders of government at subnational level. These writings on the theme of gender examined Gillard's experience from several perspectives.[22] The authors found, not surprisingly, that the gendered reaction to her prime ministership mimicked patterns encountered by women leaders internationally. For example, the negativity emanating from the way she obtained office was consistent with evidence that overt displays of ambition and assertiveness by women, by transgressing stereotypes of gender behaviour, impair their 'likeability' and popularity (a phenomenon linked to what is commonly characterised as the 'double bind' that women leaders suffer).[23]

I have already noted that I had apprehensions about the way Gillard came to office and believe that, whatever the provocations and manifest difficulties involved in being deputy to Rudd, and however irresistible the forces of party insurrection were against him, continued forbearance to prop up the partnership might have been her wiser course. Rudd has argued, not without reason, that his tearing down in 2010 established a destructive precedent and the consequences have echoed ever since.[24] Even so, it is impossible not to notice the double standard in how Gillard was made to wear her deposing of Rudd like a crown of thorns, whereas Turnbull and Scott Morrison spilt blood during their ascensions with relative impunity. Some of the other writings on the theme of gender in relation to Gillard have suggested that her treatment also reflected peculiarities of Australia's history and political culture, which served to further delegitimise and create an especially inhospitable environment for her prime ministership.[25] The overall picture arising from this literature led one international scholar to glumly conclude that 'Gillard's experience presents a cautionary tale for women seeking elite leadership roles'.[26]

Apart from the scholarly surge, have we yet witnessed the 'shades of grey' discussion about the way Gillard was treated and does it inform ongoing conversations about the place of women in Australian politics? There have been some encouraging, albeit sporadic, engagements on the subject. The most recent were piqued by the tenth anniversary of Gillard's ascension to the prime ministership, and the publication shortly afterwards of her jointly written book, *Women and Leadership: Real Lives, Real Lessons.*[27] The sense from those conversations is that Gillard's experience has become something of a chastening reference point and an injunction to do better.[28] Interviewed in mid-2019 for an extended newspaper essay about her post-prime-ministerial activities, Gillard suggested that was so: 'Women and men come up to me and say they were so taken aback by it [her treatment as prime minister], they were sort of frozen into immobility and they're critical of themselves for not having done more.' She added, 'We're in an environment now where I think if any of those things happened again, the swarm of outrage would be enormous.'[29] The essay itself argued that 'something has shifted in attitudes towards' the former prime minister; indeed, it reported she is the subject of 'fandom', pointing to the adulatory receptions she receives in many forums at which she speaks.[30]

Yet we should not exaggerate this. The view of Gillard as a wronged heroine is still likely confined to a relatively small niche. Moreover, as Paul Keating was wont to say, the political caravan moves on. From my experience of teaching an undergraduate unit on political leadership, I have been struck by how little many of the students know about the treatment that was meted out to Gillard. In a topic on gender and leadership, I show them a compilation of some of the worst bullying and sexism she suffered. The students are usually aghast (and angry) that this behaviour could have gone on in their society. And some of the young women in the class say Gillard's experience would be a disincentive to them considering a future in politics (see the chapter by Cull and Gardiner, page 145).

Finally, what about Gillard's departing expression of confidence in 2013 that it would 'be easier for the next woman and the woman after that and the woman after that': a faith she has reiterated since?[31] The number of women representatives across the Australian parliaments has increased over the past decade from 30.8 per cent to 37.0 per cent: a growth that ostensibly should improve the chances of women reaching leadership positions.[32] It is sobering to consider, however, that the two most likely candidates for the next female leader in federal politics – Julie Bishop and Tanya Plibersek – were either bypassed by their party (Bishop) or sidestepped the opportunity (Plibersek) when the possibility of their ascent presented. And neither is the drought of woman party leaders in Canberra confined to the major parties (leaving aside the eponymous Pauline Hanson's One Nation). The picture is brighter at the state level where two women premiers, one Liberal, Gladys Berejiklian, and one Labor, Annastacia Palaszczuk, have won re-election in the past two years. Yet we still seem to have trouble envisaging women as national leaders, let alone normalising it as a practice. The contrast with our trans-Tasman neighbour is stark. New Zealand recently re-elected its third woman prime minister, Jacinda Ardern (in a campaign in which both major party leaders were female), meaning that the country has been ruled by women for more than half of the past quarter of a century.

Nevertheless, my cautious answer to whether it will be easier for the next woman prime minister in Australia when she eventually does come along is yes. Not least because it is almost impossible to imagine that there could be anything quite like the same perfect storm of adversities that conspired against Gillard. The limited scholarly evidence about media representations of subsequent women leaders also indicates that they are not subject to the same negative preoccupation with their gender. A caveat is that this moderating effect may be diminished the longer the time that elapses between the first woman and the next.[33] Let's hope, then, that we don't have to wait for decades to pass before we have a woman prime-ministerial successor to Gillard.

'SHE JUST WON'T LIE DOWN AND DIE': GILLARD, MISOGYNY AND AUSTRALIAN POLITICAL LEADERSHIP

Mary Walsh

On 29 May 2012, Tony Abbott addressed a Coalition party meeting claiming he had no illusions about how hard it would be to win the federal election the following year, particularly after the Newspoll published that day showed Labor enjoyed a slight lead. He told his colleagues that their job would not be over until the next election and observed: 'Gillard won't lie down and die, and where there's life, there's fight.'[1] In this chapter, I take Abbott's phrase as a starting point to assess the leadership experience of former prime minister Julia Gillard. The phrase captures a relentless assault upon Gillard by opposition leader Tony Abbott, former prime minister Kevin Rudd, media commentators, including radio broadcaster Alan Jones, and everyday Australians emboldened by a climate of sexism and misogyny.

In an interview with Gillard, which took place six years after her prime ministership and just prior to the 2019 election, journalist Jacqueline Maley states, 'I am reminded of how many people, in the media and public life, ignored or explained away the sexism levelled against her at the time. I am reminded I was one of those people.'[2] Maley's article captures Gillard's dignity in not being the type of former prime minister that interjects in political debate or undermines her own party, something that Rudd, Abbott and Turnbull have all done:

I'd like to think people watch what I do and see dignity in how I've taken defeat, but my strongest motivation is not to have constant toxicity and poison in my own head. You know, I am not going to sit in my lounge room, sharpening an axe for Tony Abbott. No, I'm not.[3]

Around the same time in 2019, Judith Ireland wrote an article for the *Herald Sun* titled 'Can't win: Uneven balance for female leaders', which reflected on Labor's deputy leader Tanya Plibersek's decision not to run for the ALP leadership due to family responsibilities. The tone of this piece seems to imply that work/family balance is the problem facing women in leadership roles in Australian politics (see the chapter by Rowe and Alver, page 145). However, Gillard's tenure as prime minister demonstrates that the problem of female executive leadership in Australia is more complex than sexist attitudes and work/family balance. Sexism is discrimination based on a person's sex while, according to philosopher Kate Manne, misogyny is about controlling and punishing women who challenge male dominance.[4] It is not about male hostility or hatred towards women as is sometimes thought. Sexism and misogyny are not the same, and the difference matters because what Gillard experienced was not isolated cases of sexism but what appeared to be an exposition of entrenched misogyny in Australian politics that was designed to undermine the nation's first female prime minister. However, in the aftermath of Gillard's prime ministership, the issues of gender, sexism and misogyny remain largely unacknowledged, and this continuation means we are not progressing on key issues around women and political leadership in Australia.

Defending Gillard

As the chapter by Paul Strangio (page 36) also notes, Julia Gillard suffered relentless sexist-based attacks as prime minister, but the question of sexism did not really surface until towards the end of her tenure. It was unconsciously present but not publicly acknowledged by Gillard herself or Australian society more generally. In *My Story*, Gillard says 'of all the experiences I had as prime minister, gender is the hardest to explain, to catch, to quantify'.[5] Gillard made the point:

> When I became prime minister, I decided I would not campaign
> on being the first woman. It was so obvious it did not need
> constant reference. Having made that decision, I made a second
> decision – to tolerate all the sexist and gendered references and
> stereotyping, on the basis it was likely to swirl around for a while
> then peter out. I was wrong. It actually worsened.[6]

Support for Gillard during her time as prime minister was sparse. Outside Tony Windsor's defence of the Gillard government in parliament in mid-August 2012, Anne Summers' Newcastle essay, subsequently published in *The Misogyny Factor*,[7] and Jacqueline Kent's *Take Your Best Shot*,[8] little was published that defended Gillard's prime ministership. Having said that, I recognise efforts to acknowledge Gillard's legacy *after* her removal as prime minister. Her legacy has been promoted in conversations with Anne Summers in Sydney and the Victorian Women's Trust event in Melbourne. More recently, Blair Williams' work comparing Gillard and Turnbull's ascendency to the top job details how Gillard was portrayed in the media.[9] Alternatively, others have been less willing to explicitly defend her. Kerry Anne Walsh's *The Stalking of Julia Gillard* explicitly says, 'It's not a defence of Gillard',[10] while Michael Cooney's *The Gillard Project* states, 'I don't believe her record needs a defender'.[11] Where is the recognition that what happened to former prime minister Gillard should be a deep concern to all? Gillard deserves a defender. As she explains:

> The main analysis when I was prime minister was nothing that
> happened to me could be explained by gender, and if I ever
> said that, it was an illegitimate thing to say … the woman-card

argument ... now there is a general acceptance that there is this thing called sexism in politics and we have to think about it and we have to try to eradicate it.[12]

Gillard argues that the zeitgeist has caught up, and that things will be better for the second female prime minister. There is already, she suggests, a hint of this: 'Women and men come up to me and say they were so taken aback by it, they were sort of frozen into immobility and they're critical of themselves for not having done more.'[13] Gillard believes if it happened again, there would be a swarm of outrage, but I am doubtful. Her experience suggests that Australian political and executive leadership culture has entrenched sexism and misogyny, which constructs barriers for woman to be treated fairly.

Relentlessly attacking Gillard

Now I want to go back to Abbott's May 2012 comment that 'she just won't lie down and die'. In retrospect, the comment does not really capture the worst of the relentless attacks she endured. In fact, what it acknowledges is that that Gillard was under sustained attack yet would not yield. It also demonstrates Gillard's incredible resilience and strength. She never publicly complained and appeared to just get on with the job.

Throughout her prime ministership, these attacks persisted. During her tenure as prime minister, Gillard faced 150 publicly reported claims that her prime ministership would be brought to an end by a certain date or because of a certain event.[14] Perhaps most famously, at a carbon rally held in Canberra on 16 August 2011, protesters stood with a placard saying 'Ditch the Witch' and Gillard is 'Bob Brown's Bitch'. In August 2012, Gillard faced claims that she had been involved in a 'slush fund' with a 'previous boyfriend'. The story was published by Hedley Thomas on the front page of *The Australian*. Later that month, at an event with Liberal Party members, radio broadcaster and so-called 'shock jock' Alan Jones proclaimed Gillard is 'destroying the joint' and advocated throwing her out to sea. Shortly after Gillard's father died in September 2012, Jones attacked the prime minister again and remarked that her father had 'died of shame'.[15] In October 2012, Tony Abbott, in a comment regarding the appointment of Peter Slipper as Speaker, appeared to revisit these remarks when he told parliament that her government 'should already have died of shame'[16]. Abbott later claimed his remarks were not intended to be linked back to Jones's.[17] Nevertheless, by 9 October 2012, Gillard opened up in parliament to deliver her now infamous and unscripted 'Misogyny Speech'. As Gillard recalls:

> On this day, getting ready, I was fired up. I do not normally think in swearwords but my mind was shouting, *For fuck's sake, after all the shit I have put up with, now I have to listen to Abbott lecturing me on sexism. For fuck's sake!*[18]

The media coverage of the speech reveals a disjunction between what happened in parliament and how it was reported in the media. It also revealed the difference between how the Australian media reported the speech compared to international media coverage. In an October 2012 ABC *Media Watch* episode, it was observed that, 'The gallery, almost to a man and woman, focused upon the hypocrisy, as they saw it, of Julia Gillard attacking Tony Abbott for sexism while defending Slipper'. Yet, Gillard did not defend Slipper. Moreover, a decision on Slipper's Federal Court case had not been made. As Gillard said at the time, the parliament is not a kangaroo court. As it turned out, Slipper resigned of his own accord later that day. Moreover, it was Abbott who used the word misogyny first. This *Media Watch* episode did, however, highlight how Abbott was using his 'head kicker' proclivities – a description he earned while a minister in the Howard government – to enjoy what one commentator described as a 'spectacularly successful term as leader of the Opposition'.[19]

Another way to illustrate the relentlessness of the sustained attacks on former Prime Minister Gillard can be illustrated by what I refer to as 'a typical week in hell'. Monday had been part of the Queen's Birthday long weekend. On Tuesday 11 June 2013, Gillard gave the 'Blue Tie Speech' in her prime minister's address to 'Women for Gillard' where she mentioned the importance of the right to abortion for women: 'We don't want to live in an Australia where abortion becomes the plaything of men who think they know better'.[20] This was met with loud and outright condemnation by the opposition and the mainstream media, not for her statement on abortion, but for her reference to a government led by 'men in blue ties'. The next day, Wednesday 12 June 2013, the so-called 'Menu Gate' incident broke in the media. It was subsequently revealed that a menu item at a Liberal Party fundraiser event of Kentucky fried quail had been named after Gillard and referred to as 'small breasts, huge thighs and a big red box'.[21] The next day, a Perth radio host, Howard Sattler, asked Prime Minister Gillard, on air, if her partner Tim Mathieson was gay.

In late 2013, controversy surrounded Gillard for changes made by her government to the single parent pensions. The policy, which attracted a great deal of criticism and is often held up as a counterbalance to Gillard's appalling treatment, centred upon shifting single parents away from parenting payments onto Newstart. The move left single parents, mostly referred to as single mothers, with $60–$100 per week less and would save the government $728 million dollars over four years. At the time, Gillard said, 'I am going to stand up for it as a decision of the government I lead.'[22] Gillard claimed her government's motivation for the change stemmed from a 'grandfathered' class of women who received different benefits to other women due to earlier rule changes affecting the pension. As Gillard explained:

I formed the view that that was unfair and I felt we needed to have arrangements that facilitated and helped women get into work when their children were of an older age, which is ultimately better for them and better for their children.[23]

The media and public reaction to the government's decision in this case played out as a personal attack on Gillard as a woman for not protecting other women. This appears to be a double standard as male politicians are rarely personally criticised as men for policies that do not protect other men.

Double standards

Let's contrast this account with another high-profile Australian who has experienced sustained discrimination: AFL player Adam Goodes. Racism (especially between men) and the treatment of Adam Goodes has recently been taken seriously by the leadership in Australian sport. The documentary about Adam Goodes' struggle with racism – *The Final Quarter* – aired in Australia in July 2019. Another documentary about Goodes, *The Australian Dream*, aired in Australia in February 2020. These documentaries were in part a response to the racism Goodes and other Indigenous sportsmen had experienced from players, spectators and the sporting establishment throughout their careers. In 2013, Goodes was publicly called 'an ape' by a thirteen-year-old girl on the football field and subsequently endured being booed on field for weeks. Such experiences of racism negatively affected Goodes and he ended up leaving the game. In 2014, he was named 'Australian of the Year' in recognition of his leadership and dedication to the Indigenous community, and in 2015 he was described as a champion 'driven from the game he loved'. In an interview on *The Sunday Project* (14 July 2019), *The Final Quarter* director Ian Darling asked Australians to look again at what happened to Goodes 'with fresh eyes and an open heart'. He asks, 'How did Goodes survive the pressure? Why were so many Australians so fearful? ... When people say it's not about racism, they were wrong – it was racist.' In uttering these words, the director sought to ignite a serious and sober national conversation on racism, and was well supported by the AFL administration, sports players and sections of the media and public to do so. Yet there have been no equivalent efforts to encourage a national debate on sexism or misogyny, based on Julia Gillard's experiences as prime minister.

Racism and sexism have different historical, cultural and social origins and manifestations, but there are nonetheless lessons that may be learned from Goodes' experience. Perhaps the nation could similarly benefit from the initiation of a sober conversation about how gender-based discrimination impacts upon our leadership culture and reflects broader community attitudes that need to be addressed. Certainly, Gillard may have struggled to begin this discussion herself; she would have undoubtedly been accused of playing the 'gender card' and depicted as unable to handle the strains of office. This was evident with the aforementioned responses to her 'Misogyny Speech', which, while celebrated by many, was also seen by some as evidence of her supposedly incompetent leadership.

A contrast can be made with a man who – like Gillard – drew attention to institutional sexism. In 2013, then Chief of Army Lieutenant General David Morrison responded to a scandal in the Australian Defence Force that involved a group of 12 men (a self-proclaimed 'Jedi Council') who had shared on their work emails, without consent, images of a woman being filmed during sex. The group had also said all manner of vile things about women more generally. Morrison called out the sexist and unacceptable behaviours, making a three-minute video condemning the men and telling them there is no place in the defence force for this behaviour. The video was celebrated globally and he was lauded as a hero in addressing sexist cultures in the armed forces. In 2016 he was named Australian of the Year. Again, the institutional and community celebration of Morrison's impassioned response is vastly different from Gilliard's treatment.

While Gillard was subjected to horrendous sexism and appalling behaviour, I don't think her prime ministership can be understood through the lens of gender, sexism or misogyny alone. 'Gender' is an important aspect for understanding the ways in which Gillard was treated, but there are a range of other factors that worked in complex ways to bring down her prime ministership. As also noted in the previous chapter, these factors include being a progressive politician in Australia, media framings of Gillard having 'knifed' Rudd, the relentless negativity of Abbott and the opposition who felt 'robbed of government', the power of interest groups that opposed the carbon price and the Minerals Resource Rent Tax, the power of anti-Gillard commentators in the media and Kevin Rudd's simmering revenge. This latter point was not as obvious during Gillard's tenure, even though Rudd had attempted to take the leadership back three times during 2010–2013. This last factor was something that was more fully comprehended after 26 June 2013.[24]

To sum up, what Gillard experienced throughout her tenure as prime minister of Australia is beyond sexism: it is misogyny. The appalling treatment of Australia's first female prime minister, and how this amplifies the lived experience of female political and executive leaders, is deeply entrenched. In Australia, issues of discrimination in relations between men are given more credibility, as the cases of Adam Goodes and David Morrison reveal. Her treatment goes beyond the manner in which she assumed the position of prime minister, as the current revolving door of Australian prime ministers demonstrates.[25] Like Ian Darling, the director of *The Final Quarter*, I advocate that we look at what happened to Gillard during 2010–2013 'with fresh eyes and an open heart'. Something much more deep-rooted is afoot that cannot be reduced to simplistic, one-dimensional analysis.

JULIE BISHOP AND THE UNMAKING OF AN UNFEMINIST

Katrina Lee-Koo

Julie Bishop has been an enigmatic figure in Australian politics. As the nation's first female foreign minister (2013–2018) and former deputy leader of the Australian Liberal Party for over a decade (2007–2018), Julie Bishop has had an impressive political career, trailblazing a number of 'firsts' for women politicians. However, throughout her career she has shown a stubborn defiance of the feminist label. In 2014, when asked if she considered herself a feminist, she famously described it as 'not a term that I find particularly useful these days'.[1] Her resistance endured throughout her political career. Following her resignation, she continued to insist that labels were less valuable than actions. In March 2019, when asked if she felt comfortable describing herself as a feminist, she told *The Australian* newspaper: 'I prefer to be judged on what I do in pursuit of gender equality, rather than how I may self-describe.'[2]

The question of whether Julie Bishop is, or is not, a feminist is not the point of this chapter. As will be demonstrated below, she consistently pursued gender equality policies in her role as Minister for Foreign Affairs. She oversaw the introduction of measures that sought to free women around the world from violence, she worked to see women better represented and supported to participate in public life, and she directed – more so than comparable countries – Australian aid money towards women's economic empowerment. In fact, she placed Australia among the global leaders in pursuing pro-gender norms as part of its foreign policy. Certainly, arguments can be made about what kind of feminist she was throughout her political career (and whether or not she was an especially good or consistent one), but there is enough evidence to show the pursuit of a feminist agenda in her role as foreign minister.

While Julie Bishop supported women's empowerment on the global stage, she was comparatively less vocal on gender equality in her capacity as a member of the House of Representatives and as deputy leader of the Liberal Party. She occasionally lamented the lack of women in the cabinet and parliament more generally, but she was rarely an outspoken or vocal advocate of women's rights and leadership in Australia. Throughout most of her career, Bishop refused to acknowledge that she herself had experienced any gender-based discrimination or mistreatment, and she criticised former prime minister Julia Gillard's 2012 'Misogyny Speech' for 'playing the gender card'.[3] She is not a public supporter of quotas for women in politics, and throughout her career – even during her two years as Minister for Women under the Howard government (2006–2007) – she was not associated with gender equality activism. In fact, her advocacy of women's leadership in Australian politics was perhaps best shown through her own failed 2018 leadership challenge, where she clearly demonstrated her belief that women can, and should, hold the highest leadership office in the land.

Clearly, there is a disconnection here. This chapter explores how Julie Bishop's strident commitment to global gender equality ran parallel to her resistance to feminism in domestic politics. Furthermore, the chapter seeks to understand how – as a prominent woman in Australian politics – her domestic resistance to feminism shapes the nation's political leadership culture.

Julie Bishop, navigator:
Striking a bargain with patriarchy

In his recently published memoirs, former prime minister Malcolm Turnbull offered readers a frank reflection on the 2018 leadership spill that perhaps strikes at the heart of Julie Bishop's unsettling relationship with feminism. He said: 'There were too many people in the party room who wouldn't vote for Julie simply because she's a woman.'[4] This insight, if accurate, gives us a sense of what Bishop was up against within her own party. It provides some evidence that her rejection of the term 'feminist' was less about her personal political convictions than it was about her political navigation through conservative party room politics.

It further suggests that women's political survival in the Liberal Party room requires charting two inter-related courses. The first is careful navigation of the so-called gender double bind: women must demonstrate the capacity for masculinist notions of tough, impartial and strong leadership, but must do so within socially acceptable forms of (in this case) conservative femininity.[5] As foreign minister, Bishop managed this with precision. Staring down her opponents across the floor of the United Nations Security Council in her Armani suits and silver brooches, Bishop was the epitome of steely elegance. She was celebrated for her style and her poise as much as her work. Another way to think about it is that – for some – her legitimacy and success was tied to her gender performance as an elegant, professional, feminine woman. In his tribute to Julie Bishop at the end of her political career, Prime Minister Scott Morrison referred to her as 'classy', a woman with 'dignity', 'grace', and 'the best shoes in parliament'.[6] Such gendered language and focus upon personal style (rather than her achievements as a member of parliament) highlights the persistence of the gender double bind.

But while she was masterful in her manipulation of the gender double bind, she failed to successfully navigate the patriarchal bargain that she had entered into. The patriarchal bargain describes circumstances where women advance within a system on the often-unspoken understanding that they do not unduly disrupt male power and privilege. Turkish–British gender researcher Deniz Kandi-yoti describes it as when women understand the different patriarchal 'rules of the game', and 'strategize [to maximise options] within a set of concrete constraints'.[7] Bishop no doubt believes that she fulfilled her end of the bargain: she worked diligently and only seemed to strengthen the Liberal Party's brand. Within her party she deftly nav-igated party room politics to serve as deputy to leaders with divergent policy ideals (moderate Brendan Nelson, socially conservative Tony Abbott and socially progressive Malcolm Turnbull). Within domestic politics, she was not outspoken on gender issues in ways that would embarrass or disrupt male dominance. As a reward, she was allowed to advance within the party and win the widespread respect and broad affection of the electorate. But her bid for party leadership was, as it turned out, well outside the terms of the patriarchal bargain.

Julie Bishop, Foreign Minister: An advocate for global gender equality

Upon Julie Bishop's resignation as Australia's first female foreign min-ister, she was widely celebrated by her colleagues across the partisan divide. Prime Minister Malcolm Turnbull described her as 'Australia's finest foreign minister'.[8] She was also acknowledged for her trailblaz-ing role as the first woman to hold the traditionally masculine port-folio, with Liberal Party colleague Simon Birmingham calling her 'the most significant woman in the history of the Liberal Party'.[9] Even her political opponents acknowledged Bishop's impact on Australian politics. As Shadow Minister for Foreign Affairs Penny Wong put it:

> While Labor has at times been critical of the foreign policy
> directions under prime ministers Abbott and Turnbull,
> Ms Bishop's commitment to standing up for Australia both

here and abroad has never been in question. In particular I have deeply appreciated her commitment to bipartisanship, and her personal courtesy to me.[10]

Such accolades and positive reviews of her performance were focused upon her stewardship of Australia through numerous crises during her tenure as foreign minister. These included the ongoing conflicts in Afghanistan and Iraq, her diplomacy in the rising tensions over the South China Sea, her management of the early years of the Trump presidency, the amalgamation of AusAID (Australia's aid agency) into the Department of Foreign Affairs and Trade (DFAT), Australia's candidacy and election as a temporary member of the Human Rights Council, the second year of Australia's temporary UN Security Council seat, and her departmental management in the face of the successive cuts to the aid budget.

She is perhaps most celebrated for her repeated calls for an international investigation into the downing of Malaysian airlines flight MH17 over Ukraine in 2014. This tragedy killed over 280 passengers, 38 of whom were Australian, and Bishop was lauded for her management of Russian President Vladimir Putin, her ability to build an international coalition of support for a collective response, and her performance in the UN Security Council as she sought access to the crash site, and a process for justice.[11] The strength of her leadership was celebrated in newspaper headlines. *The Guardian* led, on 30 July 2015, with 'MH17: Julie Bishop Savages Russia for Vetoing UN Tribunal Proposal', while journalist Michelle Grattan reported 'Julie Bishop shows the boys how it's done' with a veiled reference to prime minister Tony Abbott's hollow threats to 'shirtfront' Putin at the 2014 G20 summit.[12] Similarly, her persistent diplomatic efforts to stay the execution of two Australian citizens found guilty of drug smuggling in Indonesia in 2015 affirmed her ability to take on regional strongmen, with her repeated appeals to President Joko Widodo for mercy.

Less celebrated in the tributes that followed her resignation, however, was her strident commitment to global gender equality in the foreign, aid and development programs. In line with those states, such as Sweden and Canada, which have loudly proclaimed a feminist foreign policy, Bishop oversaw a much quieter integration of pro-gender equality norms into policy platforms. This emerged as a consistent goal, evident across a number of aid and development policy documents that were released in 2014 and 2015. These include the 2014 'Making Performance Count', which focused upon ensuring effectiveness in aid and development spending, and the 2015 'Gender Equality and Women's Empowerment Strategy', which outlines the strategies for gender equality within the department and in its policies. Collectively, Bishop oversaw a robust commitment to 'integrate gender equality and women's empowerment into Australia's foreign policy'.[13] Under her leadership, gender equality became one of the six investment priorities of the aid program. In a National Press Club speech in June 2014 on the new aid paradigm, she described gender equality as 'perhaps the most important priority and one that is a personal passion'.[14]

As part of these policies, Bishop announced that 'over 50 per cent of our aid initiatives are directed towards women' with aid programming to focus upon three pillars: women's leadership, women's economic empowerment and addressing violence against women.[15] In defending this strategy in the 2015–2016 Appropriation Bill, she stated: 'Gender equality contributes to growth, development and stability. When women are able to actively participate in the economy and in community decision-making, everybody benefits.' Similarly, both documents make a commitment to mainstreaming gender equality principles across the aid program: 'more than 80 per cent of investments, regardless of their objectives, will effectively address gender issues in their implementation'.[16] To monitor this, all aid investments are assessed annually and 'at least 80 per cent of these investments will need to demonstrate real progress in addressing gender issues'.[17] This is a significant commitment to global gender equality. It is arguably as strong, or stronger, than that made by self-proclaimed feminist

Prime Minister Justin Trudeau in Canada's 2017 'Feminist International Assistance Policy'.[18]

Alongside these policy announcements we also saw a small, but significant, policy pivot in 2017 when, for the first time, a Foreign Policy White Paper made a commitment to gender equality as being in Australia's national interest. Up until that point, the issue of women's rights or gender equality had not been a consideration in white papers, which serve as Australia's premier strategic foreign policy doctrine. However, the only one produced during Bishop's tenure as foreign minister states that 'Australia's foreign policy pursues the empowerment of women as a top priority' and names gender equality alongside 'political, economic and religious freedom, liberal democracy, the rule of law, racial … equality and mutual respect' as a core national value.[19]

Here, it is worth highlighting that Bishop's agitation for gender equality was carefully scripted within the boundaries of the broader national interest. It was not promoted as part of a feminist agenda as has been the case in Sweden, Canada and elsewhere. Instead, the foreign minister built a case that gender equality was 'the smart thing to do' in service of the national interest. For instance, the aforementioned White Paper states: 'We promote gender equality because eliminating gender disparities in the region would significantly boost per capita incomes.'[20] Indeed, a close reading of Bishop's prominent foreign policy speeches finds that gender equality was always framed as a vehicle to pursue the national interest: it was a means to an end and not an end in itself. For many feminists, the linking of gender equality to neoliberal futures is problematic; so too is the instrumentalising of gender equality in service of the national interest. However, for the purpose of this chapter, the key point is the existence of these policies and the substance of the commitment, which represents an important foreign policy shift.

Bishop's ongoing commitment to gender equality within the foreign affairs portfolio did not, however, feature in mainstream assessments of her performance following her resignation. In fact, throughout her time in the portfolio, there appears to have been no public discussion of her ambitions to position Australia as one of the global leaders in advancing gender equality in its foreign policy. On this issue, the mainstream media and her colleagues were silent. Her committed advancements of global gender equality went under the domestic radar.

Julie Bishop, Liberal MP: Fulfilling the patriarchal bargain

In her domestic political performances, however, Julie Bishop was much less brazen in her promotion of gender equality. She appears to have struck an unspoken patriarchal bargain with those within her party. While she remained popular in the electorate, she could advance within the party and hold senior leadership positions, but she could not fundamentally upset the gendered order by publicly calling out or challenging sexist behaviour. Consequently, as previously noted, she never publicly declared herself to be a feminist, never 'complained' that she had experienced any kind of gender-based discrimination in the workplace, and she remained evasive about any domestic political issue that appeared to disruptively agitate on the issue. She seldom spoke publicly about gender issues in the parliament, the party room (as far as we know) or the broader electorate.

Bishop is, of course, not the first female politician to resist being labelled a feminist. In particular, the term has proved far from desirable for many prominent conservative women politicians. The current Minister for Women, and Foreign Affairs and Trade, Senator Marise Payne, once commented that she became a feminist at age one, but since achieving a high profile in the Coalition government, has shied away from the term.[21] Former Minister for Women, Senator Michaelia Cash, told the *Sydney Morning Herald* in 2014 that she also does not like labels. 'In terms of feminism', she said, 'I've never been someone who really associates with that movement. That movement was a set of ideologies from many, many decades ago now.'[22] Former Liberal MP and Speaker of the House Bronwyn Bishop also told a girls' school on International Women's Day in 2015: 'No, I don't consider myself a feminist, I consider myself an individual Australian.'[23] Alternatively, former Liberal Party prime minister Tony Abbott is a self-declared feminist.[24] Like his colleagues, he sees feminism as something needed in the past – not in this era where women, according to him, have smashed the glass ceilings in Australia.

When questioned in 2014, Julie Bishop disagreed with the idea that conservative women tended to reject the term because it was seen as progressive. What, therefore, drives the unwillingness for ambitious women to adopt a concept that advocates for their empowerment and equality? Arguably, resistance to the term may be driven by a belief that such an admission will lock women political leaders out of both the corridors of power and public sympathy. This social distancing from feminism is a problem not just for feminism, but for women politicians, and for the nation's politics more broadly. It undermines the country's ability to have meaningful national conversations about gender-based discrimination, inequality and violence in our society.

This was perhaps best demonstrated in the fallout surrounding Labor prime minister Julie Gillard's 'Misogyny Speech' in the parliament in 2012. In a comment directed at opposition leader Tony Abbott following his call for her to sack house Speaker Peter Slipper, Gillard famously told parliament that Abbott would lecture neither her nor her government on sexism and misogyny. The speech went viral around the world, with many adopting it as a rally cry to call out sexism in politics. In Australia, it ignited a heated debate that was fuelled by discussions regarding both the experiences and the number of women in politics.

The political fallout of the speech was polarising. On the one hand, commenters including the *Sydney Morning Herald's* Peter Hartcher described Gillard's judgment as 'flawed' and the speech as resulting in 'a serious loss of credibility'[25] while Anne Summers writing for the ABC celebrated her 'passion' as 'exhilarating' and 'electrifying'.[26]

Julie Bishop's response was harshly critical of Gillard. She accused her of presenting herself as a victim, of playing the so-called gender card, and of being a poor role model to others. She argued that Gillard used the speech as a means of deflecting debate away from her incompetence and poor leadership. She said: 'She was a woman who became the Prime Minister of Australia. She was no shrinking violet. She was no victim of a glass ceiling. She reached the highest position in public life and she was complaining about sexism.'[27] Bishop appeared incredulous at the thought that a female prime minister might experience sexism in the workplace. 'Yet those outside Canberra', she continued, 'outside Australia, probably took it at face value and thought it was factually correct and that she was portraying herself as a victim of rampant sexism, whereas I believe her motive was to deflect criticisms of her leadership.'[28] This was one of the few times that Bishop spoke publicly on domestic issues of sexism, and her response was to be critical of the woman who called it out.

In her denial of sexism and misogyny, Bishop upheld her end of the patriarchal bargain. She backed her prime minister and the patriarchal order he presided over. This appeared to come unstuck, however, when, at arguably the height of her popularity, she nominated for party leader (and consequently prime minister) in the August 2018 leadership spill. Despite her profile and popularity among Australians – a Roy Morgan poll taken the week of the spill found that she was best placed to beat then-Labor leader Bill Shorten at the 2019 federal election – Bishop secured only 11 out of the possible 85 party room votes. Declaring that she was 'Turnbull in a skirt', Tony Abbott's former chief adviser Peta Credlin claimed that Bishop was too close to Turnbull to be a credible option. Others pointed to her lack of presence on the parliament's floor, and her apparent unpopularity within her own party. The spectacular failure in her bid to be Australia's second female prime minister precipitated Bishop's exit from politics within six months.

However, speculation also turned to her gender as a contributing factor. The *Sydney Morning Herald's* Peter Hartcher posited:

Yet consider this proposition. The Liberal leadership is vacant. The party's deputy leader of 11 years contests the leadership. He is a man. He's served five years as a highly successful foreign affairs minister. He's by far the most popular candidate. Could you imagine that he would not win the ballot? Of course you can't.[29]

Arguably, Bishop had overplayed her hand, and the patriarchal bargain was now in tatters on the floor. Recognising this, Bishop came clean. As it turned out, the Liberal Party and federal politics – according to Bishop – was not free from sexism. In fact, it was quite the opposite. In a flurry of outbursts and resignations, a number of notable female Liberal Party MPs spoke out about their experiences following the spill, citing bullying behaviours, sexism, and toxic work cultures. Liberal Party colleagues Julia Banks, Kelly O'Dwyer and Lucy Gichuhi joined ranks to speak openly about the negative experiences that they had had within the Liberal Party and politics more broadly.[30]

Bishop was especially vocal. In the month following her failed leadership bid and decision to leave politics, she admitted and outlined the depth and breadth of sexism she had experienced. She noted: 'I have seen and witnessed and experienced some appalling behaviour in parliament, the kind of behaviour that 20 years ago when I was managing partner of a law firm of 200 employees I would never have accepted.'[31] In a number of interviews since her resignation, Bishop has highlighted negative experiences she's had that she believes to be rooted in gender politics. These include being overlooked and undervalued for her contributions, being spoken over, being stereotyped, and enduring sexist comments and attitudes. She famously noted that when Tony Abbott appointed himself Minister for Women – at a time when she was the only woman in the cabinet – 'it was quite clear that we have some way to go'.[32] She further noted that it was unacceptable that less than 25 per cent of Liberal Party MPs were women and argued that 'when a feisty, amazing woman like Julia Banks says this environment is not for me, don't say "toughen up princess", say "enough is enough"'.[33]

At this point, Bishop had clearly shredded her copy of the patriarchal bargain. While her star was on the rise, Bishop maintained her end of the bargain – she kept quiet about the 'appalling behaviour' she saw in her ranks and instead criticised other women who called it out. But following her failed leadership attempt, she was no longer prepared to protect male privilege. But what did this delayed decision cost Australia and its political leadership culture?

A sympathetic reading of Bishop's political career might argue that she had little choice: a vocal and strident female 'disrupter' would not advance in Australia's conservative party (for evidence of this, read James Walter's chapter on Peta Credlin, page 69). Bishop understood the 'rules of the game' and played by them. But the problem with the patriarchal bargain is that not only does it maintain the patterns of discrimination that exist, it also legitimates them. While in office, Bishop publicly denied the presence of sexism in her party and, through her rise, appeared to demonstrate that women could make it 'on merit'. But in doing so she reified the culture and arguably made it difficult for other women to legitimately call it out while remaining in politics. In a 2019 International Women's Day speech in Hobart, Bishop said that she was aware that women in senior leadership roles 'have a responsibility to make it easier, not harder for other women to follow in their footsteps'.[34] While in some ways she did make it easier (she was apparently pivotal in ensuring she was replaced in her foreign affairs portfolio with another woman, Senator Marise Payne), in other ways she made it harder for women to challenge the discriminatory elements of political leadership and for the nation, more broadly, to have serious and sober conversations on the gendered politics of Australia's political leadership culture.

Julie Bishop's political career is therefore something of a paradox when it comes to her troubled engagement with feminism. On the one hand, her actions as foreign minister demonstrate her commitment to gender equality. She embedded pro-gender norms within the structures of Australia's foreign affairs department and policies. Meanwhile, she deftly navigated the domestic patriarchal order by rejecting feminism and denying the presence of gender inequality. But this strategy worked only to a point, as she appeared to hit the Liberal Party's glass ceiling. Ultimately, this is a cautionary tale. Patriarchal bargains that are struck by women seeking to advance or even just survive within gendered orders are fraught with danger. This is because they protect and keep hidden the discriminatory cultures that by design exclude women. While some individual women may successfully navigate this, the broader culture remains untouched. As she left office, Julie Bishop was part of a small group of men and women who began to open the lid on this culture and challenge it publicly. However, there is undoubtedly more work to do before we reach the point where – to borrow from Julia Gillard's final speech as prime minister – the nation can have a sophisticated conversation about the gender politics of executive political leadership.

PETA CREDLIN AND THE 'RIGHT' ARTICULATION OF GENDERED RAGE

James Walter

Liberal democratic institutions were founded on the presumption that the political arena was a male domain. Political rights (such as the rights to vote, or to stand for election) were initially vested in men, and while the struggle to gain the right of political engagement for the other 50 per cent of the population has incrementally advanced, the residual tradition of political conflict demanding manly attributes is deep-rooted. Efficient leaders are expected to be tough, decisive and aggressive: qualities conventionally regarded as masculine. Majoritarian systems, in which winning parties gain all the spoils of office and business is conducted as government *versus* opposition, heighten adversarial approaches to the settlement of political issues.[1]

Over recent decades, there has been an intensification of partisanship as mass parties (whose positions were tempered by broad membership) have become professionalised, with small, unrepresentative and more assertive membership bases. Recent analysis of dispositions along the spectrum, from party voter to party member, party professional or elected politician, shows that at each step the pool becomes increasingly *less* representative of the general population in experience, views and demands.[2] The inner, most activist, circle is committed to leaders who will fight tenaciously for their cause. Each of these developments amplifies the tendency of political activists to engage in a hard-ball, take-no-prisoners approach to their work. Conditions are ripe for tribalism and a warrior culture.

These trends have accentuated the 'double bind' facing women in politics: namely, women have to demonstrate 'male' virtues to be taken seriously in leading roles by colleagues, but risk offending traditional 'feminine' expectations (and diminishing their broader support) by doing so. Where women do gain political traction, it is often in portfolios such as health, social services or education, which appear more aligned to 'womanly' nurturing values: care, compassion and being oriented towards people. Such values also seem to gain more credence in collectively oriented 'progressive' parties. Nonetheless, on neither side of the Australian political divide can the 'double bind' be discounted, as the fraught career of the nation's first female prime minister, Julia Gillard, demonstrates.[3] However, the task demands particular finesse in parties of the right that have many socially conservative members. Traditionally, these parties have been leader dominated and hence more prone to the 'warrior' disposition rather than being philosophically inclined.

Margaret Thatcher: Unsung feminist heroine?

Consider a woman who surmounted such challenges: Margaret Thatcher, British Conservative prime minister (1979–1990). Thatcher also served in 'caring' portfolios, as Undersecretary at the Ministry of Pensions and National Insurance during Harold Macmillan's administration, and then as Education Secretary in Edward Heath's Cabinet. But her approach was tough, decisive, non-consultative and counter to progressive trends: she reined in commitments to comprehensive schooling, supported market forces influencing research funding, and enforced a Treasury suggestion to achieve spending restraint by abolishing free milk for children in primary schools. It was a foretaste of the individualising, free-market, small government agenda her government would drive. Determination, decision and readiness to crush those who disagreed won Thatcher support in her party and eventually party leadership.[4]

As prime minister, Thatcher was even more dominating, and said to terrify those in her cabinet who were not already adulatory. Over a decade, her centralisation of executive authority and an uncompromising neoliberal agenda that emphasised its (masculine) competitive principles changed Britain's political temper decisively. In the public realm, international events also played into her hands. She was a combative ally of other 'strong men' of her era and soon a leading voice in international crusades against regimes seen as enemies of individual freedom. When Argentina attempted to seize the British-held Falkland Islands in 1982, it precipitated a war in which Thatcher performed as the central agent and that Britain won. Her masculinisation and 'warrior' leadership now reached its apogee: she concluded a celebratory postwar dinner with her generals, at which she was the only woman (spouses were kept waiting for post-dinner drinks elsewhere), saying, 'Gentlemen, shall we join the ladies?'[5]

Thatcher would, however, learn the perils of a style that won many battles but created enemies. When another controversial policy, a poll tax, caused public sentiment to shift strongly against Thatcher, her opponents within the party seized their chance to argue that the Conservatives could not win again under her, and she lost the leadership. A tirade of gendered abuse was unleashed, from feminists for her betrayal of women's causes, and from others for allegedly prioritising her career over her husband and children. Yet, in showing how power might be seized and exercised in a male-dominated realm, she arguably normalised female success. To the surprise of the feminist mainstream, Natasha Walter called her an unsung feminist heroine.[6]

Peta Credlin:
The female 'warrior' in Australian politics

There has been no elected female politician in Australia with whom one might compare Thatcher. Despite the backlash provoked when she ousted Kevin Rudd to assume the prime ministership, Julia Gillard was not habitually confrontational, did not routinely set about crushing opponents, had a gift for building working relationships and was a Coalition and consensus builder in sustaining a progressive legislative agenda in a minority government.[7] She was the obverse of Thatcher, and a person feminists were proud to claim (despite Gillard never defining herself in such terms). Coalition governments had long promoted able women into the ministry, but did nothing effective to address the continuing gender disparity among their representatives. Nonetheless, in the 1970s it was a Liberal Party senator, Margaret Guilfoyle, who was the first woman to hold a cabinet-level portfolio in Australia, first as minister for education, then social security, and finally finance. She was dubbed the 'Iron Butterfly' by the media, due to her discipline, cool nerve and style, but despite being a key member of the Fraser Coalition government's 'razor gang' in the 1980s, she contributed to an enlargement of government activity in areas such as childcare. The combination of (masculine) toughness and resolve along with (feminine) social concern, compassion, elegance and style allowed Guilfoyle to be seen as a serious player among her male colleagues, yet without compromising traditional gender expectations.[8] It was a model for Australian conservative women, but it was not the Thatcher way.

The Australian woman who best exemplifies the 'political warrior' style was not an elected politician, but a political insider credited with significant influence in conservative political circles: Peta Credlin.[9] Former prime minister, Tony Abbott, with whom she served in both opposition and in government, described her as 'the smartest and fiercest political warrior I have ever worked with'.[10] Such a designation, from a notably aggressive and confrontational leader, placed

Credlin at an extreme on the spectrum of women adopting masculine modes of behaviour for political purposes. It provoked predictable criticism from those committed to conventional expectations of gender-appropriate behaviour.[11]

Credlin was highly attuned to the nature of Liberal Party politics. In 2002, she married Brian Loughnane, who was appointed Federal Director of the Liberal Party in 2003 and served in that position until 2016. Between 1999 and 2015, Credlin worked in the offices of senior parliamentary Liberal Party figures, including those of successive party leaders Brendan Nelson and Malcolm Turnbull, before her appointment as Chief of Staff (COS) in Tony Abbott's office when he ousted Turnbull in 2009. Her ability to sustain her position in successive leadership teams, despite the intra-party conflict attending each transition, demonstrated great dexterity. Her experience and relationships gave her unusual reach into both the party organisation and the parliamentary domain.

Abbott performed remarkably as opposition leader, targeting a handful of areas in which the government was vulnerable to populist attack – the failure to control 'illegal immigration' (asylum seekers), carbon pricing as a tax that would supposedly destroy enterprise and jobs, and budget deficits – and pursuing them relentlessly. This contributed to Kevin Rudd's ouster and wore down the credibility of Gillard's minority government. Abbott himself indicated that Credlin, described by political commentator David Marr as 'a one-woman politics and policy machine', was integral in developing this strategy. Credlin, at the heart of the campaign, described herself as the 'Queen of No', and Abbott called her 'the *force majeure*'.[12] The strategy was vindicated: Abbott destroyed two prime ministers on the path to power, and gained the sobriquet 'Dr No'. On winning the 2013 election, Abbott lauded Credlin as his partner in this success.

The pattern continued in government, as Credlin made the Prime Minister's Office (PMO) the command centre of Abbott's regime.[13] She was not only the prime minister's chief adviser, but closer to Abbott than any of his ministers. She controlled access, directed the wider ministerial staff (and could veto appointments), ensured discipline, sat in on meetings of the leadership group and of cabinet and was always on call in the parliamentary chamber when Abbott was present. It was her judgment that determined when ministers, public servants, MPs and lobbyists could see the prime minister, and the questions that needed to be satisfied before they did so. In most instances she was tough but respectful, capable of considerable charm. But she was impatient with those who were ill-prepared or not sufficiently attentive to the dictates of the PMO, not above reprimanding and criticising those who were not performing, whatever their station, and was seen publicly berating and arguing with ministers, including members of the leadership group. Her intimidating mien and readiness to vent her anger when crossed were public knowledge. While she never spoke publicly in her own voice, one account suggested that insiders treated her as the prime minister's proxy, and it was a factor that media representations amplified.[14]

Nevertheless, Credlin was good at her job, at maintaining tight organisation, and focus – not least with Abbott himself. Abbott, it became apparent, was reliant upon her, insistent on her accompanying him on his travels, and anxious when she was not immediately at hand. It was said that in private he called her 'the boss'. Her gender was an asset: 'It gave her licence to take liberties with Abbott that no man could have. She treated him like an ill-disciplined best friend she had taken under her wing.'[15] Yet by reinforcing his combative partisanship, and supporting him even when party allies raised concerns, Credlin's PMO provided no bulwark against Abbott's own limitations. He was a warrior preoccupied with the next battle, but he could not build a coherent team or a policy framework attuned to the complexities of contemporary challenges.[16]

Abbott and Credlin:
The downfall of 'warriors'?

As opinion turned against Abbott and his administration, the centrality of his relationship with Credlin became a target. There was concern that an unelected individual had gained such influence and power that it undermined democratic principles. Other comments were quite scurrilous. Significantly, such criticism was voiced not only by the opposition but also among ministers. Abbott's response was to tell them they would not have been in government without Credlin.[17] But that Credlin attracted more media opprobrium than any prior COS on record could not be ignored.

In the aftermath of Abbott's deposition by Malcolm Turnbull, when Credlin also resigned, analysts explained the ill-fated administration as a product of the power duo that had seemed so invincible in opposition but ill-suited to government.[18] A persuasive article by Katrina Lee-Koo and Maria Maley compared Julie Bishop and Peta Credlin in relation to metaphorical models of the 'Iron Butterfly' and the 'Political Warrior'. They argued that Bishop, the 'Iron Butterfly' – tough, diligent, a strong voice, but consultative – was 'the "good girl" of the Liberal Party who works hard, works within the system, cooperates and does not challenge gender boundaries in an unacceptable manner'. Credlin, in comparison, was 'the "bad girl" whose ambition was too raw, approach too assertive, and use of power too unsettling for the conservative political order'.[19]

They concluded that Bishop successfully adopted the 'Iron Butterfly' model, with its 'long heritage in Australian conservative politics [of] … a non-disruptive modulation of anger, compassion, power and feminine identity', while Credlin 'deliberately flouted gender norms, challenged the status quo and combatively confronted the gender power order. The savage reaction to her behaviour, and its element of moral outrage, signifies her violation of deeply held gender norms'.[20]

Certainly Bishop was an important figure in the Coalition government, outlasted Credlin (with whom her relationship was said to be toxic) and won plaudits for her stabilising influence as deputy leader and diplomacy as foreign minister. But Bishop's defeat in the 2018 contest for party leadership triggered by alpha male Peter Dutton's challenge against Malcolm Turnbull, suggests the limitations of this model of success. Bishop was thought by former allies incapable of winning against the strong men of the party and in the forthcoming election campaign, despite being the most popular of all contestants. And it prompts one to think further about what Credlin's confrontation of the gender power order reveals.

Consider, again, the characteristics Thatcher displayed. She was highly attuned to a male-dominated order, and saw exactly how to gain leverage within it by 'joining' the men – and the same can be said of Credlin. Thatcher, like Credlin, harnessed powerful male allies, yet Thatcher's imperious control of her male associates, and Credlin's metaphorically taking Abbott 'under her wing', speak volumes about their management of such partnerships. Opposition provoked Thatcher's contempt and anger; Credlin was often represented as an 'angry woman'. Each crushed their critics. Thatcher was relentlessly ideological in promoting her cause, as was Credlin. Thatcher created many enemies, who would eventually bring her down. Compare with this the tide of acrimony Credlin also provoked. Nevertheless, it was by these means that Thatcher not only achieved many of her own ambitions, but changed the political landscape. Here, perhaps, one might conclude that their paths diverge. Abbott's failure was Credlin's failure too.

Yet to accept this may be to misconstrue the nature of Credlin's ambition. She may have chosen the ministerial staffer route as the quickest means of ascent into the inner circle where, even if she could not speak in her own voice, her influence could prove critical in what was to be done. And having exhausted those possibilities, she sought a new platform: 'I want to move on with my life and do something where I get my own voice.'[21] For her, the battle is far from over, and now she *can* speak in her own voice as the *diva* of, and a 'thought leader' on, *Sky News*. Direct political engagement is one path to achieving what one believes to be socially desirable, but changing the way a meaningful proportion of people think is another. 'Thought leaders', US political professor and commentator Daniel Drezner argues, 'develop their own singular lens to explain the world, and then proselytize that worldview to anyone within earshot.' While public intellectuals traffic in complexity and criticism, thought leaders burst with the evangelist's desire to 'change the world'. Moreover, the right has made significant gains in this sphere.[22] Credlin has leapt from one realm of political influence to another.

Medusa's legacy

The difficulty in coming to terms with figures like Credlin, for those intent on changing the nature of the gender power order itself, is that neither the 'Iron Butterfly' nor the Political Warrior model alters politics as a domain where masculine behaviours prevail – even if, as feminist writer and activist Natasha Walter argued, women who succeed in gaining power and influence within it normalise conceptions of women in leading roles. Rather, these might be thought instances of achieving the symbolic power that cultural theorist Angela McRobbie deems 'post-feminist', replacing feminism 'with competition, ambition, meritocracy ... and the rise of the "alpha girl"'.[23] Still, there is more to be said about the way female assertion is both transformational and yet demonised in cases like that of Credlin, and even Thatcher. These were women who would not let anyone, let alone men, get in the way of what they thought was needed. Credlin's anger was, and is still, directed against the 'authority' of (sanctimonious) progressives on the left and within her own party, and those who are thought to be dominant in cultural and educational institutions. Yet men who adopt these familiar tropes in promoting 'cultural rage' are not subject to the degree of acrimony directed at Credlin.[24] The reason may be that she has triggered a complex that has its origins deep within Western culture, and is metaphorically rendered in the myth of Medusa.

Medusa and the reformulation of women's anger

I turn your face around! It is my face.
That frozen rage is what I must explore–
Oh secret, self-enclosed, and ravaged place!
This is the gift I thank Medusa for.
(May Sartor)[25]

Medusa, in Greek legend a fearsome Gorgon woman with snakes for hair, whose gaze turned onlookers to stone, was decapitated by Perseus, but even the severed head petrified those who saw it. Athena, goddess of war (hence *uber* political warrior), had the image of Medusa on her shield. Over many centuries, Medusa became the go-to figure for those seeking to belittle and demonise assertive women (monsters who did not know their place). Others, however, saw the power implied by the myth. Sigmund Freud, in a brief essay, argued that the fear of Medusa (that is, the potential of assertive women) was that the monster 'froze' or rendered impotent the (male) observer – an implicit threat to masculine models of power.[26] Feminist writer Hélène Cixous' much-cited essay, 'The Laugh of Medusa', has been read as a call to arms for women to reclaim their identity by acknowledging their rage (against patriarchal constraint) and turning it against society's internal prohibitions and voices of authority.[27] Doing so would enable them to laugh at the constrictions of gender: 'Women have wept a great deal ... but once the tears are shed, there will be endless laughter instead ... And her first laugh is at herself.'[28]

Cixous' essay precipitated ongoing debate in psychoanalytic and feminist circles about women accepting their anger and acting on what it was telling them.[29] In addition, works that captured a wider audience – novels (e.g. Fay Weldon, *The Fat Woman's Joke*, 1967, and *The Life and Loves of a She Devil*, 1983), bestseller polemics (e.g. Harriet Lerner, *The Dance of Anger*, 1985) and even poetry such as that quoted above – celebrated female rage and the disruption generated by 'unruly women' as weapons of social change and political power. The argument has not only continued, but intensified, with the popularity of recent novels (from the angry women of Elena Ferrante's Naples to the raging anti-heroine of Gillian Flynn's *Gone Girl*, 2012), works of non-fiction (such as Brittney Cooper's *Eloquent Rage*, 2018) and performance art (such as Hannah Gadsby's Netflix sensation, *Nanette*, 2018) – all of which have been amplified by the #MeToo movement.[30]

Credlin: An unruly woman

Few would claim Credlin for the feminist cause, although she has spoken about the forms of gendered discrimination she encountered in politics, and she has attempted to encourage the Liberal Party to address the gender disparity in its ranks.[31] Credlin was heedless of the norms of gender-appropriate behaviour, surely a form of challenging the conventional gender order (the laugh of Medusa). Rather than seeing her as unable to control her anger (emotional laxity as a 'woman's problem'), she was arguably adept at mobilising rage (think of the image of Medusa cowing opponents).

It would be a mistake to subsume Credlin's rage against authorities as merely an element in the cultural war of the right against what they see as the march of the left through social institutions. Undoubtedly, it feeds into that battle, but with the added complexity that she is clearly a woman whose anger is directed against anyone – and they are mostly men – who would seek to frustrate or demean her ambitions. It accords with political scientist Harold Lasswell's famous proposition that powerful political activism may be driven by the suppression and projection of deeply personal impulses onto public causes.[32] Thus, the frustrations of a clever woman of conservative disposition, but implicitly subject to gender constraints, may find an outlet for action (in joining the men) and public expression (in the cultural rage of the right) against the supposed leftist impositions on individual action and enterprise.

Credlin certainly figures as an 'unruly woman' given to disruptive activity – it was crucial to Abbott's success in opposition, though less so in influencing governmental practice. Within Abbott's leadership regime, for around six years (in opposition as well as government) she exercised a degree of control that affronted many influential men and rendered them (politically) impotent. A striking image of Abbott in defeat is one of Credlin leading him away from the lectern though crowds of reporters: he was finished, but she would march on ahead into her own media niche, to speak in her own voice. Her story is not yet over.

One need not agree with Credlin's politics, nor conclude that she is a feminist heroine, but it should be acknowledged that she presents an example of how female agency can be exercised that – in scorning conventions of gender-appropriate behaviour – can achieve powerful influence and resist the impositions within which women are expected to work. Laughing off suggestions that she was intimidating, she remarked:

> If you're a cabinet minister or a journalist and you're intimidated by the chief of staff to the prime minister, maybe you don't deserve your job … If I was a guy I wouldn't be bossy, I'd be strong. If I was a guy I wouldn't be a micromanager, I'd be across my brief, or across the detail. If I wasn't strong, determined, controlling (and got them into government from opposition I might add), then I would be weak and not up to it and should have to go and could be replaced.
>
> So, it's very binary when it comes to women.[33]

That she was pilloried for her methods, her unstinting commitment to the warrior mode, was irrelevant. She gave politics her best shot, and then moved on, remarking that, 'No career goes in a straight line and I think it's really important for women that if you hit a period where resilience and stress is required then we don't give in'.[34] Political editor Katharine Murphy, an acute observer, remarked that Credlin left politics 'refusing to shrink, rolling on, stoking her own mythology like a little sustaining campfire, owning a persona she invented for a purpose, refusing to defer'.[35] It is this – owning a persona invented for a purpose, recognising that careers are not linear, scorning conventional impositions, and refusing to defer – that is Credlin's most important message to women in politics.

II
INSTITUTIONS
AND STRUCTURES

THE POWERS AND PERILS OF WOMEN IN MINISTERS' OFFICES

Maria Maley

On days when federal parliament is sitting in Canberra, the foyer of Parliament House is full of besuited young men striding briskly across the marble floors. These are the political advisers sometimes derided as 'the boy scouts' in ministers' offices. Yet they provide a false picture of Australia's political staff. The minister's office is an important site of power in Australian politics, and many of the political staff wielding that power are women. Australian women are more likely to be found working in ministers' offices than as MPs in federal parliament or as ministers in the cabinet. Australian parliaments are spaces dominated by men, yet historically, the minister's office is a space heavily populated by women. In many ways, the position of political adviser is an easier place for women to gain access to power in Australia's political system. However, they also face strong limitations on the power they wield and can find themselves subject to gendered tropes and expectations. While the subsidiary nature of the political adviser role conforms to traditional gender role expectations for women, the role can also be subject to harsh gender-based scrutiny.

Women in ministers' offices

Australian ministers' offices today are large, influential and politicised; over 440 ministerial staff worked for federal ministers in February 2020.[1] Historically, women have been strongly present in Australian ministers' offices, usually outnumbering men. In studies conducted in the 1970s and the early 1980s, the proportion of all staff in ministers' offices who were female ranged from 59 per cent to 66 per cent.[2] However, they were mainly found in administrative roles such as assistant private secretaries, receptionists, diary managers, typists and office managers. It is important to distinguish administrative staff from those who provide political and policy advice to ministers. These advisory staff today have titles such as assistant adviser, adviser, senior adviser and chief of staff, and they are the focus of this chapter.

More than 30 years after the original studies, data was collected on 1275 ministerial staff who worked in federal ministers' offices in 2010, 2013, 2014 and 2017.[3] It shows that there are now almost equal numbers of men and women employed in ministers' offices, but women still dominate the administrative positions (over 90 per cent are female). Overall, women comprised 52 per cent of media staff and 43 per cent of the advisory staff. This presents a significant increase compared to earlier studies: women comprised only 15–16 per cent of advisory staff in the 1970s and 20 per cent of advisory staff in the early 1980s.[4] The highest position in a minister's office is the chief of staff. In his research, Walter found no offices were headed by women in 1981 and only 8.6 per cent of these top positions were held by women in 1983.[5] Today, women occupy more than 35 per cent of chief of staff positions.

Table 1 shows that women are present in large numbers in the positions involved in policy and political decision-making in ministers' offices, and this is true of both Labor and Coalition governments. They now represent 40–47 per cent of all advisory staff and between 35–45 per cent of the powerful chiefs of staff. In comparison, women comprised only 37 per cent of federal parliamentarians and just

26 per cent of cabinet in 2020.[6] Table 1 also shows that there was a sizeable group of women working in key advisory positions close to decision-makers in the period 2010–2017. In each year studied, they were a cohort of around 80–100 people.

TABLE 1

Female advisers and chiefs of staff in four governments 2010–2017

	2010 Labor	2013 Labor	2014 Coalition	2017 Coalition
Number of all staff				
Advisers#	189	172	191	212
Chiefs of staff*	33	31	31	33
Percentage who were women				
Advisers	47.1	42.4	40.8	44.3
Chiefs of staff	36.4	35.5	45.2	39.4
Number of female advisers and chiefs of staff	101	84	92	107

These staff have the following titles: assistant adviser, adviser, senior adviser, principal adviser, research officer, policy adviser, senior policy adviser, chief economist, deputy chief of staff.

*These staff have the title chief of staff, which is the top position in a minister's office.

Tony Abbott's 'Amazons'

It is notable that in 2014, over 45 per cent of ministers' offices were headed by a female chief of staff, the highest rate ever (see Table 1). In October 2013, as the newly elected Coalition parties were forming government, the *Daily Telegraph*'s headline announced 'Abbott's Amazons to Steer Coalition', explaining that 'Prime Minister Tony Abbott has hired a crack team of female political warriors to spearhead the Coalition's reform agenda and manage his most senior colleagues'.[7] There are several possible reasons for the high proportion of female chiefs of staff in 2014. Political staff were recruited *en masse* at the start of the new government, and appointments were vetted by a high-level committee (the Government Staffing Committee) dominated by Abbott's chief of staff Peta Credlin, who is the subject of focus in the previous chapter by James Walter. It was said she had a 'tight grip on appointments' through this 'star chamber'.[8] A female chief of staff employed at this time reported that Credlin set the bar high for chiefs of staff and sought experienced and mature people, many of whom were 'formidable' women: 'She was a big promoter of women. She was looking for quality. She wasn't prepared to use party hacks.'[9] Many of the female chiefs of staff recruited at this time were senior public servants or experienced political staffers who had worked for ministers in the Howard government (1996–2007). Except when a new government is formed, opportunities for recruitment to ministers' offices are intermittent; winning a position is often based on personal contacts, political loyalties and advantageous timing. But it appears that when recruitment is more deliberative, and prioritises experience, women can reach the most senior staff positions in almost equal numbers to men.

Among staffers, power is concentrated in the offices of cabinet ministers and, especially, in the Prime Minister's office.[10] Women were well-represented in these positions of influence: more than one-third of the chiefs of staff to cabinet ministers in the 2010–2017 dataset were women (35.2 per cent). At times they headed the most important offices, such as those of the ministers of finance, defence and foreign affairs, prime minister and deputy prime minister. In the outer tier of the ministry, women were chiefs of staff to junior ministers, parliamentary secretaries and assistant ministers in almost equal numbers to men (48.7 per cent).

At the apex of power, there are many women working as advisers in prime ministers' offices. Women occupied 43 per cent of all advisory positions for the prime ministers in the 2010–2017 study (Kevin Rudd, Julia Gillard, Tony Abbott and Malcolm Turnbull), ranging from a low of 35 per cent for Abbott to a high of 54.5 per cent under

Turnbull. Four of our last six prime ministers employed a woman as one of their closest and most trusted advisers: Nicole Feely (chief of staff to John Howard 1996–1997); Amanda Lampe (chief of staff to Julia Gillard 2010–2011); Peta Credlin (chief of staff to Tony Abbott 2013–2015); and Sally Cray (principal private secretary to Malcolm Turnbull 2015–2018).

While women now occupy advisory positions in almost equal numbers to men and can reach the topmost positions, they remain under-represented as chiefs of staff. This may be because the conditions of work are difficult. One former staffer described her job this way: 'the hours were long, the demands never-ending, the stress phenomenal, and the fear of stuffing up overwhelming'.[11] Such intensity and long hours are not family-friendly conditions. The age profile of political advisers in the study shows that female advisers tended to be younger than their male counterparts. The data shows that fewer women take up these jobs after 30, while men keep working in ministers' offices into their 40s and beyond. At ages when men are recruited to chief of staff positions, women may find the hours do not suit family responsibilities.

Work as a political adviser requires both traditionally masculine and traditionally feminine skills. The milieu of the ministerial wing in Canberra is combative, cut-throat, hostile and competitive.[12] Tony Abbott's chief of staff Peta Credlin described Parliament House as 'the toughest, most masculine, most exclusionary place'[13]. For some, aggression is part of the job. John Howard's chief of staff Nicole Feely described herself as 'the battering ram' and said 'I've had my head kicked in by some of the best'[14]. The work of political staff often involves contest with others and the raw exercise of power, warrior behaviour traditionally associated with masculinity.[15] However, it also involves alliance-building and persuasion, as relationship management is at the core of the job. To be successful, political staff need street-fighting skills but also communication and interpersonal skills. These 'softer' skills are traditionally associated with the female gender role.

The powers of female advisers: Hidden power players

Ministerial advisers in Australia can be very influential in policy making. They manage ministers' relationships with departments, stakeholders and other ministers, and they can play key roles in cabinet decision-making processes. The most powerful offices (especially the prime minister's office) can be decisive in negotiations, resolving disputes and exerting authority over other offices to help ministers coordinate and make collective decisions.[16] Yet while ministers' offices are increasingly powerful, they remain hidden from the public eye. Ministers refer to their 'private office' and their 'personal staff', and the names of advisers are not published or referred to in parliament. Their shadowy existence and unaccountable power are a source of great concern in Australian politics.[17]

The backstage nature of the political adviser role in Australia gives women a certain freedom of action not enjoyed by female politicians. The hidden nature of their influence and actions means that female advisers are less likely to provoke public outrage for acts of dominance or combative behaviour that transgress expectations of women's gender roles. Their power-seeking and power-wielding behaviour, which is so problematic for women in political life, is screened from public and media scrutiny since they are not public actors.[18] The careful negotiation of the gender double bind that is required of female politicians – where they must be seen as tough enough for the political sphere while maintaining their feminine legitimacy – is a tightrope that female political staff usually do not have to walk in public.[19] Being hidden from public view, the minister's office is a space where women may assume powerful roles in political life, free from the scrutiny and criticism often faced by female parliamentarians.

For women, there are both advantages and disadvantages in the adviser role. Working as a political adviser provides an opportunity to move close to centres of political power without the long, hard road of seeking preselection, winning a seat in parliament and doing time on the backbench before ultimately reaching a ministerial position. Along the way, women ministers face institutional barriers inside their parties and the harsh scrutiny of the media. The status of advisers as auxiliaries to powerful actors resonates with the traditional female role of the hand maiden – an assistant who plays a subsidiary role to the principal, sublimating her own ambitions to advance the interests of the power holder. The supporting and ancillary role of the ministerial adviser means that women can occupy these roles without disrupting traditional power relations.

Yet while the job of political staffer may represent an easier route to power than seeking public office, there are limitations on the powers that staffers can wield. Australian ministers cannot legally delegate their powers to political staff; under the *Members of Parliament (Staff) Act* 1984, advisers may only act as agents of the minister. They are the surrogates of power holders and do not possess their own legitimate power. Key advisers in the most powerful ministers' offices do, however, have considerable authority over others and often operate autonomously from their principals.[20] Yet this behaviour is in tension with their status as agents and auxiliaries. If their power-wielding comes under the public spotlight, female advisers can find themselves in a perilous position.

The perils of female advisers: 'Never become the story'

A successful political adviser in Australia is one who remains in the background and does not become the subject of media stories. If an adviser does move from backstage to centre stage, they can be judged harshly, and this can involve gender-based criticism. When female political advisers become the focus of political events, it is often a sign they have transgressed gender role expectations. This can be seen in the case of Peta Credlin, Prime Minister Tony Abbott's chief of staff from 2013–2015.

A survey of media coverage over 20 years (1995–2015) found that Peta Credlin attracted more media attention than any previous chief of staff and that media commentary about her was far more negative than positive or neutral.[21] Internal criticism from ministers, MPs and other staffers leaked into the public domain where she was pilloried for her 'command and control' style[22] and her 'uncompromising pugnacity'.[23] Tony Abbott praised her as 'the smartest and the fiercest political warrior I have ever worked with'.[24] Yet her political warrior approach violated feminine norms of conduct, which prescribe communal and caring behaviour.[25] Political scientists Elizabeth Gidengil and Joanna Everitt found that displays of combative behaviour by women in politics are seen as more newsworthy, attract greater attention and are reported negatively, because they violate these gender norms.[26] Credlin's behaviour involved a double norm break: her political warrior approach violated gender norms – attracting media attention – and she was also criticised for becoming the story, breaking the norm that political staff should remain in the shadows.

Credlin's position was difficult: she faced intense media attention, which she did not seek, and she could not control the way she was portrayed. While often accused of leaking stories to the media during her period as the prime minister's chief of staff, she never spoke on the record. As a political adviser, Credlin had no public voice with which to craft her image. Not a political figure in her own right, she was unable to control public perceptions of her as a woman, as female politicians might do. They often are able to skilfully deflect criticism and modulate their performance of femininity on the 'tough and tender' range. Credlin's political voicelessness left others free to write her dissonant gender performance.

Peta Credlin was not the first female political staffer to face scrutiny and criticism for her use of power. In 1968, Liberal prime minister John Gorton scandalised his critics when he appointed 21-year-old Ainsley Gotto as his principal private secretary. She was the first female principal private secretary of an Australian prime minister. She attracted intense media attention and was one of the most talked about people in Australia at the time.[27] When appointed, she was described as 'pert, freckled and bubbling with self-confidence' and photographed cradling a kitten.[28] The media mainly focused on her youth and physical appearance and questioned her legitimacy as a young woman occupying a position so close to power. When Minister for Defence Dudley Erwin was sacked by Gorton, Erwin accused her of being responsible for his demotion: 'The political manoeuvre used to get me out of office wiggles, it's shapely, and its name is Ainsley Gotto.'[29] He also claimed she was 'cold blooded' and 'ruled with a ruthless authority' in controlling communications with the prime minister.[30] After Gorton resigned, one headline read: 'PM listened to girl more than to his cabinet'.[31]

Handmaidens or 'swallowers of virile men'?

One of the strongest criticisms Peta Credlin faced was that she inverted the proper power relations between a minister and their chief of staff. She was criticised for being Abbott's alter ego rather than his assistant, exceeding the power a political staffer should wield. The media reported that Abbott, in private, called Credlin 'the boss'[32] and that MPs believed 'she could make him do or not do pretty much everything'.[33] Powerful staffers, in close and co-dependent relationships with ministers, are not unusual.[34] But this dynamic is problematic for female political staff as their power can be seen as diminishing their male principal, and even emasculating them. It touches on deeply rooted cultural fears of women devouring men's strength. Instead of being 'loyal handmaidens', powerful female staff can become, in the words of historian Simon Schama, 'swallowers of virile men'. Schama suggests the ancient myth of Delilah (who cuts off Samson's hair, robbing him of his power) is difficult to transcend and haunts Western cultures even today.[35] When there were calls for Credlin to be sacked, Tony Abbott's loyalty in defending her was seen as evidence of his weakness and dependence, and her power over him. Similar dynamics were at play in 2018–2019 when a female adviser to aged care minister Ken Wyatt was accused of bullying and 'inappropriate influence' over him. When he allegedly threatened to quit parliament to protect her, this seemed to prove his excessive dependence.[36] In this way, subordinate women may appear to threaten established hierarchies when a powerful man is overly dependent on them.

'Affairs' and affairs

Both Ainsley Gotto and Peta Credlin also faced persistent rumours that they were having affairs with the prime ministers they worked for. There is no evidence of the affairs, and it is not scuttlebutt that male chiefs of staff would encounter. These rumours suggest there is a deep suspicion that the power female advisers wield stems from their sexual identities. The sexuality of female political staff can be perceived as threatening to the political and social order.

When deputy prime minister and treasurer Jim Cairns appointed 41-year-old Junie Morosi to head his ministerial office in December 1974, a scandal immediately erupted. Questions were raised about her suitability for the role, her looks and her relationship with Cairns. Though they denied it, they were accused of having an affair (both were married). There was a storm of sensationalist media coverage; it splashed across newspapers as a 'bombshell sex story'. A press gallery journalist of the time recalled that Morosi was 'a stunning beauty, slender, with beautiful black hair – in short, a knockout … The media could not get enough of the yarn'.[37] The media attention was relentless, with strong sexual overtones, and the scandal was even given a name: 'the Morosi Affair'. In parliament, Cairns defended her appointment as principal private secretary:

> I am quite satisfied that Miss Morosi is a person of very
> considerable ability, character and integrity … I suggest to
> honourable members that if I had chosen a man or even a
> woman who was not good looking, perhaps nothing would
> have happened.[38]

Morosi was also unsettling because of her ideas: she held radical ideas about women's rights and sexual politics, and had strongly influenced Cairns' thinking about these issues. Whitlam's speech writer Graham Freudenberg concluded: 'she was the most disturbing thing – a woman with influence'.[39] Rather than back down and sack Morosi, as he was urged to, Cairns went on the front foot and they appeared frequently in the media. Morosi's attempts to speak publicly to correct misrepresentations and promote her ideas were seen as mistaken, and only fed the media frenzy. Some argue the Morosi Affair contributed to Cairns' eventual dismissal from office six months later and, along with the Loans Affair, to the eventual fall of the Whitlam government.[40]

The 'bonk ban'

In 2018, sexual relationships between ministers and their staff hit the media spotlight when it was revealed that deputy prime minister Barnaby Joyce had been having an affair with his 33-year-old media adviser, Vikki Campion, while he was married. The affair was undeniable – she was now carrying his child. Prime minister Malcom Turnbull reacted angrily to the story, speaking of

> the terrible hurt and humiliation that Barnaby, by his conduct, has visited on his wife Natalie and their daughters and indeed, his new partner. Barnaby made a shocking error of judgement in having an affair with a young woman working in his office. In doing so he has set off a world of woe for those women, and appalled all of us. Our hearts go out to them.[41]

The prime minister moved immediately to rewrite the Statement of Ministerial Standards to ban sexual relationships between ministers and their staff in what came to be known as the 'Bonk Ban'. The ministerial code now makes it clear: 'Ministers must not engage in sexual relations with their staff. Doing so will constitute a breach of this code'.

Turnbull's moral outrage was directed towards the male minister involved, and he portrayed the wives and families as victims: 'Ministers should be very conscious that their spouses and children sacrifice a great deal so they can carry on their political career. Their families deserve honour and respect.' He also framed female advisers as the victims of such consensual sexual relationships. Turnbull criticised 'the culture of this place', stressing the need to create 'workplaces where women are respected'. He stated: 'I think many women who work in this building understand very powerfully what I am saying.'[42] In contrast to the way Junie Morosi was portrayed in the 1970s, moral judgments of Vikki Campion were muted. Instead of being demonised, she was infantilised as a 'victim' of the affair.

Turnbull's comments allude to the reality that young female advisers are vulnerable to sexual harassment and bullying, and this problem has a long history. Elizabeth Reid, who was appointed Gough Whitlam's women's adviser in 1973, recently recalled her experience of an unwanted sexual advance by the (then) governor-general.[43] In 2019, two female advisers complained that their reports of sexual assault in the workplace received little support from the Liberal Party, with the expectation the women would remain loyally silent.[44]

While Malcolm Turnbull's language cast female staffers as victims in their consensual sexual relationships with ministers, in another sense the Bonk Ban can be seen as a way of controlling the possibly disruptive power of women's sexuality. Monica Lewinsky, whose affair with US President Bill Clinton while she was a young intern almost destroyed his presidency, has complained that she was portrayed as a temptress who initiated the affair, rather than it being a mutual relationship.[45] Young women are, today, numerous in ministers' offices and many work closely with their ministers. At a deep level, female staffers can be seen as possibly threatening the social order in their ability to lure powerful men away from their wives and families. The boundaries that the Bonk Ban sets can therefore be seen as designed to protect men as much as their female staffers. As well as shielding young women, it is also a way to control women's behaviour.

Shedding light on the hidden world of the Australian ministerial office reveals that women are found in significant numbers in policy and political adviser positions, almost reaching parity with men. Even though they are still under-represented as chiefs of staff, they lead more than one-third of ministers' offices.

For women, the position of ministerial adviser offers a pathway to power and opportunities to exercise influence without the intense scrutiny of the public gaze. It allows them to avoid the barriers and hurdles women often face in seeking political office. Their backroom role gives them a freedom of action not enjoyed by female politicians. They can be hidden power players who are less constrained by gender norms than women in the public eye. However, their power is formally limited and practically perilous. If they do move into public view, they can find themselves subject to unwanted attention and strong criticism for not adhering to norms of feminine behaviour; for wielding power and for transgressing the boundaries of the loyal handmaiden role. As advisers, they have no public voice with which to craft their public image. They can find themselves subject to moral outrage and deep suspicion. A powerful woman in a close inter-dependent relationship with a male principal can evoke deep-seated fears about female power over men and the threat posed by female sexuality to the social order. At these times, they can be seen as disruptive figures who need to be controlled.

THE POLITICAL PARTIES: THE GENDERED POLITICS OF PRESELECTION PROCESSES

Narelle Miragliotta and Anika Gauja

The representation of women in Australian parliaments fares poorly by international standards. In 2019, just under 30 per cent of House of Representative seats were held by women. Although an historic high for the lower house of the Australian parliament, this ranks Australia only at 50th of 191 nations – well behind comparable states such as New Zealand, the United Kingdom, France, Italy and Scandinavian countries.[1] Political parties are a key element in this story of chronic under-representation. In Australia, parties are essentially the gatekeepers to public office due to the prominent role they play in elections. While there are some independent members of parliament, to have a realistic chance of gaining political office, an aspiring politician must be endorsed by a political party to run as its official candidate. Political parties also serve as training grounds for future leaders, and are important institutions in socialising political elites. While this creates opportunities and pathways for entry into legislative office, it also creates impediments. Globally, a persistent barrier for women is that political parties disproportionately nominate male candidates.[2]

In this chapter, we examine the extent to which Australian political parties perpetuate the systemic under-representation of women, reinforcing the gendered nature of political leadership. In particular, we focus on the mechanism of candidate selection, which is the primary way in which parties facilitate the election of women to parliament and foster the political careers of future leaders. Analysing new data compiled from Australian federal elections from the House of Representatives from 2007 to 2019, we examine party-based representation and selection, assessing the differences between political parties and trends that have emerged over time in the nomination of women to different types of seats. In doing so, we engage directly with two of the key questions that guide the analysis in this collection: How does gender politics govern access to political leadership? And how does gender shape organisational cultures? We find that women continue to be under-represented as party candidates for the federal parliament. While the Australian Labor Party has achieved some gains in promoting gender equality, the preselection practices of the Liberal Party and other conservative/right parties continue to perpetuate the systemic under-representation of women in the legislature.

Political parties, gender and candidate selection

Events leading up to the 2019 federal election once again high-lighted some of the gender politics that underscores partisan political culture in Australia. Three high-profile Liberal women resigned from the parliament – Julie Bishop, Kelly O'Dwyer and Julia Banks – amid allegations of bullying in the party.[3] More recently, Victorian Labor President Hutch Hussein has called on party members to call out bullying and support women who have launched complaints of sexual harassment within the party.[4] Both major parties are aware of this negative culture, with comments from former prime minister Malcolm Turnbull exemplifying the issue:

> The Liberal party does have a women's problem in the sense that we do not have enough women in parliament. And it is one that the party is acutely aware of … I am a very, very strong critic of

the culture in Australian politics … the culture with respect to women and with respect for women and attitudes to women in Australian politics is more like the corporate world in the 1980s, maybe a bit earlier.[5]

As several studies of Australian partisan politics have shown, this culture has been notoriously difficult to shift. This has been due – in part – to the gendered norms that permeate adversarial politics and parliamentary debate, the operation of party factions, the traditional influence of unions, a lack of institutional rules to support women and/or critical actors to champion their cause, and a disparity between men and women in the resources (time and money) required to enter into politics.[6] The problem is also reflected in the institutions and processes of candidate selection, which are uniquely controlled by political parties and determine entry into the parliament. The actions of parties can either perpetuate – or alter – norms of gender representation.

Gender and partisan representation in the Australian Parliament

In order to understand the gendered role of political parties in governing access to leadership, it is necessary to examine the long-term pattern of representation in the Australian parliament. The data presented in Figure 1 displays the percentage of women in parliament following each federal election between 1943 and 2019.[7] Three points are worth making. The first is that women did not win seats in parliament until 1943, even though they gained the right to contest federal elections in 1902. The second is that for the first four decades following the election of the first women to parliament, the number elected remained chronically low, with extended periods of time when the House of Representatives did not include a single female representative. Even when women became a more permanent physical presence within the national parliament, they remained a scarce

FIGURE 1

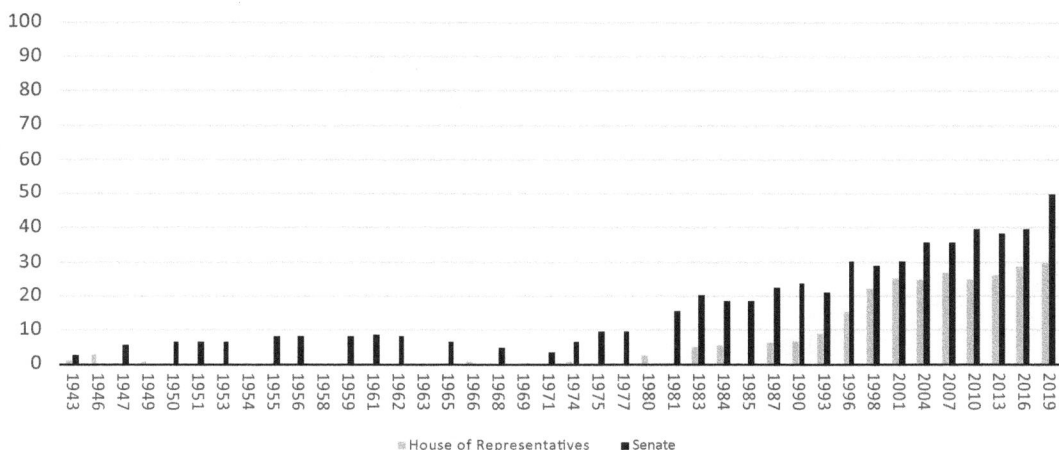

House of Representatives ▪ Senate

presence, consistently occupying fewer than 10 per cent of seats until the 1980s. It has only been since the 2000s that the number of women in either house have reached 30 per cent of the total. The third point of note is that women have generally achieved higher levels of representation in the Senate compared to the House of Representatives. This trend is reflective of the proportional representation electoral system used to elect senators – which differs from that used for the House of Representatives – and which research has shown advantages women.[8] Following the 2019 federal election, women attained representational parity with men in the Senate, while in the House of Representatives, the proportion of women in the 151-strong chamber remained at only 30 per cent.

While Figure 1 presents a vivid picture of the under-representation of women in the national parliament, this data does not reveal a great deal about women's interest in pursuing a career in legislative politics. In order to better understand women's efforts to gain entry to parliament, we now turn to data on electoral candidates.

Table 2 provides data on women candidates from the five most recent elections – 2007, 2010, 2013, 2016 and 2019. The data shows

TABLE 2

Women candidates for the Australian Parliament (2007–2019)

	House of Representatives			Elected as proportion of nomination		Senate			Elected as proportion of nomination	
	Total candidates	Women candidates	Women elected	*Male*	*Female*	Total candidates	Women candidates	Women elected	*Male*	*Female*
	n	%	%	%	%	*n*	%	%	%	%
2019	1056	32 n=341	30 n=45	7	12	458	39 n=178	52.5 n=21	7	12
2016	994	31.3 n= 312	29 n=43	10	15	631	36 n=228	45 n=34	10	15
2013	1188	28 n=327	26 n=38	7	9	529	27 n=143	33 n=13	7	9
2010	849	27 n=230	25 n=36	10	14	349	35 n=123	42.5 n=17	10	14
2007	1054	26 n=272	27 n=40	11	11	367	37 n=135	37.5 n=15	11	11

SOURCE Calculated from AEC data (2007–2019)

that women are significantly less likely than their male counterparts to contest elections. Of the total number of candidates who nominated over the last five federal elections, women made up 29 per cent of the field for the House of Representatives and 35 per cent of all Senate nominees. While women were a minority of candidates, they were – on average – more competitive than their male counterparts. In 2019, for example, women were almost twice as likely to be elected as men – with 12 per cent of women candidates elected compared to 7 per cent of male candidates. Although the number of women who nominate to contest elections is low, those who run for election seem to enjoy stronger prospects for success than male candidates. This finding corroborates international research that has shown women perform just as well as men during general elections and are not discriminated against by voters.[9]

'Gatekeepers' to public office: The role of parties

The dynamics of candidate nomination are closely connected to the preselection practices of political parties. As noted earlier, parties are the 'gatekeepers' to legislative office.[10] Elections are typically contests waged between party candidates, with non-aligned and independent candidates a comparatively small numerical presence. Australian political parties vary in the way they select their candidates (between parties and even within parties, across different states and for different houses of parliament). Cross and Gauja note that there are three main ways in which candidates are selected: by a vote of local party members, by a central party committee, or by a combination of the two methods.[11] There is some debate as to which of these methods is most favourable to women,[12] but the key point to note is that irrespective of who decides, candidate selection is an intra-party matter. Given parties' control over the selection of candidates for election (preselection), it is instructive to examine the patterns of preselection by first exploring variation in gender nomination by party family type.

To do this, we have sorted 26 Australian parties into six broad but established categories of party family types that share similar (but not identical) organisational instincts and ideational preferences. We include a mix of major and minor parties in the analysis, selected because they satisfied one or more of the following criteria: contested a significant number of seats, have a track record of contesting elections, managed to elect at least one candidate, and/or have achieved more than 4 per cent of the primary vote. The categories are:

- Anti-establishment: Australia First Party, Fraser Anning's Party, Katter's Australian Party, One Nation, Rise Up Australia Party and United Australia Party/Palmer United Party.
- Socially conservative: Australian Christians, Christian Democratic Party, Citizens Electoral Council and Family First.
- Mainstream right: Liberal Party, National/Liberal National Party and Liberal Democrats.

- Centrists: Centre Alliance/XEN, Derryn Hinch's Justice Party, Reason Party/Australian Sex Party.
- Green/Progressive: Animal Justice Party, Australian Democrats and the Australian Greens.
- Social democratic/Left: Australia Labor Party, Democratic Labour Party, Socialist Alliance and Socialist Equality Party.

A party's 'family' is a useful lens to examine the gendered dynamics of candidate nominations because party ideology and party organisation are known to impact nomination outcomes for women.[13] Some party families are more receptive to women candidates, as most acutely reflected in their adoption of (or failure to adopt) gender quotas.[14] Social democratic and progressive parties are more likely to have quotas for women, while right-tending parties, and anti-establishment parties especially, are often hostile to the use of quotas, preferring strictly merit-based selection of candidates. At best, parties on the political right rely on in-house women's networks to recruit women to stand, leading to frequently poor nomination outcomes for female aspirants. Labor, for example, first established quotas for the preselection of women in 1994, and in 2015 revised the target to 50 per cent of all elected representatives by 2025. The Liberals, by contrast, rely on training seminars, mock presentations, assistance in developing campaign material and public speaking training to promote female candidates.[15]

Figure 2 shows the proportion of women candidates who nominated for a House of Representatives seat. In order to even out differences in the number of candidates selected by individual parties within each of the six categories, the data is presented as an average of the proportion of female candidates by party, as against the total number of female candidates per family type.

Although the graph presents descriptive aggregate data, it does point in the direction of the assumed relationship between party

FIGURE 2

Percentage of women candidates for the House of Representatives by party family,
2007–2019

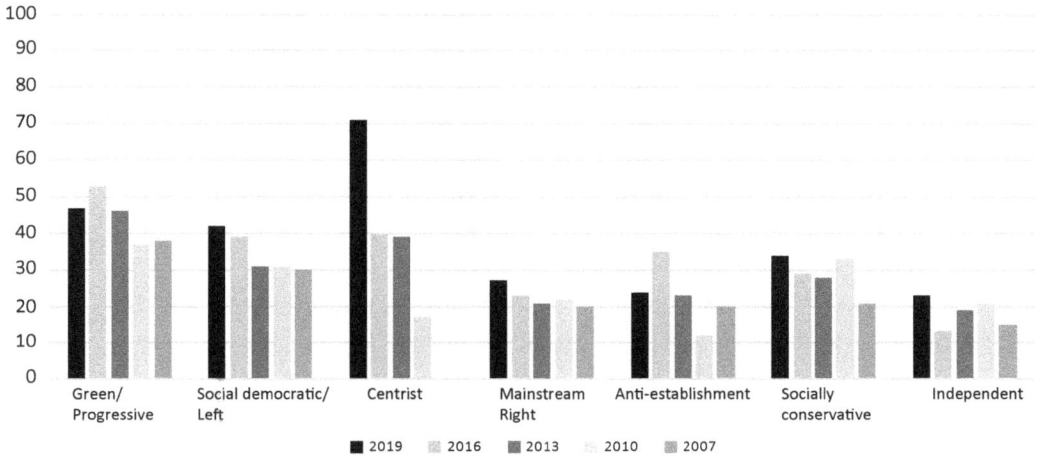

SOURCE AEC election data (nominations by gender)

family type and gendered nomination outcomes. Essentially, parties on the left and those on the more progressive end of the ideological spectrum, such as the Greens, consistently nominated more women candidates. In contrast, parties located on the right of the ideological divide tend to select far fewer women candidates, especially mainstream right-tending parties. Other Australian and international comparative studies have also showed this trend in recruitment.[16]

One factor that might affect our findings is that the parties that make up our sample vary significantly in their size, resourcing, and electoral and legislative prospects. This, in turn, is likely to have implications for a party's capacity to recruit women nominees and even the party's attractiveness to women candidates interested in electoral or legislative politics.

The Labor and Liberal parties

In Australia, the two largest and best resourced party vehicles for facilitating the election of candidates to parliament are Labor and the Liberals. These parties typically field the largest number of candidates, dominate the contest for House of Representatives and Senate seats, and win the vast majority of all seats (see Table 3). It follows that these parties are likely to be among the most attractive destination for women keen to pursue a legislative career, and they are worthy of further, more focused analysis.

Given that Labor and the Liberals are electorally dominant, their recruitment practices and preselection outcomes are particularly important for shedding light on women's prospects for gaining entry into parliament. The number of women candidates nominated by these parties, and the seats or vacancies that female candidates are selected to contest, is critical to the final gender composition of parliament.

We begin by examining the nomination outcomes of the two parties for the Senate. The first finding to draw attention to is the combined total of women on the parties' state and territory Senate tickets over the five election periods we surveyed. Table 3 shows that Labor has a more consistent record of returning tickets, which contain more or less equal numbers of women, demonstrating the effectiveness of Labor's quota system. In contrast, women candidates on the Liberal's Senate tickets typically make up only a third of all candidates.

A more pointed indicator of parties' commitment to the election of women to the Senate is to examine the placement of women on the party's state and territory tickets. Under the proportional representational system used to elect senators, parties submit a ranked list of candidates in the order in which they expect these candidates will be elected. The order in which candidates are listed on the parties' ballot papers largely determines whether the candidate will secure election. The safest position on the voting ticket is the number 1 placement, although both parties easily elect their second named candidate on

TABLE 3

Candidate distribution in Labor and Liberal Senate tickets

	Labor				Liberals[+]			
	All candidates (n)	Women candidates (%)	Number 1 position (%)	Winnable* position on the ticket (%)	All candidates (n)	Women candidates (%)	Number 1 position on ticket (%)	Winnable position on ticket (%)
2019	38	55 n=21	50 n=4	63 n=5	31	45 n=14	50 n=4	25 n=2
2016	49	55 n=27	50 n=4	50 n=4	50	38 n=19	13 n=1	13 n=1
2013	31	42 n=13	50 n=4	63 n=5	33	36 n=12	13 n=1	13 n=1
2010	29	48 n=14	38 n=3	50 n=4	31	32 n=10	25 n=2	13 n=1
2007	27	56 n=15	50 n=4	63 n=5	33	33 n=11	13 n=1	13 n=1

SOURCE AEC election data

+ Here, Liberals refers to those tickets that contained the Liberal Party label, even when the party is running a joint ticket with the National Party or, as in the case of Queensland, the Party contests as the Liberal National Party. It further includes the Country Liberal Party.

*Winnable position is defined as two women in the top three positions on the party's state ticket in a half Senate election, and four women in the top six positions in a full Senate election. For the ACT and the NT, which each return only two senators per election, these tickets were classified as winnable if a woman candidate was in the number 1 position.

their state tickets. The parties' success in electing their third named candidate is more variable, and more so in the case of Labor, which is typically only successful in securing its top two candidates on most of its state Senate tickets. The columns labelled 'women candidates' contains the percentage of women from each party placed in the number one position on the Senate ticket. The figure is calculated by averaging the number of state and territory Senate tickets where the party had a woman in the number one position.

In the case of Labor, and excepting the 2010 election, women led the Senate ticket in at least half of the state and territory tickets. In stark contrast, women are much less likely to have been placed in the number one position on the Liberal's Senate ticket. Only in 2019 were 50 per cent of candidates for the number one spot on Liberal Senate tickets women. In 2013 and 2016, only 13 per cent of the number one positions were held by women. Women candidates have also fared poorly in being awarded a winnable position (top three candidates) on most of the Liberal's state and territory Senate tickets.

Next, we turn to the House of Representatives. While both chambers of the parliament are critical law-making and deliberative bodies, the House of Representatives enjoys the distinction of being the seat of government. This is the chamber that selects the prime minister; it is also the chamber from which most ministers are drawn. Consequently, it is often the higher-profile house in terms of media coverage and public awareness, making it crucially important to the culture of political debate and leadership in Australia.

Figure 3 provides a summary of the candidates selected by the major party groups and by gender over the five most recent elections. It shows that both Labor and the Liberal Party candidate pool is over-whelmingly made up of male nominees, and only a comparatively small number of female candidates. Of the two, Labor tends to con-sistently nominate a greater number of female candidates than the Liberals, but still well short of gender parity. Again, this reflects the effect of Labor's gender quota over time. When it was first introduced in 1994, a quota of 35 per cent of all preselected candidates in win-nable seats was set (to be achieved by 2002). In 2012 this was raised to 40 per cent, and in 2015 it was lifted again to 50 per cent (to be achieved by 2025). It is worth noting that in 2016 and 2019, both parties selected more female candidates than they had in the previous three elections.

It is conceivable, although admittedly unlikely, that the low num-bers of female candidates that a party nominates might reflect a lack of interest by women party members to nominate for a lower house

FIGURE 3

Percentage of major party candidates (men and women) for the House of Representatives, 2007–2019

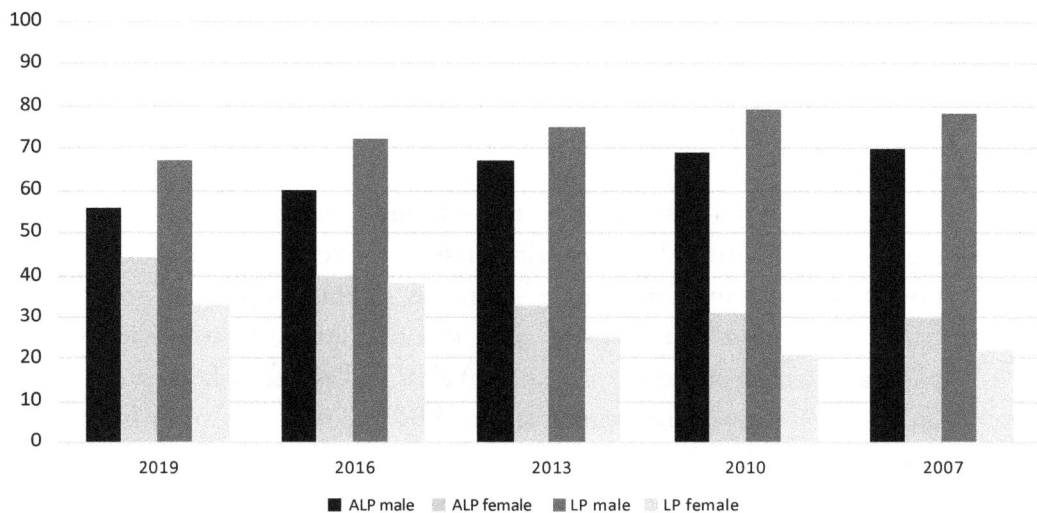

SOURCE AEC election data

seat. It might be that both parties genuinely desire to select more female candidates, but only very few women nominate. In Australia, we lack the data on political party members that would enable us to understand the motivations of women party members (including the incentives and constraints to nominating for public office). We know, however, that women are less likely than men to become a member of a political party.[17] Given that party membership is a prerequisite of nomination, this automatically lowers the number of potential women candidates that parties might preselect.

An important study of political recruitment in Denmark examined the effect of several factors that affect women's propensity to nominate, such as education, income, family obligations, party office, political interest and self-perceived political competence.[18] The study found that while these factors do explain lower nomination rates, they do not completely account for the difference in nomination rates between men and women, and that there is a separate gender story in play. In policy terms, bridging the political representation gap in terms of political representation not only involves minimising differences in income and education, equalising childcare responsibilities and raising women's political interest and self-perceptions of competence, it also involves actively recruiting women as political party members and creating internal party processes that encourage women to nominate.[19]

Another way to assess the parties' commitment to female candidates is by exploring the competitiveness of the seats that they were nominated to stand for.[20] For a candidate seeking election to parliament, the most desirable seats are those that are (a) held by their party at the time of the election and (b) classified as safe or fairly safe. Such seats are considered winnable seats[21] by the defending party but uncompetitive for the major party challenger, even though electoral upsets can occur. Marginal seats, however, are notionally competitive for a challenger party candidate, although the electoral outcome mostly favours the incumbent party. Thus, we should expect that even if only a small number of women nominate for election, both parties should, at least, ensure that these nominees are selected to secure and winnable seats.

To get a sense of the parties' respective commitment to the selection of women candidates, we have sorted candidates for both major parties based on the competitiveness of the seat they have been selected to contest. Four categories of seats were created based on the Australian Electoral Commission's (AEC) pre-election designation of electorates: (a) secure seats, consisting of safe and fairly safe party-owned seats prior to the election, (b) winnable seats, comprised of marginal party-owned seats prior to the election, (c) competitive seats, made up of marginal seats that are not party-owned, and (d) uncompetitive seats, made up of safe and fairly safe seats that are not party-owned. The data was then averaged across the five elections by gender, and then again by party.

TABLE 4

Candidates by gender and by seat, by percentage nomination

	Labor men (%)	Labor women (%)	Liberal men (%)	Liberal women (%)
Secure seats	31	26	31	24
Winnable seats	14	20	17	18
Competitive seats	18	18	16	26
Uncompetitive seats	37	29	37	32

Table 4 shows that the parties do not do a particularly good job of selecting women candidates to secure seats. Beginning with Labor, male candidates tend to be marginally favoured for secure seats (31 per cent of male candidates were placed in secure seats compared to 26 per cent of women), while female candidates are more likely to be awarded winnable seats, or party-owned marginal seats (20 per cent compared to 14 per cent of male candidates). Leaving aside the chronically low numbers of women selected by the Liberals, their record of selecting women to secure seats is on a par with Labor, as is their selection of women to winnable seats. The Liberals are, however, more likely to preselect women for competitive seats, defined as marginal seats owned by their rival party.

Women candidates are less likely, as a proportion of their overall numbers, to be selected to uncompetitive seats than their male counterparts in both Labor and the Liberals. Overall, while the major parties do not place more women than men in secure seats, they also do not 'dump' women candidates in uncompetitive seats. However, it is important to underline that the number of women candidates selected by both parties remains woeful.

Final thoughts

Through their effective control of the selection of candidates to parliament, political parties in Australia are the 'gatekeepers' to political office and hence political leadership. As this chapter has demonstrated, both the major parties have been unable to achieve gender parity in representation, though Labor – assisted by a system of quotas introduced in 1994 – has made significant gains in the last 20 years. The Liberals, who have relied on merit-based selection and intra-party mentoring and support for women candidates, lag behind. In this chapter we have focused predominantly on the effect of institutional mechanisms and electoral processes, but their relationship with broader party cultures is inseparable. Until more women are preselected by Australia's political parties, and consequently elected to parliament, the culture of partisan politics in Australia will not change. However, partisan culture currently places more impediments on women securing preselection than it provides for supportive opportunities. Until both these elements are addressed, Australian political parties will continue to be largely unsupportive arenas for women in politics.

BARRIERS FROM WITHIN: THE AUSTRALIAN CONSTITUTION AND WOMEN'S PARLIAMENTARY REPRESENTATION

Zareh Ghazarian and Jacqueline Laughland-Booÿ

In 1902, Australian women first won the right to vote and stand for national parliamentary elections.[1] However, it was to be another 40 years before Australians elected their first female parliamentarians. The entry of two women into parliament in 1943 might have been considered a watershed moment for Australian history – one that would open the way for fair and equal gender representation in Australia's highest levels of government. Fast-forward to 2020 and we see that this ambition is still to be realised. Although policies have been implemented to reduce gender imbalance in the Australian parliament, the problem still exists. We argue that this is, in part, due to institutional arrangements that serve to disproportionately discourage women from seeking, and keeping, a seat in federal parliament.

Since the first women were elected to the Australian parliament almost 80 years ago, the number of women in the parliament has remained low. The 2011 United Nations General Assembly resolution on women's participation recognises that 'active participation of women, on equal terms with men, at all levels of decision-making is essential to the achievement of equality, sustainable development, peace and democracy'.[2] At the same time, it acknowledges that, worldwide, women still face significant obstacles to achieving fair and equal political participation – including systemic barriers that discourage women from holding office.

Although many may like to think that Australia is a society where Canberra's glass ceiling has been systematically broken and that our political systems are without gender bias, this is simply not correct. Over and above the many cultural and attitudinal barriers Australian women must navigate on the path to becoming a federal parliamentarian, we argue that rules remain embedded within the Australian Constitution and parliament itself that serve to disproportionately discourage women from wanting to become members of the national legislature. Specifically, we highlight how Section 44 (iv) of the Australian Constitution and the current operations of the national parliament present unacceptable disadvantages for women. If Australia is to see more women in Canberra, then it is critical that these barriers be dismantled.

The Australian Constitution

The conditions under which citizens are disqualified from becoming a member of the national parliament are set out in Section 44 in the Australian Constitution. This includes, for example, Section 44 (i), which disqualifies any Australian citizen who holds, or is entitled to hold, foreign citizenship, while Section 44 (ii) does not allow those who have been convicted of crimes that are punishable by imprisonment for at least one year to be a member of parliament. Furthermore, Section 44 (iv) bars those who 'profit under the Crown' from running for parliament. The intention of this exclusion is to prevent government employees from being politically active.[3] The practical impact, however, is that Section 44 (iv) constructs a substantial barrier for public sector employees from running for parliament and, while unintentional, has a gendered dynamic as it acts to curtail the political aspirations of a sector where there are more women than men.

Over two million Australians are currently employed in the public sector[4] and the majority of those are women. At the national level, women comprise 59.7 per cent of the Australian Public Service.[5] Similarly, at state level, women make up the majority of public sector employees. In the two most populous Australian jurisdictions, for example, women comprise approximately 62 per cent of the New South Wales Public Service[6] and 61 per cent of the Victorian Public Service.[7] Furthermore, women make up the majority of professions that are largely engaged by the public sector. Of the 288 294 full-time equivalent of teachers working in Australia in 2019, nearly 72 per cent were women.[8] Moreover, of the total 421 167 individuals in Australia who held general registration as either a nurse or midwife in early 2020, 89 per cent were female.[9]

The public sector wields significant authority and has proved to be an invaluable conduit by which women have been able to lead public decision-making.[10] The high proportion of women in the Australian public service, however, can act as a double-edged sword. This is because, unless they are prepared to leave their position, those who work in the public sector are excluded from running for political office.[11] In recent years, some arrangements have been made to allow public sector staff to temporarily step back from their employment if they wish to participate in a parliamentary campaign and then be re-employed if they are unsuccessful. There is, however, variation in rules across jurisdictions, and running for election still comes at a high price. In the federal public service, for example, staff who choose to contest an election must resign within six months before the close of nominations and return to their role within two months after the election if they wish to keep their position.[12] Furthermore, some states depend on the discretion of managers to decide whether a candidate who was unsuccessful at a federal election should be reappointed or not – meaning that while there is a mechanism for re-employment, it is not guaranteed.[13] As a consequence, the aspiring candidate must be prepared to risk their career, income and capacity to save for their retirement in order to contest a national election. This is particularly challenging for women who traditionally earn less than men and therefore have less capacity to take a break from regular income.

There are examples that illustrate how this component of the Australian Constitution plays out in contemporary society. For instance, the political aspirations of Liberal Party member Helen Jackson were curtailed by this constitutional rule in 2019. Jackson was preselected by the Liberal Party to contest the lower house seat of Cooper in Victoria. She was, however, employed by Australia Post and as such was asked to withdraw by the Liberals. After refusing to do so, she was disendorsed by the party.[14] In another instance, Liberal member Hollie Hughes was selected by her party in New South Wales to replace the National senator Fiona Nash in 2017. Nash had won a seat in 2016 but had been ruled ineligible when it was discovered that she was entitled to British citizenship. Hughes had also been on the 2016 Coalition Senate ticket, but had won insufficient votes to be elected. She was, however, the next candidate in line to replace Nash.[15] After the election, Hughes had accepted a part-time position with the Australian Administrative Appeals Tribunal, but after the removal of Nash, Hughes immediately resigned from this job with the view to filling the Senate vacancy.[16] A decision from the High Court, however, found that because Hughes had accepted a position within the public sector during a period of time ruled by the court to be still within the election period, Hughes had rendered herself ineligible for the Senate.[17] The vacancy was eventually filled by Jim Molan, though Hughes was subsequently elected at the following election as a senator for New South Wales in 2019.

There have been debates about clarifying Section 44 (iv) of the Constitution. In 1981, for example, a parliamentary report noted that this section needed to be revised to better help public sector employees understand their rights and responsibilities.[18] There were no changes made, however, and in 1992, the High Court reaffirmed the broad definition of profiting 'under the Crown' in a watershed case when it determined that a school teacher from Victoria, who had been on unpaid leave, could not be elected to parliament.[19] In

1997, the House of Representatives Legal and Constitutional Affairs Committee made further recommendations to clarify this part of the Constitution to no avail.[20] This has contributed to the current understanding of Section 44 (iv) that teachers, nurses and police, among others who are considered to be working in the public service, are disqualified from running for office.[21] This rule, however, does not apply to serving ministers in the government.

Perhaps it is time to revisit the true intention of this constitutional clause and consider whether the risk posed by allowing the country's teachers, health workers, administrative workers, and others who 'profit under the Crown' to run for election, supersedes the need to achieve balanced gender representation within parliament. Furthermore, this constitutional rule appears to go against current Australian Government guidelines concerning the rights of citizens to contest elections.[22] In providing guidance to those involved in designing public policy, the Attorney-General's Department emphasises the need to consider whether policy decisions may limit 'the ability of a category of individuals to stand for office or to vote in elections'.[23] Moreover, it asks policy designers to consider whether their decisions may potentially impact on the eligibility of citizens to be appointed to public office.

Changing the Australian Constitution is notoriously hard as it requires a majority of voters in a majority of states to agree to the proposed alteration. In fact, since federation, only eight of 44 referendums have been approved by voters. As a result, changing Section 44 (iv) of the Constitution to allow public sector employees to be eligible to contest elections would be difficult to achieve. At the very least, this hindrance could be navigated through the adoption of a standardised national approach that provides public sector staff the opportunity to contest elections without unduly jeopardising their job and income. This would involve keeping the obligatory time required to leave the service prior to nomination to a minimum and agreeing to safeguard the employee's position until the election process concludes. In doing so, a key obstacle for women considering a run for parliament would be dismantled.

Parliamentary operations

Another factor that serves as a massive disincentive for women to become parliamentarians is the way in which the Australian parliament operates. Australia is the sixth largest country in the world with an area of 7 692 024 km². When parliament is sitting (which on average occurs 67 days across 20 sitting weeks per year), federal parliamentarians must be in Canberra.[24] They must also be in Canberra to undertake many ministerial or parliamentary committee duties.[25]

In recent years, as discussed in the chapter by Rowe and Alver (page 135), the tension between law-making obligations and commitment to family has motivated female parliamentarians to leave their jobs. Kelly O'Dwyer, Minister for Women in the Morrison Coalition Government, decided to leave politics prior to the 2019 election. Citing the need to spend more time with her family, she explained, 'I no longer want to consistently miss out on seeing my children when I wake up in the morning and when I go to bed at night'.[26] At the same time, Labor's Kate Ellis, the Shadow Minister for Early Childhood and Development, also left politics due to the strain that travel to and from the nation's capital was causing. As Ellis explained, she 'did not want to be spending 20 weeks of the year in a different state to my child'.[27] She continued, 'When I thought about all the things that I would miss, I just decided that it would make me quite miserable.'[28]

While men also undoubtedly find that parliamentary and family responsibilities are difficult to juggle,[29] former Victorian MP Margaret Fitzherbert, who had prepared a report for the Liberal Party on gender representation, identified that women often had to clear a 'double hurdle'.[30] The first hurdle was 'a woman's own self-assessment of her readiness for preselection and whether she has what it takes to be an MP', while the second was 'a preselection process that often treats men and women very differently, with motherhood identified as a key issue'.[31] These challenges remain for many women and play a role in the gap in gender representation in the Australian parliament.

In a blunt assessment, former prime minister John Howard suggested that the goal of gender balance in parliament might never be achieved:

> I'm not sure that you will ever have a 50/50 thing because it's
> a fact of society that the caring role, whatever people may say
> about it and whatever the causes are ... women play a significantly
> greater part of filling the caring role in our communities, which
> inevitably will place some limits on their capacity.[32]

There are, however, ways in which the tensions between family and parliamentary roles can be addressed. In particular, we can take lessons from responses to the COVID-19 pandemic. As the virus spread across the globe, industries and their employees found innovative ways of operating.[33] It also caused some temporary changes to how parliamentary work was carried out around the world. Members of the House of Commons in the UK, for instance, agreed to allow MPs to vote from home.[34] In this hybrid model, parliamentarians could make statements and contributions by being physically present in the chamber or through online video platforms.[35] The European parliament also adopted procedures to allow representatives to 'vote from distance' which meant physical attendance was not needed.[36]

The pandemic also forced some temporary changes to the functioning of the Australian Parliament. For example, the overall number of parliamentarians in the chamber was reduced to facilitate social distancing.[37] The operation of parliamentary committees was also altered in response to the coronavirus. In particular, committees began to use online technologies and live video streaming to continue their inquiries. This allowed MPs to remain in their local communities while undertaking parliamentary work that would otherwise have them travelling around the country.

In contemporary society, it can be considered unreasonable and unnecessary for any parent to be forced to be separated from their family for long periods of time, as is the case currently for Australian parliamentarians, especially when existing technology may ameliorate key problems. As a result, some of the changes brought about by the response to coronavirus may actually enable women, particularly those who may have previously been put off by the struggle to balance family and parliamentary roles, to consider a run for the national parliament if they were adopted permanently. As has been demonstrated during the pandemic, there appear to be no constitutional or other regulatory reasons that would stop parliament from being able to perform its functions online.[38] Issues concerning privacy or security of these debates are also redundant as parliamentary proceedings and voting are open, broadcast and made available on the public record. Winding back the requirement that parliamentarians must travel and be away from home for some 20 weeks of the year would go some way in dismantling a key obstacle many women confront. As the Australian Broadcasting Corporation's chief political writer Annabel Crabb noted, 'a virtual Parliament ... would address some of the most stubborn barriers that currently keep women out of the joint'.[39]

Advancing greater gender balance in the Australian Parliament

While the constitutional and parliamentary rules examined in this chapter are also disadvantaging men, the lack of women in parliament illustrates there is a gendered dynamic to their impact. Despite Australia being an early leader in allowing women to be able to vote and participate in national elections, more must be done to undo barriers that still confront them in national politics.

The provision in the Constitution concerning the capacity of public servants to stand for election has inadvertently become highly problematic for more women than men in contemporary society. The existing patchwork of rules across Australian jurisdictions concerning how and, in some cases, if public sector employees can return to their roles after contesting an election needs revision. In particular, there is a requirement for uniform rules across governments to provide certainty and facilitate the ability of more women to participate in national elections.

The requirement that federal parliamentarians must spend so much time away from home is also in need of reform. Responses to maintaining the operation of parliamentary business, both in Australia and abroad, during the coronavirus pandemic has highlighted how this could be done on a more permanent basis. Using technology to facilitate virtual attendance in the federal legislature would dismantle an important barrier that has stopped women from participating, or even considering participating, in national politics. Addressing these obstacles would go some way to advancing the number of women in the Australian Parliament.

AM I AMBASSADORIAL ENOUGH? GENDER AND AUSTRALIAN INTERNATIONAL REPRESENTATION

Elise Stephenson

I spent a lot of time worrying that I wasn't ambassadorial enough, I wasn't like some of the people I'd seen in [foreign affairs and trade], particularly the men I have to say, because there's more of them to look at.[1]

Australian international affairs has a gender problem. Women represent only one-third of the country's international postings across the field on average.[2] As discussed in the previous chapter, this is dramatically lower than the proportion of women working in the state and public sectors. While the number of women on international postings is low, in Australia's Department of Foreign Affairs and Trade (DFAT), the number of women civil servants is now verging on parity for the first time. Furthermore, Australia now has a number of high-profile female political appointments in the defence and foreign affairs policy area. However, certain formal and informal rules of the game[3] influence who represents Australia on the world stage, with the field clearly remaining a bastion of elite forms of masculinity, heteronormativity and cultural homogeneity. International representation by way of ambassadors, high commissioners, diplomats and international advisers requires individuals to conform authentically to the values, citizenship and embodiment of the nation they are charged with representing. Who represents the state on the international stage is an exercise of authority, identity and state control – the personal is political.

This chapter attempts to understand why there is a paucity of women representing Australia in international affairs. It explores the experiences of women leaders across four of Australia's core international affairs agencies – the Department of Foreign Affairs and Trade (DFAT), Defence (including the Australian Defence Force (ADF) and Department of Defence (DoD)), the Department of Home Affairs (DHA), and the Australian Federal Police (AFP). Drawing on ideas from feminist institutionalism, the chapter argues that much of the leadership in this space is governed by both formal and informal rules that are biased against women.[4] Understanding these explicit and implicit rules of the game highlights an international context that not only positions heterosexual white men as the 'ideal' international representatives, but also reveals the ways in which women are often ignored, undervalued and invisible in the field.

Gender and Australian international representation

The representation of women in Australian international affairs is at a critical juncture. All federal public sector departments are now working towards 50/50 gender parity in leadership, and most government agencies have embraced gender equality strategies, inclusive of targets and/or quotas. The 2017 Foreign Policy White Paper committed to pursuing women's empowerment as a top priority. Recently, Australia appointed its first female foreign minister (2013), defence minister (2015) and shadow foreign minister (2016), marking the first time that women have led these portfolios. Furthermore, the subsequent defence and foreign ministers have been women, and the nation's first female departmental secretary for foreign affairs and trade was appointed in 2016.

In recent years, women have also been holding a large proportion of positions in the public sector; however, the most significant gains have occurred in domestic-facing agencies. In international portfolios, Defence was noted to be one of the largest agencies with the lowest representation of women overall, and DFAT as one of the largest departments with the lowest representation of women at senior levels.[5] Further, progress has stagnated across other core international government agencies, with women's overall representation falling in home affairs (and its predecessors) since 2009 and remaining stagnant in overall sworn populations in the AFP.[6]

Given that informal norms and rules, once made, are difficult to change, considerable gendered 'rules of the game' evidently remain to influence legitimate representation and access in Australian international affairs. This explains why there are very few women representing Australia internationally, despite the key leadership from women in related ministerial portfolios (such as Julie Bishop, Marise Payne, Linda Reynolds and Penny Wong) or secretary roles (Frances Adamson in DFAT or Rachel Noble in the Australian Signals Directorate). Understanding why women remain under-represented in the field is critical, particularly in the context of rising international challenges.

Women leaders in Australian international affairs agencies

In 2017–2019, I interviewed 57 women leaders in executive level (EL) and senior executive service (SES) roles from the four case agencies, and spoke with a further 27 associated leaders, politicians and managers. All interviewees were de-identified. Interviews were conducted face-to-face or via phone, Skype or email, and were undertaken in-person both domestically and internationally over the data collection period. Additionally, the Australian Public Service Employee Database (1984–2018) and unpublished raw data from the case agencies was considered.

Who represents Australia overseas?

Contemporary Australian diplomatic leadership remains male-dominated. Foreign policy think-tank, the Lowy Institute, found that gender diversity in Australian international affairs lags significantly behind the broader Australian Public Service (APS) as well as the foreign services of other comparable countries (US, UK and Canada).[7] Overall, women remain under-represented in the roles of ambassadors, high commissioners, diplomats and international advisers, and more militaristic agencies and intelligence agencies are generally considered the worst performing in terms of gender representation. As far as data can be sourced, women have *never* been equally represented to men internationally. While some progress has been made, Australia's largest and most strategically or economically important posts are much more likely to be headed by men. Appointments continue to be gender segregated around 'feminised' and 'masculine' portfolios. Women tend to occupy lower status positions when posted, and tend to be posted to lower status countries. Further, women remain under-represented, particularly in SES leadership levels across all agencies.

While Australia is recognised as 'strikingly culturally and ethnically diverse',[8] international affairs remains stratified along lines that are not just gendered, but also racialised. Not only was little ethnic diversity found in senior leadership and overseas representation, but women of colour, Indigenous women and those with non-Australian accents were particularly absent. In fact, Australia only appointed its first Indigenous woman ambassador in 2018, Julie-Ann Guivarra, over 100 years after the establishment of what was then Australia's Department of External Affairs.

Notions of the 'elite' are also bound up in Australia's international representation. Within the agencies today, the increase in professionalisation has allowed merit-based appointments (rather than politics and connections) to increase the diversity of representation across class. There are still challenges, however, especially for women from diverse backgrounds. Furthermore, those identifying as Lesbian, Gay, Bisexual, Transgender, Intersex or Queer (LGBTI+ or 'queer') face deep and entrenched forms of marginalisation.[9] While diplomatic privileges do offer forms of protection for sexually diverse envoys, challenges remain in providing opportunities to work in contentious global spaces, particularly given the dual role that international representation often requires of individuals and their spouses.

Across participants of this research, the low numbers of women with spouses and/or children indicate that international affairs roles are particularly onerous and present significant challenges for women seeking to have it all – leadership, international representation, family and children. Respondents frequently noted that the challenges for women in international affairs were too high and too often, and the rewards too few and too late.

'Rules of the game'

Throughout my interviews with women leaders in these departments and agencies, it became clear that there were specific accepted modes of behaviour and rules that women had to negotiate in order to progress and be recognised in their work. Rules-in-use are described by economist Elinor Ostrom as a distinctive ensemble of 'dos and don'ts' that one learns on the ground'.[10] Rules were distinct across the agencies, but reinforced similarities in gendered treatment. This had effects on both women's vertical segregation (whether they were represented in leadership) and horizontal segregation (whether they were represented across different countries and portfolios).

Formal and informal rules coalesced around three key themes: whether and in what circumstances women were listened to; how women remained systemically undervalued; and whether they were seen, and therefore taken seriously, or not. There was tremendous conflict between informal norms versus formalised rules, given that all government departments currently have varying levels of gender equality policy. Informally, gendered bias and discrimination continued to occur. In lieu of formal rules or institutions, informal rules and norms were more likely to affect women's access to power and therefore opportunities for representation.

The quest to be heard

Gendered rules guide Australian international affairs, dictating whose voice is heard, when, and in what circumstances. Within the past decade, policies across the agencies foreground equality and reinforce that everyone – regardless of gender, ethnicity, (dis)ability, sexuality – is part of a dynamic and inclusive government workforces. Yet, women's voices are frequently marginalised in international affairs, and at least historically, have remained tied to women's assumed knowledge or specific role. Their assumed knowledge was (and is) subject to bias in which women's knowledge is often of lesser perceived value compared to men's. Women have also been subject to longstanding and deep vertical and horizontal segregation, and therefore their voice was often only asked for in relation to their duties – typically areas such as secretarial duties, human resources or welfare.

More recently, women represent Australia in multilateral and bilateral settings. In multilateral settings, such as in the United Nations or other international forums, women noted that protocol formally guaranteed that they were able to speak and be listened to, as each country is given a set amount of time in which to speak and in a set order. However, in bilateral meetings or within women's own agencies, women told me that they were often ignored or had their contributions marginalised. The lack of formal rules around who speaks and when resulted in the suppression of women's voices according to an informal hierarchy of whose voice mattered most. Higher ranks were able to exert their voice more. However, among men and women of the same rank, women's voices were more likely to be overridden by mansplaining and silencing that restricted who and when individuals could speak. Women were often not automatically recognised as the voice or authority on a topic – even if they were –

and were frequently overlooked in group meetings. One participant noted, 'lots of mansplaining goes on ... People talk over you all the time',[11] with women's opportunities to contribute to 'hard' or operational topics particularly affected. Another participant, who was five feet tall and had a slight frame, found that she was frequently ignored in meetings or, literally, not even given a seat at the negotiating table.

Mackay explores why 'new' policies like those around gender equality often revert to old practices, signalling a regression in gender norms that is apparent when considering women's ability to speak and be heard. The combination of 'newness' and 'gender' makes the institutionalisation of reforms even harder. 'New rules' often go in direct opposition to the prevailing 'old norms' within international affairs in which women's voices were often marginalised or entirely absent. Further, many contexts in which participants had to work were outside the strict purview of their agencies, resulting in a reliance on more universally experienced (global) gender bias. In fact, a United Nations report noted that almost 90 per cent of people worldwide have a deeply ingrained bias against women.[12] The implications of women's (in)ability to be seen and heard have significant personal and professional ramifications, particularly as career progression is often marked by how much and how well individuals contribute to certain topics – the loudest voices are most rewarded. Critically, international affairs relies on the skilful use of voice to negotiate, and women are at a disadvantage when their voices are not equally heard or expressed.

The fight to be valued

After spending long periods talking with women leaders, I found that women were often perceived as being secondary or subordinate to men in the same role, emblematic of a systemic devaluing of women's contributions. Formal gender reviews and strategies have attempted to institutionalise equality, particularly in recent years. Yet, internally to agencies and externally to the world, my research shows that women were perceived as less authoritative, less senior and less legitimate as leaders – even in the same rank or role as men. Women of colour felt they had to work even harder again to be recognised. One participant sums up her experience:

> I'll never forget, in one country, which I shall not name, but they had a stream of very excellent women high commissioners year after year and the prime minister, male, said to me, 'When are we going to be upgraded?' I said, 'Excuse me?' He said, 'Well, when are we going to get a man high commissioner?' He was having a go, but for him to have raised it, he was also a bit sincere, you know? When are we going to get a real ambassador?[13]

Constant reminders about women's gender and their uniqueness or unexpectedness within the field reinforced women's outsider positioning. Further, notions of being upgraded to a man were common, and clearly suggested that women were perceived as a downgrade, or inferior.

Trying to combat these biases or assumptions is difficult. Unlike agency-based discrimination, there is little recourse to combat discrimination and harassment in the international field. This is particularly so because much of the work of international affairs is based around minimising diplomatic incidents – potentially reducing the chance of justice for women 'when things go wrong'. While 'valuing' women as equal to men may not be viewed as high-level discrimination, it does reinforce an existing gender order in which women are at the bottom. In addition, concepts like 'real ambassador' were spoken about by the women interviewed and suggested that only men can embody what it means to be a *real ambassador* – women were sometimes perceived as 'pretend playing' in the role until the next man came along.

To illustrate what it means to be a 'real ambassador', the guiding international document for international representation that is still in use today, the Vienna Convention on Diplomatic Relations (1961),[14] *only uses male pronouns* to describe the roles and responsibilities of a diplomat. The word 'his' is used 35 times throughout the Convention, and 'he' is used 12 times, with no references to 'she' or 'her'. Despite Australian policies that now use gender-neutral language and act as the more immediate policies for the selection of representatives, the weight and prestige of the Vienna Convention still holds, establishing an overarching diplomatic architecture in which, even if unintentional, references to women are missing. Male pronouns are used if not explicitly to refer to men, then as ungendered or gender-neutral pronouns. At least contemporarily, this is problematic given the discursive role language has in shaping social reality. Such language maintains a gender imbalance 'by obscuring male advantage as simply a gender-neutral standard'.[15]

The struggle to be seen

The third factor influencing legitimate international representation centred around the conditions in which women were visible or made to feel invisible. Whether and in what circumstances women were seen was highly conditional. In important formal negotiations and women's work generally, women frequently felt invisible and often not taken seriously. The *lack of visibility* that women experienced in these settings was deeply entrenched and had crushing results where women missed out on promotion opportunities or putting themselves forward for international roles. Alternatively, for diplomatic events, one-on-ones and non-work-related downtime, women were *highly visible* in a way that limited their range of acceptable actions. They were socially prohibited from drinking with counterparts (or even alone, or with their partner in their own time), or joining golf and other such typical informal activities. One participant noted:

> One of the things I'm learning in this role, that still has an impact on your life and maybe that impact is slightly gendered, is the public nature of the role. I can't go to the bar and have a beer because that would attract a lot of attention here, I'm a very

public figure. That has an impact on how I behave ... there's no 'off' switch in this role ... it has different implications I think for men than it does for women ... you have to manage differently, I guess. And that is a gender thing because men can go and you know, they can rock up at a golf club and find someone to play a round of golf with or hit a few balls, they can have a beer at the bar or whatever. I think that would be – you know, here that would be very much commented upon, and I don't feel comfortable doing it.[16]

Informal events, drinks, dinners or social sports often provided undocumented knowledge relating to contemporary issues, politics and relationships, as well as inside information on negotiations and opportunities. This was frequently inaccessible to women due to norms around their acceptable behaviour in public.

Crucially, women indicated that their visibility or lack thereof acted to limit and control women's representation, and in some cases was emblematic of women being seen only as they reached the 'glass cliff'[17] – particularly in sensitive or very public international negotiations, when the chance of failure was highest. This is indicative of a diplomatic double bind for women that has a compounding effect on the other factors shaping their representation and experiences.

Ideas of legitimacy remain to reinforce heterosexual, white men as the 'real' face of Australia internationally. Rules remain around who can represent Australia overseas, with women of colour, those with accents and sexually diverse women particularly affected. Further, women were frequently silenced in their work, undervalued for their contributions, and either too visible or not visible enough on the international stage. While formal multilateral settings provided women with the most opportunities to be heard, participant experiences highlighted how women's voices continued to be lost or disregarded as unauthoritative, particularly in agency and bilateral settings. Women reported being systemically undervalued, often perceived as 'less than' their male counterparts. Additionally, the ability to be visible (or not) had a severely limiting effect on women's range of action on the international stage. Women were often only seen in times of heavy scrutiny, and completely marginalised when it mattered to their career progression or claiming accomplishments. It is clear that women's increasing representation on the world stage, while significant, is still not equal. Progress often masks the considerable gendered challenges that remain. The pressure is now on to ensure that equal gender representation leads to true gender equality. As one diplomat noted:

> We always talk about how proud we are of our multiculturalism, about our broadmindedness. All of those things, right? ... if we say that and then our overseas presence is the white, heterosexual man, then how is that reflective of who Australia is? Not that I've got anything against white, heterosexual men, but it's only one part of the Australian identity.[18]

III
CULTURES

UNPAID LABOUR: GENDER AND THE UNSEEN WORK OF POLITICIANS

Pia Rowe and Jane Alver

In 2016, former prime minister John Howard raised eyebrows, and predictably triggered a backlash on social media, when he claimed that gender equality in parliament is never likely to happen due to women's caring roles. As Howard observed, 'women play a significantly greater part of fulfilling the caring role in our communities which inevitably place some limits on their capacity'.[1] Jarring as his statement might be for many people, in one way, Howard was – and still is – right. The rather grim state of affairs for women in Australian politics is indeed a reflection of the current society. Women continue to carry a significant amount of the burden of household labour, including caring for others. As also noted by Ghazarian and Laughland-Booÿ in their chapter (page 113), it is clear that these caring roles continue to negatively impact both women's workforce participation and their economic security, among other things. However, Howard's argument implies that the status quo is a permanent state of affairs – one that defies deliberate action to attempt to change things. In essence, it perpetuates traditional gender stereotypes based solely on sex: if women do the majority of caring, it is not just because they choose to, it is because they are somehow destined to fulfil an apparent biological imperative of womanhood.

Partly because of the persistence of these attitudes, politics in Australia, as well as around the world, has been a male-dominated field. The image of the perfect politician perpetuated in the media features the male breadwinner, supported by his spouse, almost exclusively a wife, who performs significant amounts of unpaid labour behind the scenes. For instance, we might picture Prime Minister Scott Morrison declaring victory in the 2019 federal election flanked at the podium by his wife and two daughters, or former prime minister Tony Abbott's frequent references to 'Margie and the girls'. The wife cares for the family, manages the household, supports her partner's campaigning and community commitments, and allows her husband to focus upon his political career. In her book, *The Wife Drought,* Annabel Crabb argued that having a spouse who can perform such unpaid work creates significant advantage to the careers of those in political leadership and elite professions.[2] Crabb further argued that even in modern times, this advantage was enjoyed by vastly more men than women.

In this chapter, we investigate the lived experiences of female parliamentarians and explore how their careers are impacted by their unpaid care responsibilities. We argue that the persistent social expectation that women undertake the bulk of unpaid labour creates both structural and cultural constraints on female parliamentarians. We do this by first exploring the concept of unpaid labour, and the gendered dimension of caring roles in Australia. We then discuss the experiences of both federal and state female politicians who have managed a political career alongside care responsibilities. Here, we draw upon six structured, in-depth interviews we conducted in 2019 and 2020 with sitting members of both state and federal parliaments across the political spectrum. These were female MPs of various ages and stages of their careers, from those starting out to those on the cusp of retiring from political life. The data from these interviews is illustrative only, and as such provides a snapshot of the challenges confronted by women parliamentarians. It also serves to unearth current blind spots, both in theory as well as practice, regarding the impact that unpaid labour, particularly care work, has upon the careers of women politicians. Finally, we explore opportunities to address the cultural and structural constraints identified in the chapter.

Making the invisible visible: Unpaid labour in Australia

Unpaid labour is pivotal to the functioning of families and our society more broadly, but it is often unacknowledged within our community. The Workplace Gender Equality Agency (WGEA) estimates the monetary value of unpaid care work in Australia at around $650.1 billion, the equivalent to 50.6 per cent of GDP.[3] This issue has come to the fore more recently with many Australians spending more time working from home. The 2020 lockdowns associated with COVID-19 have shone a spotlight on the gendered division of care and household labour. The data shows that women perform most of the unpaid labour in the private sphere, including cooking, cleaning, household management, caring and family logistics. Research shows that Australian women do 311 minutes of unpaid domestic work and care per day, compared to the Organisation for Economic Co-operation and Development (OECD) female average of 262 minutes.[4] When it comes to caring duties specifically, on average women spend 64 per cent of their weekly working time on unpaid care labour, compared to 36 per cent for men.[5] In real terms, for every hour Australian men commit to unpaid care work, women perform 1 hour and 48 minutes.[6]

This data suggests that even though women's labour force participation keeps increasing, they still spend more time on unpaid care work than men.[7] The gender gap is at its widest during the child-rearing years, when mothers are more likely than fathers to reduce work to part-time (37 per cent against 5 per cent) and consequently spend more hours performing domestic duties.[8] This gap partly reflects structural constraints such as rising childcare costs, combined with the existing gender pay gap and the fact that women are less likely to be the main breadwinners than their male partners.[9] But these constraints are not just structural; they are cultural. A recent national survey of Australians' attitudes towards gender equality showed that more than one in three of all men believe that 'it is important to maintain traditional gender roles so that families function well and children are properly supported'.[10] What's more, such views weren't limited to the older cohorts, with 35 per cent of Gen Z males (aged 18–23) believing that 'caring for children is best done by women'.[11]

It is important to consider gendered expectations and experiences of caring when thinking about women's participation in elite professions, such as political leadership. For instance, as Miragliotta and Gauja explore in their chapter (page 98), women have been significantly outnumbered in the national parliament. And the higher women climb the proverbial leadership ladder, the lonelier it gets for them. Since federation in 1901, Australia has only had one female prime minister (Julia Gillard AC), and one female governor-general (Dame Quentin Bryce AD CVO). Currently, the Inter-Parliamentary Union ranks Australia as 51st out of 191 countries in terms of its female representation in parliament.[12] Similarly, the World Economic Forum's *Global Gender Gap Report 2020* ranks Australia as 57th out of 152 countries for the 'political empowerment' of women.[13] These outcomes are matched by women's presence in senior leadership roles in elite professions within the private sector. In 2019, only 29.5 per cent of board members on ASX200 companies were women.[14]

The pressures of unpaid labour are often referenced by politicians who have decided to end their time in parliament based on 'family reasons'. Such decisions suggest that politics is an inherently unsuitable career for those with significant care responsibilities. In recent years, the number of MPs who have reportedly made that decision appears to be increasing, yet it has not prompted deeper consideration among current political leaders about how the situation could be remedied. Tim Hammond (Labor Party, Member for Perth), Kelly O'Dwyer (Liberal Party, Member for Higgins and minister), and Kate

Ellis (Labor Party, Member for Adelaide, former minister) have made
the decision to step down for 'family reasons'. While initially portrayed as the woman who 'has it all' after giving birth while in office,
former Minister for Women Kelly O'Dwyer's 2018 resignation was
largely presented as doing what's best for her family.[15] Her resignation
led Senator Linda Reynolds to request changes in the scheduling of
parliamentary sittings and committees, and to ask 'do estimates hear-
ings have to be from 9 am to 11 pm every day?'[16] In 2019, the deputy
leader of the opposition, Tanya Plibersek, referenced the challenges of
balancing work and family as the reason for not contending the Labor
leadership. 'I cannot reconcile the important responsibilities I have
to my family with the responsibilities of the Labor leadership', she
argued.[17] Comments such as these may indicate to other women that
in the Australian context, family responsibilities and political careers
are not compatible. As the chapter by Ghazarian and Laughland-Booÿ
(page 113) demonstrates, the hours are long and the workload can be
immense and – particularly at the federal level – it requires time in the
parliament, away from home.

Internationally, there have been some encouraging developments,
with Jacinda Ardern in New Zealand and Sanna Marin in Finland
successfully combining their roles as parents of young children with
their public duties. There are a number of contributing factors, ranging from various levels of structural support (for example, in New
Zealand, the prime minister and ministers can travel with a nanny
on overseas assignments and have the costs covered by taxpayers,[18]
while in Finland all citizens have access to affordable childcare) to
cultural expectations regarding shared parenting and private support
from their families. Both leaders have acknowledged the role of their
male partners in caring for their children, whether as primary or equal
carers. So how does the structure of the job, and the parliament, affect
women with caring responsibilities in Australia?

Women as the 'life support system'

Our interviewees identified a number of cultural and structural issues that created strain on their ability to maintain a sustainable work/life balance. Culturally, our respondents observed significant gender differences in the parental duties among their own colleagues. This shed some light on the traditional divisions of labour still prevalent within the political system. One interviewee noted the 'significant sacrifices'[19] of her male colleagues' partners, who were often left to raise the children on their own as the male politicians took on multiple duties and spent a lot of time away from home. Speaking candidly, this interviewee went further to argue that her male colleagues were essentially treating their wives and partners as their own personal 'life support systems' – which she noted was 'wholly inappropriate in 2019'.[20] Another respondent similarly noted that the experiences of men and women in political life differed greatly in federal politics. Taking a broader societal view, she argued that having household support is far more likely for those with a female partner.[21] However, one respondent argued that the supporting role was hard regardless of gender: 'Yes, this is hard on my husband, but it's no harder than it's usually on the wife. You just make it work.'[22]

Other female parliamentarians we interviewed also recognised the support they had received from their own mothers during campaigning, noting that they relied on their parents for basics such as providing them with nutritious meals.[23] While the respondents didn't directly acknowledge the gendered dimension of this arrangement, it still ought to be highlighted, as the reliance on their own mothers reinforces the gendered norms of women as caregivers and nurturers.

In contrast, only one person discussed her male partner's part-time paid work status, which enabled him to do 'the shopping and the cooking.'[24] The support from male partners was often discussed in terms of being an optional extra – nice to have, but not one that had any real expectations attached to it. Rather, the women were quick to acknowledge the demands of their partners' careers as a reason for not having an active support role in their own lives. In the absence of proper structural support, the jurisdictions with better gender balance – as was the case with the ACT – were seen as creating a more supportive environment for women.[25]

Finally, Australia's vast geography was seen to impact women's experience of politics. Members of state and territory parliaments did not have the same demands of travelling outside of their home jurisdiction to attend parliament in Canberra. As one female MP explained, 'The ACT is better than other jurisdictions. Part of this is the proximity as we all can sleep in our own beds at night. Federal politicians are away for much longer and that has to work for the household. To make it work you either need to be single, have no dependants, or you need to have help.'[26] The time spent away from home is amplified in the case for rural MPs whose electorates may cover vast areas of land and require extensive travel to visit constituents. For instance, the seat of Durack in Western Australia, currently held by the Liberal Party's Melissa Price, covers more than 1.6 million square kilometres.

Politicians who have traditionally enjoyed the support from their spouses may not fully grasp the forms of support that are needed to maintain families and households in their absence. Combined with the cultural acceptance of the belief that a political career places significant demands on leaders who 'get back what they put in', it is easy to see why Australian politics has remained so male-dominated. Until there is structural support as well as social change in the gendered expectations of unpaid work for men and women alike, there will remain significant barriers to diversity in politics.

Babies are OK: The unfinished business of unpaid work

There is, however, some evidence of positive change. Our interviews with female politicians suggested that there is an increasing amount of support for women from within the political system itself to help those with children to combine political and unpaid work. The legislature in the ACT, for example, tries to avoid scheduling meetings during the school holiday period, as well as school drop off times. At the federal level there have been some changes too, with policies and efforts to make parliament more 'family-friendly'. This includes childcare facilities being established in parliament, as well as the implementation of leave entitlements and breastfeeding policies for parliamentarians. These reforms are a significant improvement from the days when Senator Hanson-Young was made to remove her two-year-old from the chamber during a division in 2009, and when Minister Kelly O'Dwyer was asked in 2015 by the Office of the Chief Whip about why she couldn't simply express breast milk in order to avoid missing her parliamentary duties. The reforms to try and make parliament more accommodating for those with young children were celebrated by MPs when they were tabled in 2016:

> No member, male or female, will ever be prevented from participating fully in the operation of the Parliament by reason of having the care of a baby (Minister Christopher Pyne, February 2016).

> It will be a long time and possibly never, before this job is truly family-friendly, but this is a sign of ways of trying to improve (Manager of Opposition Business, Tony Burke, February 2016).[27]

However, while care responsibilities for babies is often seen as something that is increasingly supported within the political system, there is little recognition of caring roles beyond children at the federal level. In particular, these policies neglect the care of others, such as parents or older relatives. In the context of the increasing public awareness of the 'sandwich generation', which often sees middle-aged women caring for both children and ageing parents simultaneously, this presents a significant problem. As one of our interviewees noted: 'I have no kids so there's this assumption that I don't have a family ... there is no acknowledgment for those caring for their parents.'[28] Yet this is not consistent across jurisdictions, with a member of a state parliament noting: 'I can ask for leave [to care] for my elderly parents and it's given … The federal parliament is not so easy at granting leave.'[29]

Given the complex nature of the challenges associated with caring roles, there are no quick and easy solutions for effecting sustained change. Challenging the traditional gender stereotypes, which still hold a significant foothold in Australian society, requires both a cultural shift, as well as structural reforms – and both need to be addressed simultaneously for either of them to work. In addition, since unpaid labour constitutes far more than simply caring for children, the solutions need to be adequately diverse so as not to come across as tokenistic or discriminatory. In the first instance, creating a family-friendly environment through measures such as adjourning sittings after 6 or 7 pm (as has been done in Luxembourg and Peru), and suspending divisions on Mondays and Tuesdays to allow members and senators longer periods of time in their constituencies (and with their families), would address some of the constraints associated with the job.[30]

However, one of the biggest challenges will be addressing the prevailing cultural attitudes that cut across society as a whole. Two of the key things to address are the gendered nature of caring roles, and supporting the increased participation of men in those roles through parental leave and other employment structures. Ultimately, these measures need to be implemented at all levels of society, not just parliament, for them to be effective. Here, it is important that politicians, researchers and practitioners work together to co-generate a blueprint.

The structure of parliaments, created at a time when men left the house with hearth and family cared for in very separate spheres, is today still evident in the long sitting hours and absences that parliamentary work demands. However, on a positive note, some of the reforms adopted over the years are making a difference. These include breastfeeding in the chamber, on-site childcare centres in parliaments, and concessions made for breastfeeding mothers who cannot make the chamber at a moment's notice.

However, much of the unpaid care labour undertaken in our society still remains invisible. What's more, much of the unpaid labour remains gendered in Australian politics. While politics remains as it is, and women continue to perform the bulk of unpaid labour, it will remain difficult for women to succeed in politics. As such, it is clear that much more needs to be done. If we want equal representation of men and women in Australia's legislatures, we need to make parliament more accessible and better catch up with flexible workplace practices being introduced beyond the corridors of power.

THE DREAM GAP:
HOW GENDERED POLITICAL CULTURE
AFFECTS GIRLS AND YOUNG WOMEN

Hayley Cull and Jane Gardner

In November 2019, the former senator David Leyonhjelm from the Liberal Democratic Party was found to have defamed Greens Senator Sarah Hanson-Young after making comments in the media that amounted to what she argued was 'slut-shaming'. He was ordered to pay Hanson-Young $120 000 plus interest.[1] Federal Court Justice Richard White agreed that Leyonhjelm's comments in a series of interviews carried the imputation the Greens senator was a misandrist and a hypocrite. His remarks about Hanson-Young's sexuality were but the tip of a large and ever-present iceberg of gendered behaviour towards women leaders. She is certainly not the first woman whom a male politician has attempted to humiliate in the parliament, and she will probably not be the last. However, in her response, Hanson-Young made her point loud and clear: this behaviour has to stop.

In an opinion piece following the ruling, youth activist Ginette Villasmil noted the frequency with which powerful men used slut-shaming to disgrace and bully women. It is part of a broader series of tactics employed to silence and control women's speech and behaviour through intimidation.[2] At the same time, Villasmil suggested that Hanson-Young's victory sets an important precedent, empowering women to speak out. Immediately after the verdict, Hanson-Young fronted the media to highlight the importance of the decision for all women 'who ha[ve] ever been told to stay silent, made to stay silent'.[3] She suggested that the verdict would help to make sure that 'every young girl knows they have the right to be treated with respect ... in the classroom, the workplace, if she works in a shop, the front bar, or here in the nation's parliament'.[4]

Public disrespect towards, and unequal treatment of, women are primary causes of what we call the dream gap. Our research has shown that while there is intense desire among girls and young women to lead and become involved in politics, this ambition fades as they get older. A key reason for this is the belief that their gender will stand in their way. In this chapter, we outline the causes of the dream gap, drawing on the experiences of girls and young women. In their formative years, girls and young women are building a perception that Australia still has too narrow a view of who can, and should be, in politics. This perception is formed when they see female politicians being treated unfairly by the media and their male colleagues. We explore the findings of our data and conclude by presenting ways in which a more inclusive and representative political culture can be achieved. We identify policy directions to forge a path so girls who want to lead can feel confident to follow their ambition.

The data

In 2017, the girls' rights non-government organisation Plan International Australia (which the authors work for) released two reports exploring the dream gap phenomenon as part of its mission to support and empower girls to lead. The first report, *The Dream Gap: Australian girls' views on inequality*,[5] provided a detailed analysis of Australian girls' ambitions to lead, their experiences of inequality and their views on gender stereotypes as they grow into adolescence and young adulthood. The second report, *She Can Lead: Young people in Australia share their views on women in politics and leadership*,[6] extended the analysis of young women and girls' experiences. The reports drew on surveys conducted by Essential Research for Plan Australia. The first used the online platform Qualtrics to survey 1742 Australian girls aged 10 to 17. Of these girls, 817 were aged between 10 and 14, and 925 were aged between 15 and 17. The confidence level was set at 95 per cent with a margin of error of 3–4 per cent. A second online survey of 530 young Australian women and men aged 18–25 gathered their views on women in politics.[7] The confidence level was again set at 95 per cent with a margin of error of 3–4 per cent. A summary of the key finding from this survey is found in Table 5 below.

TABLE 5

Findings of gender surveys by Plan International Australia

Statement	Men (agree)	Women (agree)
My gender is a barrier to a career in politics	4%	35%
Wanting to start a family is a barrier to a career in politics	11%	41%
Female politicians are treated unfairly by the media	31%	57%
Female politicians are talked over more than male politicians are	27%	52 %
Political parties should do more to increase female representation	42%	63%
Female politicians are treated unfairly by male politicians	36%	56%
There are not enough opportunities for me to enter politics	26%	45%
It is harder for women to become politicians than it is for men	45%	62%
Women should focus on family life before political life	26%	13%
Men make better politicians than women	19%	8%

SOURCE Plan International, 2017[8]

Together, these surveys produced unique insights into how girls as young as 10 through to young women up to the age of 25 make decisions about their own futures based on the inequalities they see and experience around them. Of the girls surveyed, 40 per cent identified gender as the single largest barrier to their chances of becoming a leader. While 69 per cent of girls aged 15–17 wanted to become a leader in their chosen field one day, the vast majority felt discrimination and scrutiny would be a major hurdle to overcome. The research also reveals how girls, as they progress through adolescence, become increasingly aware of how women are treated in politics and public life. This affects their own career ambitions. While 56 per cent of girls view themselves as being confident at age 10, this decreases to 44 per cent by the time they reach 17, and just 27 per cent when they reach adulthood (18–25). They become progressively aware of inequality in all areas of their lives, feel scrutinised for their appearance, and their self-confidence drops.

At all ages, and in all spaces, girls think they are not treated equally to boys. Almost all (98 per cent) of girls surveyed said boys and girls receive unequal treatment – this is most profound in sports, followed by in the media (TV and magazines), at school and at home. A large number of girls surveyed felt it would be easier to get ahead if they were treated in the same way that boys are (91 per cent). When asked what change they want to see in the world, 50 per cent of girls aged 10 to 14 said – unprompted – gender equality, including equal pay. Above all else, girls just want to be treated as equals. After inequality, girls are most concerned with being scrutinised for the way they look rather than appreciated for their abilities and talents. Almost all (93 per cent) of girls aged 15–17 said it would be easier to get ahead in life if they were not judged on their appearance.

The dream gap has specific implications for political ambitions. One in three young women (34 per cent) surveyed said their gender was an obstacle to becoming a politician, compared to just one in 20 men (4 per cent). Further analysis of the data showed only 2 per cent of girls aged 10–14 listed politics as a future career option, rising to 5 per cent for girls aged 15–17 and then dropping to 0 per cent of young women aged 18–25. Almost half the women (45 per cent) surveyed said there were simply not enough opportunities in politics for them. Men's perception of women's role in politics and society contributes to this. Men were more likely to be unaware of, or comfortable with, existing inequalities. When it came to how female politicians are treated in the Australian Parliament, the differences between young men and women was stark. Women were twice as likely to agree female politicians were treated unfairly by the media and talked over by male politicians. Outdated views regarding political leadership also persist among young men. When asked who is better at being prime minister, one in five men (20 per cent) answered 'men'. At the same time, twice as many men believe women should focus on family life before political life (26 per cent men agreed, versus 13 per cent of women). The pressure to focus on family life further dampens young women's ambitions. Young women were over three times more likely to say starting a family would hinder a career in politics (41 per cent versus 11 per cent of men).

Girls of colour, with a disability or those facing other intersecting barriers find themselves almost entirely unrepresented by the political role models they have. The following quote from 18-year-old Varsha Krithivasan from Sydney highlights how the dream gap functions in this regard:

> I want to believe that glass ceilings and disadvantages will not hinder me when I finally reach the workforce, but as an 18-year-old Indian girl interested in Australian politics, there are times when I am forced to think more realistically. I am a young, woman of colour, who also has a stutter ... If I had leaders who I could relate to, who exhibited that they could reach what I believed I couldn't, it's no doubt I would be filled with more confidence, hope and aspiration ... Despite being born and brought up in Australia, the fact that I and many Australians are still excluded from what leaders look and sound like is

disheartening … Representation means allowing different voices
and experiences of being human to guide our conversations and
debates. Representations means every Australian can grow up
thinking they can be a leader.[9]

The evidence that girls initially show some interest in politics and
then give up on it entirely as they enter adulthood is not surprising.
Furthermore, it shows that there remains a narrow view of who can,
and should be, in politics. This has implications for the operation
of broader society as it leads to people self-selecting out of a role in
civic leadership, and our representative democracy is poorer for it.
The context for girls is key to understanding their reluctance to enter
politics and leadership. When a staggering 98 per cent of girls believe
they do not receive equal treatment to boys in pop culture, in sports,
at home or at school, it shapes their view of the world and the opportunities that will be afforded to them. When 40 per cent of girls see
gender as the single biggest barrier to their chances of becoming a
leader – a more significant obstacle to overcome than their education,
ambition or ability – it becomes clear that for pathways to leadership
to be opened up, we need to work harder to overcome the gendered
notions that girls and boys are forming so early in life. Girls want
to lead, but they do not believe they will have the same opportunities that boys do. They see a career in politics as being incompatible
with being a mother. They are not given confidence by what they see
around them and start to believe that, because of their gender, they
will not be able to achieve their dreams.

Girls' perceptions of leadership in Australia are strikingly similar
to what our research has uncovered on a worldwide scale. A large
study involving 10 000 girls in 19 countries conducted by Plan International showed that nine out of ten girls surveyed felt that they
would suffer from discrimination and harassment should they occupy
a position of leadership in the future. The report *Taking the Lead:
Girls and Young Women on Changing the Face of Leadership*[10] was the
first of its kind to shed light on girls' and young women's leadership

aspirations, perceptions and real experiences across diverse societies and economies worldwide. Of all girls and young women surveyed, 76 per cent said they aspired to be a leader. At the same time, 94 per cent believed that being a leader involved being treated unfairly as compared to men. Alarmingly, this perception was stronger among young women who had some experience of leadership than those who had none. The report provided evidence that deep-rooted stereotyping and widespread discrimination influence and shape girls' ambitions, limiting their sense of what is both possible and appropriate for them. The harsh reality cuts across continents, cultures and economies. In all countries where Plan International works, girls and young women are forced out of equal opportunities before their adult lives have even begun, with girls making up 70 per cent of out-of-school youth and 82 million girls each year in developing countries being married before their 18th birthday.

In the Australian case, while we saw a drop in female representation in parliament following the 2019 federal election, there has also been progress. The first senator to breastfeed in the national legislature made front-page news around the world and, as the chapter by Miragliotta and Gauja (page 98) shows, some parties have edged towards having gender parity in parliament. When it comes to young women's opportunities to lead in Australia, however, we are still failing and even going backwards on many fronts. On current estimates, the girls who participated in Plan International's research will be due to retire by the time the gender pay gap is closed in this country alone.[11] It is unlikely they will live to see gender equality in other areas of life, with the World Economic Forum predicting that the global gender gap will take 108 years to close.[12] Progress is happening, but it is too slow.

Supporting young women to become leaders

From our research with girls in Australia, we have identified three practical steps that can be taken to encourage and support them to become leaders. First, we argue that all political parties should aim for gender parity. Political parties should review their candidate selection procedures, putting in place specific measures to encourage female candidates to stand for election and to increase the number of women selected in winnable seats. The Australian Labor Party adopted an affirmative action quota in 1994 with the view of increasing the number of women in parliament. The Liberal Party, on the other hand, has been highly resistant to adopting such rules.[13] As parties are ultimately responsible for selecting the candidates who will represent them at elections, we believe they will play a critical role in raising the proportion of women in parliament.

Second, we need to address pressures that force women to choose between leadership and family life. Too many girls are deterred from pursuing a political career or having leadership aspirations because they do not believe it can coexist with family life. Indeed, following the 2019 federal election, Tanya Plibersek, who was deputy leader of the Labor Party, ruled out running for the party's leadership, stating that she couldn't reconcile this role with her family responsibilities. Plibersek later stated that she hoped 'there aren't people out there who take this [decision] as a sign that politics is incompatible with family life or that women can't have three children and operate at the highest level of their organisation'.[14] She further noted that each woman needs to make her own career decisions. However, this does suggest that we need to ensure that politics and workplaces more generally are designed to work for young women. As detailed in the previous chapter, parliament, for example, can extend flexible working arrangements, such as remote participation, to address the challenges of balancing leadership with family life. Additionally, all employers should take steps to encourage parents to share childcare equally.

Finally, steps need to be taken to nurture girls' leadership ambitions. Too many young women are growing up to believe that they will not have the same opportunities as men to become leaders, or that they do not possess the qualities of a great leader. We need to equip girls with the skills, networks and role models that will unlock their potential. This can be done, for example, by promoting and supporting workplace learning opportunities, such as internships with parliamentarians and business leaders, as well as investing in leadership programs for young women at Australian high schools.

We keep telling girls that they can achieve anything they desire, but there is a dream gap between what girls aspire to early in life, and what they believe is realistic for them as they become young adults. The inequality they perceive in adolescence weighs directly on their dreams. We cannot let this go on. Only by breaking down the gendered culture of Australian politics can we truly nurture the aspirations of every adolescent girl who has the desire to lead. When we do, we will unlock the extraordinary potential of Australia's young women, and everyone will benefit.[15]

TROUBLING ELITES: GENDER AND PARADOXES OF POLITICAL IGNORANCE

Jim Jose

For feminists and non-feminists alike, the challenge is to think about leadership in an ungendered way. This is not just because leadership has been traditionally (and continues to be) marked by masculinist tropes. We also need to avoid the trap of treating gender, whether as noun or adjective, as if it captured some definitive masculine or feminine essence, a point made in a different but related context by Carol Johnson.[1] Ideas about manhood and womanhood, about masculinity and femininity, about what it means to be a woman or a man in specific socio-political contexts, nurture and support each other, as do the practices they inform and appear to validate. Neither operates in isolation, but in relation to each other.[2] Finding a non-gendered way of thinking about and confounding the gendering dynamics that shape perceptions of leadership is, however, easier said than done.

In this chapter, I use the lens of 'the paradox of political ignorance' to explore the gendering of populist leadership and expose the hidden gender dynamics that translate into masculinised forms of knowing. This paradox is an aspect of political leadership that is little appreciated, hiding gender dynamics that reproduce and legitimise the masculinist gendering of leadership.

For the purposes of this essay, I am using 'paradox' to mean a juxtaposition of seemingly contradictory ideas or actions. This is distinct from understanding paradox as a logical contradiction deployed in the Aristotelian sense to confound an argument,[3] or as a type of aphorism used in a literary sense.[4] Understood in this way, a paradox serves to arrest our attention and possibly point the way towards a new or different way of knowing.[5] In the context of gender and leadership, I use paradox as a means of addressing some of our ignorance about that question. The broad argument is that paradoxes of political ignorance, at least those identified in this chapter, are marked by gendered practices and masculinised forms of knowing that are not accidental to the question of leadership.

Troubling elites

We can define 'elites' as people who 'occupy the highest rank in [their] society' and who wield significant 'economic, political, administrative, media, and intellectual' power.[6] This is a fairly mainstream definition. However, another meaning of elites has entered the popular imagination over the past three decades in Australia (and elsewhere in the Western world). Indigenous people, migrants, LGBTQI, women, the disabled, welfare recipients, and others, have had their struggles for equality re-presented as special interests at odds with the mainstream and hence deemed as enjoying privileges not available to ordinary folk. The rise to prominence of this way of understanding elites is part of an anti-elitist discourse[7] that has been important in nourishing populist sentiment and the emergence of populist leaders. Even so, populist critics make use of both senses when it suits them.

By 'populist' I mean a way of understanding politics that positions the will and unity of the people against the power and privileges of elite groups. For populists, elites (in both senses) are troubling because they are identified as being removed from the needs and concerns of ordinary citizens. They exercise power either for their own benefit or that of narrowly defined special (self-serving, if not selfish) interests. Such elites determine political and social outcomes, if not directly then by proxy through elected members of parliament. In this way, populists position whatever they deem to be 'the elite' as alien to ordinary people because their decisions, policies and values are out of step with the wishes and concerns of the people.[8] Articulating a cleavage between 'the elites' and 'the people' is a value-laden distinction that sets populism apart from other political ideologies or ways of interpreting the world.[9]

On the other hand, elites (in the traditional sense) are troubled by populists for two reasons. First, populism threatens to undermine or remove the ability of elites to get their own way because it privileges the will of the people. Second, once unleashed, populism threatens to spin political power out of the control of the elites. On both counts, populism poses a political threat to the power of elites,[10] whether from the right or the left. As one political scientist put it, populism could be considered a 'democratic disorder', or at least 'the dark side of democracy'.[11]

Hostility to populism can be attributed to many theorists/advocates of (liberal democratic) representative democracy since all versions of such democracies are designed to minimise the political power of ordinary citizens in favour of already-powerful political elites. Yet despite this hostility, the fact remains that democracy presupposes populism. Populism is a necessary part of democratic practice.[12] This is because conceptions of representative democracy, at least since the seventeenth century, have based the legitimacy for sovereign political power on the consent of the governed.[13] By the end of the eighteenth century, 'the governed' began to be understood as 'the people'. This is why a central feature for the legitimacy of representative democracy is the idea that the people are sovereign, that their will authorises both government and what governments do.[14]

Populism draws much of its strength, and a good deal of its rhetorical power, from this key idea that the people are sovereign. Almost without exception, every variant of populism posits a conception of 'the people' as singularly special, as real, the 'heartland', as Taggart termed it.[15] Populist leaders claim a special relationship with the people. Only the populist leader knows the needs of 'the people' and how to represent them and, conversely, citizens 'who do not share their conception of "the people" ... should have their status as belonging to the proper people put into doubt'.[16] These so-called 'proper people' do not actually exist, but are rather an 'imagined community' along the lines formulated by political scientist Benedict Anderson in his discussion of national identity.[17] Within the populist imagination they are 'a mythical and constructed sub-set of the whole population'.[18] It therefore follows that the relationship between a populist leader and 'the people' is similarly a mythical construct. And both imaginaries rely on paradoxes of ignorance.

Appeals to whatever is imagined as 'the people' form part of the ideological pronouncements of populist parties like Pauline Hanson's One Nation (PHON) or possibly Bob Katter's Australia Party. But such appeals can also find a place in the rhetoric of mainstream political parties, for example the Liberal Party and Robert Menzies' invocation of the 'forgotten people' or the ALP and Kevin Rudd's deployment of 'working families'.[19] Even if we only consider the imagined 'people' articulated by PHON, there is still no consistency in its conception of 'the people' as to who should be included.[20]

On paradoxes of leadership

In a democracy, political leaders of all complexions have to negotiate what political scientist Kane and Patapan have called the 'paradox of the democratic leader', broadly framed as a 'tension between leadership and the democratic principle of popular sovereignty'.[21] Specifically, the leader, in order to lead, has to be someone whose political skills mark them out as not ordinary (i.e. not just like those who vote for them), while at the same time positioning themselves to be popular enough to gain the confidence of the voters. This means that leaders have to create the means for citizens to be able to identify with them in positive ways, usually through emphasising popular sovereignty. This opens the way for populist leaders to emphasise whatever qualities might be appropriate to win citizens to their particular political position.

Populist leaders emphasise their 'popular sovereignty' by playing up their ordinariness and playing down the possibility that their political skills mark them as not ordinary. By doing so, Kane and Patapan's 'paradox of the democratic leader' morphs into the 'paradox of the populist leader'. On the one hand, populist leaders emphasise their lack of political skills by proclaiming that they are not professional politicians (i.e. not part of some unspecified elite); on the other, they project themselves as having the knowledge to solve whatever crisis or problem that has created the opportunity for their rise to political prominence. As one scholar of populism wrote, not without irony and while not explicitly acknowledging it as a paradox, populism 'requires the most extraordinary individuals to lead the most ordinary people'.[22]

The 'paradox of the populist leader' could also be understood as a 'paradox of (political) ignorance'. That is to say, that the leader presents as not-knowing (or un-knowing) while also presenting as having the answers. This was certainly how then-Liberal Party candidate Pauline Hanson presented herself both during and after her election in 1996. On her second successful effort as a One Nation candidate in 2016, this was no longer a plausible strategy despite her efforts to keep exploiting the paradox of ignorance. The same might also be said of her strategy of representing herself as powerless in the face of elitist disparagement.[23] Representing oneself as powerless undermines any rationale for political support (except perhaps from sympathy) since it undercuts any claim to knowing how to tackle the problems of others, and hence undercuts the very appeal of being a leader. This is another paradox of political ignorance.

The question of knowing the answers (or not) is central to how we construct our understanding of what defines good or successful leadership, and in particular how assumptions about gender are woven into such understanding. Related to this is the capacity for good or sound judgment, understood as the capacity for weighing up relevant evidence and choosing alternatives based on that weighing-up process. The question of evidence is also a question of degrees of knowledge and, conversely, degrees of ignorance. The more evidence we have for a given issue, the less our ignorance is assumed to be, and the better our capacity for good judgment. While having a capacity for good judgment might not guarantee success as a leader, its absence guarantees failure, as the political fortunes of former prime ministers Kevin Rudd, Mark Latham, Tony Abbott and Malcolm Turnbull attest. For example, in 2016, prime minister Malcolm Turnbull called a double dissolution election in which all seats in both houses were declared vacant. Part of the rationale was to reduce the presence of the crossbench parties and improve the position of the Coalition parties. However, in a double dissolution, parties campaigning for election to the Senate need only half the quota of votes required in a half-Senate election. Turnbull's political strategy made it easier, not harder, for independents and minor party candidates to be elected. The outcome was an increase in the number of crossbench senators, and in the House of Representatives, the Coalition saw its 20-seat majority reduced by 19 seats. This was clearly a poor judgment call, one that did nothing to consolidate his authority within his own party.

A successful leader does not necessarily have to know much about a topic or issue because they can always surround themselves with those who do. However, choosing advisers still requires an exercise of good judgment. The negative experience of Pauline Hanson at the hands of several of her men advisers during her leadership in the 1990s illustrates the need for good judgment. Despite her claims that she has always been her own woman, during the 1990s she deferred to several men advisers, such as David Ettridge, David Oldfield and John Pasquarelli, all of whom let her down politically.[24] Indeed, in the 1998 election, she was probably ill-advised about standing for a lower house seat, instead of making a bid for the Senate where her chances of election were far stronger (it being a state-wide electorate).

A successful Senate bid would have given her a six-year term from which to build a strong political presence and entrench her leadership position. But perhaps this was not an outcome to be welcomed by her key advisers given their own political ambitions at the time.

On knowing ignorance

As important as the capacity for good judgment might be, the key point is that populist politicians like Hanson pitch themselves as not-knowers, in contradistinction to the 'knowing elites'. Not-knowing is a form of ignorance, and it comes in many forms. Knowing ignorance might appear to be an oxymoron. As soon as we begin a discussion of ignorance, we are by definition making ignorance an object of knowledge and engaging in a process of trying to know about ignorance.

There are many kinds of ignorance and numerous ways of classifying them. For example, 'ignorance' denotes a lack of knowledge where something is often understood as 'in need of correction, a kind of natural absence where knowledge has not yet spread'.[25] This is ignorance interpreted as a 'native state' or 'resource', perhaps the most common form of ignorance where we recognise a gap in our knowledge and seek to fill it. This form of ignorance spurs us towards some form of enlightenment. We seek to overcome ignorance by producing knowledge about what we do not know. In this respect it serves as a resource for developing knowledge. For example, in the area of research funding, the principal justification for funding projects is the identification of an area of ignorance that needs to be overcome.

A different form of ignorance concerns loss of knowledge. Such a loss might arise through different ways of organised forgetting. This may be due to a lack of interest in maintaining or reproducing that knowledge, or result from budgetary and other funding decisions, whether public or private. Alternatively, decisions might be taken to destroy particular repositories of knowledge and social memories, whether held in buildings or maintained by specific cultures. Organisational change often results in loss of corporate memory, in particular forms of tacit knowledge upon which successful administration often depends. Or a natural disaster may result in loss of species, knowledge repositories or artefacts that cannot be replaced.

Another form of ignorance, and one more at home in the domain of politics and leadership, is the deliberate fostering of ignorance where not-knowing is actively sustained or produced. This may involve deception where people are deliberately kept in the dark or misled. A variation on this theme is the creation of doubt about particular phenomena. The campaigns waged by the global tobacco companies over the health consequences of tobacco use is a stark example, as are current campaigns aimed at discrediting the science informing interpretations of climate change. A different form of deception involves the selective deployment of information by governments to achieve their policy goals, or the use of secrecy to ensure that only selected knowledge is publicly available. In some cases, the resulting ignorance might be necessary for the greater good; in other cases, it might be done to prevent successful challenges to government or company policies, or to advance a country's strategic interests. Whichever means is deployed, the key point is that ignorance is actively crafted to foster varying levels of not-knowing.

Not-knowing presupposes knowing. In order not to know something there must be prior knowledge of it so that it can be not-known. This is distinct from a more potent form of ignorance, namely that of structured non-knowing. The idea of 'non-known' was developed by philosopher Charles Mills in his essay 'White Ignorance'. In Mills' view, 'white racism or white racial domination and their ramifications' were central to the origins of non-knowing.[26] 'Non-knowing' is not simply a matter of white people lacking knowledge about some aspect of racism (and which therefore can be fixed through some form of education or enlightenment). For Mills, the problem goes much deeper. Non-knowing is the outcome of an active process of not just excluding particular forms of evidence, but of ensuring that there could be no recognition of the possibility of that evidence. As political scientist Mary Hawkesworth explains, an epistemology of white ignorance shapes 'perceptions, public memories, and imaginative possibilities around what is sayable, doable, and thinkable'.[27] If something cannot even be thought, it cannot be known or not-known; it is a non-known.

Something similar occurs with gender. A system of knowing shaped by a masculinist epistemology of ignorance operates to shape perceptions, interpretations and understandings through which some things get to be known (whether true or not) and others remain in the realm of the non-known.

Gender and the paradox of ignorance

The masculinist epistemology of ignorance fosters particular forms of non-knowing, especially those informed by an anti-feminist politics aimed at sustaining ongoing forms of backlash.[28] In some respects, backlash is a direct consequence of the more visible successes of feminist efforts to change (at least some) masculinist privileges and practices. These successes are often widely acknowledged, and sometimes exaggerated, by supporters and opponents alike to suit their respective political purposes. But paradoxically, these successes are often forgotten. Overt knowledge becomes absorbed into everyday commonsense that is itself mediated by the masculinist epistemology of ignorance. This is a form of commonsense involving hierarchies of intellectual originality in which a few are recognised as the leaders in their field and the rest merely as supportive but subordinate contributors.[29] Feminist knowledge, not to mention feminist achievements, recedes into the domain of ignorance as the non-known. This was very ably illustrated in the 2017 movie *Hidden Figures*, which brought to public awareness the unknown and ignored contributions by three women mathematicians who were crucial to the success of the US space program. So for women aspiring to leadership, this is a paradox that must be handled carefully because a feminist sensibility does not form part of a masculinist epistemology. This is just one of a number of troubling paradoxes of political ignorance aspiring women leaders must negotiate.

Another paradox concerns the tacit knowledge that is part of every leadership position (and the means to get there). While it might be that men, too, experience this ignorance, they are more likely to be closer to knowing than most similarly placed women. This is partly because such knowledge is rarely shared openly, and partly because the extracurricular social activities where such knowledge is shared usually excludes women (even if they are physically present!). This kind of ignorance is cultivated and protected within what is sometimes referred to as the 'locker room' aspect of a leadership mindset that must be mastered by aspiring leaders.[30] Women aspirants cannot admit that such knowledge exists. To admit that it does might signal a troublesome demeanour or someone unwilling or unable to fit in. On the other hand, to act as if such knowledge does not exist places them at a disadvantage.

The paradox is further underscored by another related feature of the masculinist epistemology of ignorance. The systemic gendering of leadership is treated as a problem to be overcome by individual women, rather than an outcome of perceptions and practices that posit and sustain a disjunction between women's assumed gender roles and the capacities required for leadership.[31] Failure to succeed is seen as a personal attribute, rather than a product of men's failure or inability to recognise their own non-knowingness. Moreover, systemic structures remain (mostly) unaffected by women changing their individual behaviours. Effective change usually only occurs when measures are implemented on a structural basis (though whether it is lasting is another matter). Non-knowing is sustained because what is deemed to be appropriate knowledge for leadership remains focused on individuals rather than systemic structures.

Another form of this paradox of ignorance is what we might call the 'who knows?' paradox. On the one hand, individual women might be unaware of each other's experiences on any number of issues (even when they have experienced the same event). On the other hand, this individualised ignorance combines with that of the wider community to further sustain the state of non-knowing. Gender biases (discrimination) flourish through the (re)production of this form of ignorance. The consciousness-raising strategies of the feminist upsurge in the late 1960s and early 1970s made possible a range of knowledges that proved effective in counteracting this form of ignorance for a time. But the rise of a neo-liberalised political culture in the following decades enabled the individualising dynamic within the masculinist epistemology of ignorance to reassert its influence.

Finally, there is the paradox of what we might call 'the survival form of ignorance'. Women have to become 'strategically ignorant' by presenting themselves as ignorant or feigning ignorance relative to men. In order not to be contained within the domain of non-knowing, a woman has to assert herself as one who knows enough, but not too much. Every assertion of being one who knows immediately positions women as legitimate targets for political and social approbation. As a result, women have to deny and affirm the ignorance that makes them politically acceptable and possible leaders. Yet not to do so means that women cannot gain political prominence, let alone the credibility, to be considered proper leadership material. This is one of the many ways in which women, as distinct from men, are expected to perform gender. For example, both Julia Gillard and Julie Bishop, their party and ideological differences notwithstanding, carefully worked at presenting themselves in ways that did not position them as outshining their men colleagues. Similarly, Pauline Hanson, pursued a strategy of defiance and deference as part of her 'manning up' approach.[32]

The systemic dimensions of the masculinist mindset and its various and multiple practices are not accidental. It is not just that it suits men to leave this mindset unchallenged, though that is an important dimension. It is a function of the masculinist epistemology of ignorance. Aspects of it might 'trouble' elites from time to time because of concerted challenges to their authority and privileges, but elites can and have lived with making occasional adjustments. Some of these adjustments might even challenge this or that aspect of the masculinist epistemology of ignorance but, to date, the viability/longevity of its systemic nature remains mostly undisturbed. Elites may be troubled from time to time, but not to the point where they fear their elimination.

IV
MEDIA
REPRESENTATIONS

THE RIGHT ROYAL DILEMMA: WOMEN AS JOURNALISTS AND SOURCES IN THE MEDIA

Jenna Price

I have been writing for Australian news organisations my entire adult life. For the past 20 years, I have also had the privilege of being both an academic and the writer of an opinion column for the *Sydney Morning Herald* and the *Canberra Times*. When I look at my columns over any 12-month period, they have been almost exclusively about what might be called 'women's issues': domestic violence, reproductive rights, child rearing and child care, families and women at work.

When I started to look at who wrote what in the Australian media, I was concerned that I had become an outlier. Had I pigeonholed myself by writing about 'women's issues'? Were other women journalists doing a better job of how they engaged with their work? And what of sources? When women were interviewed as experts, what were they talking about? I had been asking myself these questions my entire professional life, but it became a research project after a brief interaction on Twitter with Australian philanthropist Carol Schwartz. She, too, wanted to know the answers to these questions. The data showed stark gender differences in terms of who the reporters were, what they wrote about, who the sources for their stories were, who took and appeared in the photographs, where stories were placed in the media outlet, and who wrote the editorials.

As it turned out, I was not an outlier. Journalism is a highly gendered industry, and this is no less the case when it comes to reporting on Australia's politics and political leadership. This chapter provides an overview and analysis of who is writing what in Australia's media, and considers the impact this has on opportunities to embrace diversity, particularly in leadership. The findings are significant for a number of reasons: they show that Australia has an established cultural norm of male journalists reporting on political leadership (arguably seen as 'men's issues'); despite some important advances, institutionalised structures of gender-based discrimination remain; and finally, there is a paucity of women as both political leaders and political journalists. This constrains our ability to challenge leadership norms and imagine a gender-inclusive leadership culture.

Analysing Australian media

To get an understanding of these issues, I undertook research with my colleague Anne Maree Payne, supported by the Trawalla Foundation, to take a snapshot of Australia's most influential news sites on four consecutive Thursdays in October 2018. The report used seven of the ten sites that Nielsen, which measures digital performance by publishers, ranks highest for traffic for digital content. As we were looking at news media, we used 9news (which focuses on news headlines) in place of the broader nine.com.au site (which focuses on celebrity, fashion and other lifestyle content). Similarly, we used Yahoo!7 in place of Yahoo. We also added *The Australian*, the *Australian Financial Review*, the *Courier Mail*, *Herald Sun*, the *West Australian* and BuzzFeed for a range of reasons, including audience and geographical variation. Below is the full list of news sites analysed:

- 9news
- ABC
- BuzzFeed
- *Courier Mail*

- *Daily Mail Australia*
- news.com.au
- *The Age*
- *The Australian*
- *The Daily Telegraph*
- *Financial Review*
- The *Guardian*
- *Herald Sun*
- The *Sydney Morning Herald*
- The *West Australian*
- Yahoo!7.

We chose Thursdays because that is traditionally a high-traffic day with big audiences, and we targeted the peak times between 12 pm and 2 pm. From those sites we selected the top five stories from their position on the homepage of the publication. In February 2019, we analysed the top five opinion pieces on each site across Tuesday to Saturday in one week. Again, we looked at what was on offer between 12 pm and 2 pm.

Furthermore, we analysed 300 news stories across four separate data collection dates, and we then categorised them into one of nine separate topic codes: government and politics; law, crime and justice; business, finance, and economics; science (defined broadly to include a range of scientific fields encompassing areas as diverse as meteorology, climate change and medicine/health sciences); disasters and accidents (including 'near misses'); media/arts/entertainment; celebrities/royals; sport; and what might be described as the 'weird and the wonderful, the odd and unusual'. We also conducted interviews with key editors for their insights into the gender dynamics at play in the media. In summary, this approach provides a snapshot into what Australians are reading on popular and prominent news sites, and what Australian journalists are writing about.

Who writes what?

For decades, men have outnumbered women in newsrooms across Australia. Now, according to the Workplace Gender Equality Agency (WGEA), the news industry is nearly at parity.[1] This, however, does not necessarily mean that women have achieved equality in the news media. Our research showed Australians are reading more stories about men, written by men, who quote men, with stories by male journalists often positioned in the top spots on the home pages of these websites in what journalists call a 'better run'. As Table 6 shows, the coverage of government and of politics, together with the category of law, crime and justice, made up nearly half of all the stories in our sample. Men wrote 60 per cent of the stories in both of these topic categories (the most male category is sport, where 88 per cent of the stories were written by men). The next most frequently represented topic was business and finance. Again, this was a section in our sample that was dominated by male reporters as they wrote 60 per cent of the stories. It is important to note that these topics – government, politics, business, finance, crime and justice – are the ones where national policies are highlighted, critiqued and debated. These are the stories that shape the national politics.

TABLE 6

Gender of journalist by story code[2]

Topic	Male (%)	Female (%)
Sport	88	12
Other[3]	71	29
Government and politics	61	39
Business and finance	60	40
Law, crime and justice	59	41
Disasters/accidents	50	50
Media/arts/entertainment	48	52
Science	41	59
Celebrities/royals	24	76

Women journalists, on the other hand, dominated the celebrity and arts categories. The sample of stories for our research was taken during the official 2018 royal visit to Australia of Prince Harry and Meghan Markle. We classified those stories in the celebrity/royals category. While there might have been a time when writing about the royals meant engaging in world affairs, this hasn't been the case in this century. Women's bylines, at more than three-quarters, dominated this category, although that's not quite as strong as the male domination of sport. As Table 6 demonstrates, women also wrote slightly more media, entertainment and arts stories; and three-fifths of the stories about science. However, this last finding may be an anomaly. In our data set, only 19 stories, accounting for 6 per cent of all the stories in the sample, related to science. This was another broad category, and included stories ranging from weather (meteorology) to climate change and the health sciences. Climate change is a hot topic, but only two stories in the sample directly addressed it, although there were a number of stories about 'wild weather'. While we found that female journalists wrote 59 per cent of the science-related stories, science remains a male-dominated field and other research into science journalism has suggested that male journalists continue to dominate the reporting.[4]

Who's the source?

We also saw a gender bias in who journalists approached to be their expert sources in stories. Our research shows that men's voices are far more prominent than those of women, as outlined in Table 7. Across our data set from all of the sites analysed, the average representation of female sources was just over one-third. However, we found that male journalists were more likely to quote men as their source, while mixed teams and women journalists were more likely than men (but not guaranteed) to quote women as their source. The use of male sources by male journalists ranged from 93 per cent at the *Australian*

Financial Review to 62 per cent on BuzzFeed. Men constituted 95 per cent of direct sources in sports-related stories (despite the rise in coverage of women's sport), 82 per cent in business and finance stories, 79 per cent in law, crime and justice stories, then dropping to a low of 41 per cent in stories relating to celebrities/royals. The representation of male indirect sources (sources mentioned in the story but not directly quoted) was even higher in most story topic categories.

TABLE 7

Gender of sources quoted (direct and indirect) by story code[5]

Topic	Direct sources		Indirect sources	
	Male	Female	Male	Female
Government and politics	159 (68%)	76 (32%)	46 (72%)	18 (38%)
Law, crime and justice	73 (79%)	29 (21%)	22 (76%)	7 (24%)
Business and finance	80 (82%)	18 (18%)	17 (89%)	2 (11%)
Celebrities/royals	31 (41%)	45 (59%)	3 (60%)	2 (40%)
Media/arts/entertainment	32 (62%)	24 (38%)	4 (57%)	3 (43%)
Science	35 (67%)	17 (33%)	1 (100%)	0 (0%)
Sport	18 (95%)	1 (5%)	8 (89%)	1 (11%)
Disasters/accidents	14 (70%)	6 (30%)	1 (100%)	0 (0%)
Other	5 (65%)	3 (37%)	2 (100%)	0 (0%)

Only the stories on one news site – BuzzFeed – quoted more women than men. BuzzFeed stood out both because of the number of bylines by women journalists and the number of women quoted. Female journalists on this site were the most likely to use female sources (65 per cent), closely followed by 9news (63 per cent). BuzzFeed, which is American owned and has since closed its Australian news outlet, says it targeted 'a new generation of news consumers looking for something new' and was, when the research was undertaken, a frontrunner in terms of gender equity in news reporting. It had the highest epresentation of both female journalists and inclusion of female sources across all of the news sites analysed. However, an analysis of its stories showed that nearly half of the articles in the sample related to celebrity, royals, media, arts and entertainment, which have traditionally been more likely to be written by women and to quote women as sources. Outside BuzzFeed and 9news, female journalists approached gender parity in the sources they cited at *The Age* (53 per cent) and the *Guardian* (47 per cent). At the other end sits the *Australian Financial Review*, where women made up only one in seven of the sources.

In terms of topics, we found that women were 32 per cent of direct sources quoted and 28 per cent of indirect sources in stories on government and politics that were written by women. However, it should be noted that some political stories – such as those on the campaign to decriminalise abortion in Queensland or the sexual harassment allegations made by Dr Christine Blasey Ford against Trump Supreme Court nominee Brett Kavanaugh – had a much higher representation of female sources than others. Women appeared as sources when the subject of the stories was specifically about women's experience or women's political battles.

However, while women are more likely than men to quote female sources, this wasn't consistent. For example, our research found that 100 per cent of the sources cited by female journalists at the *Herald Sun* were male, and female journalists also used a high proportion of male sources at the *Australian Financial Review* (82 per cent), the ABC (78 per cent), and the *Daily Telegraph*, the *Courier Mail* and the *West Australian* (each at 75 per cent). These figures suggest that the gender of the journalist alone is not a reliable predictor of the likelihood of female sources being cited. But it's important to note that the choice of source is constrained by the fact that there is often little choice. This is particularly the case in political leadership roles where women are under-represented and therefore simply not an option in terms of being a journalist's source.

The then-education editor at *The Age*, Henrietta Cook, told our researchers that she constantly considered gender diversity in her sources. 'It is something at the back of my mind, but my round also has a lot of women academics. Most of the principals' associations are headed up by women and I often feel that it's mothers who are much more likely to contact me about issues at schools than fathers', she said.[6] Joanne Gray, managing editor of the *Australian Financial Review*, recognises that capturing women's voices as sources is an issue for her publication. She explained:

> What we would love to do is constantly track how many articles we have about women, quoting women. We do pay attention to the pictures of women. But quoting women directly and indirectly, I don't think we've been getting the data on that. So, I'm wondering if we can get our product people to come up with a tracker for us; I think that would be really useful.[7]

In summary, the figures from this sample show female journalists are significantly more likely to use female sources (40 per cent) than male journalists (24 per cent). Articles co-authored by male and female journalists are also significantly more likely to use female sources (37 per cent) than articles written solely by male journalists (24 per cent). In other words, if you want more diverse sources, a good tip is to have more diverse writers.

Who is taking the photos, and who is in them?

In our research, we also found that images of women were scarce. Women were absent from the photos that accompany the top stories. As explained earlier, this data collection coincided with the 2018 royal visit. If photographs of Meghan Markle and female victims of crime had been omitted from the data set, the representation of female subjects in photographs would have been even lower. Moreover, women had poor representation behind the camera – just under 80 per cent of the bylines on photographs belong to men. When it comes to celebrity photos, again we see domination by male photographers. Members of the paparazzi are mainly men, and we found that 81 per cent of the photos in the celebrity story topic were taken by male photographers. The majority of the photos attributed to female photographers were taken by female journalists themselves, and they were not of the celebrities or royals but of 'local colour'; that is, street shots of royal well-wishers.

In the government and politics category, just under a quarter (24 per cent) of the photographers were women, and women were the subjects in just 29 per cent of the photos. This may, of course, reflect the low numbers of women in elected political roles. Law, crime and justice was the second most prevalent topic in these high-profile spots on the home page, and women did appear in more of the photographs and were the subjects in 32 per cent of photos. However, it is important to note that the majority of the women in these photographs were victims of crime. While women made up 59 per cent of photo subjects relating to science stories, a number of these were photographs of women in bikinis accompanying weather-related stories.

Who writes opinion pieces?

Opinion pieces are important in shaping both leadership and political debates on policy. We therefore looked at opinion pieces to see if topics or authorship were gendered. In February 2019, we analysed the top five opinion pieces on each of the 15 chosen sites across Tuesday to Saturday in one week. Again, we looked at what was on offer between 12 pm and 2 pm. Of the 282 pieces in our opinion data set, nearly two-thirds were written by men (see Table 8). In the *Australian Financial Review*, 18 of the 25 opinion pieces collected were by men, two by women and a further five had no byline, in keeping with style for the publication's editorials. Across our entire data set, a higher proportion of opinion pieces on the topics of government and politics, and business and finance, were written by men compared to news stories on these topics. For example, the *Australian Financial Review* had gender parity in the representation of male and female journalists on the top five new stories, but 90 per cent of opinion pieces in our data set from the *Australian Financial Review* were written by men. Similarly, *The Australian* had close to gender parity (slightly more men than women) in the representation of journalists who wrote the top five stories on its news site, but over 80 per cent of opinion pieces were authored by men. So, you could say that while women were trusted to report the information, they were not trusted to interpret it. However, while nearly 90 per cent of news stories on sport were written by men, well over half of the opinion pieces on sports-related issues were by women.

TABLE 8

Opinion pieces and gender of journalist[8]

Topic (no. of opinion pieces)	Male	Female
Business and finance (47)	18 (90%)	2 (10%)
Government and politics (103)	21 (84%)	4 (16%)
Science (8)	17 (74%)	6 (26%)
Sport (8)	20 (74%)	7 (26%)
All other (33)	17 (71%)	7 (29%)
Law crime and justice (8)	18 (69%)	8 (31%)
Total	165 (62%)	103 (38%)

In all likelihood, if you read an opinion piece from the two national publications, *The Australian* and the *Australian Financial Review*, they will nearly always be written by men. Diversity in opinion writing matters because those columns undertake what researchers Kelling and Thomas (2018) call 'the evaluation, explanation, analysis and contextualization that journalists involved in daily reporting may not necessarily have the capacity to do due to time and space constraints'.[9] Commentary not only makes sense of what author Hulteng called 'the glut of events',[10] but it also shapes public opinion.[11]

Consistent trends

The findings from our research are consistent with other analyses of Australian media. For example, Streem, an Australian media monitoring service, completed a similar analysis to ours in November 2019 and highlighted similar trends.[12] They found that the *Herald Sun* once again featured many more male voices, written by male journalists, despite having some of the best women reporters in the country. Media analyst Conal Hanna described Streem's method in November 2019: 'We decided to celebrate the journalists who have produced the most page-one stories this year in print, or homepage-leading stories in digital.'[13] There were 212 journalists who made the Streem list: 16 of the top 50 were women, and women were 37 per cent of journalists overall. In the highest profile rounds, such as federal politics, there were 15 reporters and six of those were women (40 per cent). Both of the sports reporters in the top 50 were men. The combined economics/business/finance reporters numbered eight, and of those, only one was a woman. Do women choose to do other rounds or become socialised to do other rounds? It would require a different kind of research to discover why men write in these rounds, and we would have to do longitudinal studies from the first time reporters set foot in a newsroom to discover how news round choices are shaped.

Gaven Morris, the director of news, analysis and investigations at the ABC, gave an interview to one of our researchers. He said he thought the gendered nature of rounds was a

> generational thing, and starts with the culture of those areas. The more the cultures change in areas such as the business and finance sector, or politics, or sport, I think the more interesting

and diverse the coverage of those areas will be, and the more interesting and diverse the journalists who want to work on those stories will be. If it's seen as a bit of a boys' club – because the people who work in the area are predominantly men – it's not a particularly welcoming place for women to be.[14]

Sport is a great example. The rise of women's sport as a mainstream, prominent area of interest for all Australians in the past five years has been extraordinary. It isn't just netball anymore; it's football and other sports that we've seen as being male domains. The more we see women's sport rise – and the broader the issues have become – the more we see a diversity of journalists interested in covering it, and the better the coverage has been.[15]

Lessons for the future

As long as politics, sports, economics and other areas remain male-dominated, then the representation of these issues will remain male-centric. When men write, they tend to interview men in stories about men. It's men who are often seen as both journalists and experts in the media, so it is men who are prominent in shaping the national debates and agendas. And if you can't hear women's voices represented in leadership debates, then this has an impact on our understanding of whose voices matter, what leadership looks like, and who can be our leaders.

American activist Marian Wright Edelman reportedly said: 'You can't be what you can't see'. There is a direct link between media representation and leadership, and the importance of role models has consistently been demonstrated. As researchers Morgenroth and colleagues noted, we need role models because they represent the possible, they are inspirational, and they tell us how to behave.[16] Of course, it's not just good for women and girls to have women role models, it's also good for boys and men to see this diversity.

Well-managed diversity matters, from the boardroom to the class-room and beyond.[17]

If we are to see a positive change in the current gendered climate of voices and sources in the media, then we should first acknowledge the problem and then actively encourage greater gender diversity in news. Reading a diverse range of sources will allow news consumers a broader picture across business, politics, law and justice. News managers need to recognise the benefits of gender and other forms of diversity, and this requires deliberative hiring practices and a conscious move to support women to report on areas that are now largely occupied by male reporters. That's the only way to change the picture in the long term.

THE MURDOCH PRESSES:
REPRESENTATION OF MASCULINITY
AND FEMININITY IN LEADERSHIP

Blair Williams

The Murdoch press has long held political and cultural influence in Australia, in part due to its dominance of national daily newspaper circulation and its monopoly in multiple states and capital cities.[1] Murdoch-owned papers have been criticised by some as promoting conservative economic and social views that are hostile to women, especially those women who threaten the political status quo by ascending to the upper echelons of national politics.[2] To explore this claim, this chapter examines how three of the most prominent products of the Murdoch press, *The Australian*, *Daily Telegraph* and *Herald Sun*, reported on parliamentarians over the last decade who challenged a sitting prime minister – Julia Gillard, Kevin Rudd, Malcolm Turnbull, Scott Morrison, Peter Dutton and Julie Bishop – to identify whether gendered double standards can be found in such coverage, and to assess their impact on women in politics.

Five of the six prime ministers who have served since 2010 were deposed by a challenge to their leadership, and a prime minister hasn't served a full term in office since John Howard in 2007. The frequency of these challenges has led many Australians to joke that leadership spills should be considered a national sport, or that paramedics can no longer expect patients to name the current prime minister because it's all just too confusing! While it might seem chaotic and unpredictable, the appointment or removal of prime ministers by their party is a time-honoured privilege of the Westminster parliamentary system. Yet such a move is highly newsworthy and can be negatively received, with accusations of the challenger's disloyalty, egotism and even murderous motives frequently appearing in news headlines.

The recent round of leadership spills started when Julia Gillard, then deputy prime minister, challenged sitting Labor prime minister Kevin Rudd for the leadership in June 2010 and subsequently became Australia's first woman prime minister. Many were excited by this 'historic' moment, but the path by which Gillard gained leadership brought out the full wrath of the Australian press. She was accused of treachery for 'backstabbing' an incumbent (male) prime minister, and, as noted in previous chapters, was forced to endure explicitly gendered and misogynistic media coverage throughout her prime-ministerial term.[3] Rudd regained the leadership with a successful challenge of his own in June 2013 that followed two previous, unsuccessful spills in February 2012 and March 2013. The federal election in the same year saw the Labor Party lose to the Coalition led by Tony Abbott who, after years of ridiculing Labor's leadership challenges, was himself replaced by former leader Malcolm Turnbull in September 2015. Finally, Turnbull was unsuccessfully challenged on 21 August 2018 by cabinet minister Peter Dutton, who announced a second spill on 24 August, which Turnbull did not contest. This spill saw deputy prime minister Julie Bishop and treasurer Scott Morrison competing with Dutton for leadership. Bishop, although more popular with the electorate, was eliminated in the first round, leaving Morrison to defeat Dutton in the second round.

Despite the bipartisan regularity of these spills, Gillard endured the most vigorous media backlash for challenging a sitting prime minister, spearheaded by the Murdoch press.[4] Some might attribute this to the novelty of her actions, yet leadership challenges weren't an unusual event in the Australian political landscape before 2010, and, moreover, the male challengers who followed her example received a very different reception from the media.[5] The primary point of distinction here, then, seems to be Gillard's gender, and these more recent leadership spills provide a valuable opportunity to examine the specifically gendered differences in Murdoch press coverage of leaders and their challengers.

Parliament – a space for men only?

Parliament is a highly masculine domain created for and dominated by men.[6] The results of the 2019 election show that women remain a minority in the House of Representatives at 30.5 per cent of total MPs (46 women versus 105 men). Despite these numbers, many still refuse to acknowledge the extent to which the political process is far from gender-neutral.[7] A 'masculine blueprint' shapes the very idea of what it means to be a politician, privileging men and granting them an advantage while disadvantaging women.[8] This blueprint ties political leadership to personality traits traditionally viewed as masculine, such as authority, strength, determination, rationality and decisiveness, while stereotypically feminine traits like compassion, warmth and sensitivity are considered antithetical to leadership.[9] Women politicians are therefore relegated to an almost inescapable gendered double bind, compelled to display the masculine traits traditionally viewed as crucial for success, even while doing so exposes them to critique as 'unwomanly' and unrelatable for the general electorate. While men hold the bulk of positions in the Australian parliament, women politicians are more likely to be scrutinised, especially if they challenge a sitting leader – an act seen as hypermasculine.

Women in politics are also subjected to a different standard of heavily gendered media coverage. Mainstream media tend to reinforce gender norms through articles, editorials and online pieces that present male politicians as the norm and women as a political novelty, focusing on their gender, appearance and personal lives to an extent that can delegitimise and trivialise their public personas.[10] While this is a general trend, the Murdoch press, as detailed below, seems to be a particularly consistent purveyor of such gendered coverage.

Despite the rise of social media and online news platforms, newspapers continue to define what we consider to be 'newsworthy' – often setting the news agenda for the day – and therefore remain an important focus for media analysis. Furthermore, News Corp Australia dominates the Australian media landscape and enjoys ownership of the only daily local newspaper available in multiple capital cities, wielding significant political influence. How, then, does the Murdoch press cover women politicians who threaten the status quo by challenging a sitting leader? And does this coverage differ for men who commit the same act?

To answer these questions, I have collected a representative sample of articles published in three Murdoch-owned newspapers: *The Australian*, as our only national broadsheet, and the *Herald Sun* (Melbourne) and the *Daily Telegraph* (Sydney), as two of News Corp's most widely circulated tabloids. Leadership challenges generate a high volume of media coverage, often occupying the front page for several consecutive days, so I have restricted the scope of my study to the first four days following the public announcement of each challenge (see Table 9). Dutton alone among the six politicians analysed challenged

TABLE 9

Number and dates of newspaper articles selected per leader

Challenger	Leader	Date	Number of overall articles	Number of relevant articles
Julia Gillard	Kevin Rudd	23–27/06/2010	93 (36 duplicates)	48
Kevin Rudd	Julia Gillard	26–30/06/2013	59 (33 duplicates)	20
Malcolm Turnbull	Tony Abbott	14–18/09/2015	101 (27 duplicates)	36
Peter Dutton	Malcolm Turnbull	21–25/08/2018	131 (54 duplicates)	64
Scott Morrison	Malcolm Turnbull	24–28/08/2018	58 (17 duplicates)	39
Julie Bishop	Malcolm Turnbull	24–28/08/2018	33 (13 duplicates)	19

for the leadership twice in one week, so I have included coverage of both spills, though it should be noted that this subsided considerably the day after his second challenge.

Lady Macbeths and triumphant men

My analysis exposed three principal manifestations of gender bias in the Murdoch press. First, I discovered that women challengers for the prime-ministerial role (Gillard and Bishop) experienced a greater quantity of gendered coverage than their male counterparts. For example, women were far more likely than men to draw comment for their gender or aspects of their gendered identity. Second, and more surprisingly, I found that the political affiliation of the challenger didn't impact their coverage as much as I had anticipated. Finally, I noticed stark qualitative differences in the discussion of a woman's gender, appearance and family life than that of her male counterparts.

A closer analysis shows that Gillard's and Bishop's gender, appearance and family lives were frequently discussed and emphasised in news stories whose focus had little relevance to their personal lives (see Figure 4). Unsurprisingly, Gillard's gender was often mentioned to emphasise the historic consequence of her status as Australia's first *female* or *woman* prime minister, while Bishop's gender was emphasised by her frequent description as a 'trailblazer' for Liberal *women*.[11] Such coverage, although predictable, celebrates their achievement as the first women to enter these roles, but also emphasises deviation from a masculine political norm, 'reinforcing the notion of women as out of place and unnatural in the political sphere [with] important political consequences'.[12] As men are the assumed norm as prime ministers and challengers for leadership, gender was rarely noted in coverage of Rudd, Turnbull, Morrison or Dutton, and mostly used when describing their actions. Dutton, for example, was referred to as 'the man who brought Turnbull to his knees',[13] while Morrison

FIGURE 4

Percentage of articles that mentioned gender, appearance or family

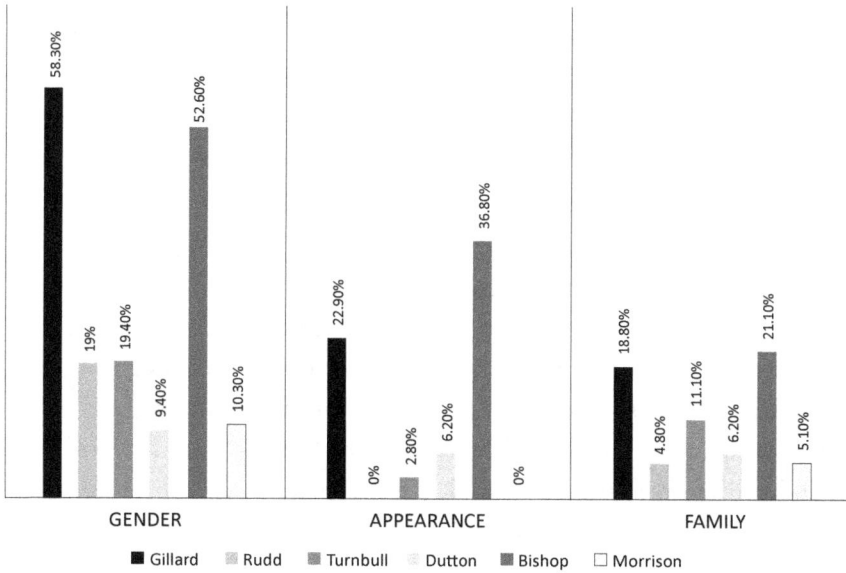

| | GENDER | APPEARANCE | FAMILY |

Gillard values: 58.30%, 22.90%, 18.80%
Rudd values: 19%, 0%, 4.80%
Turnbull values: 19.40%, 2.80%, 11.10%
Dutton values: 9.40%, 6.20%, 6.20%
Bishop values: 52.60%, 36.80%, 21.10%
Morrison values: 10.30%, 0%, 5.10%

■ Gillard   ▨ Rudd   ■ Turnbull   ▢ Dutton   ■ Bishop   ☐ Morrison

was described as 'the man who stopped the boats'.[14] While the term 'woman' in the examples above serves to emphasise Gillard's and Bishop's femininity as a point of difference and deviation from the norm, 'man', though often a universal label for humanity in general, is used here to play into the association of masculinity with action; it casts them as 'action men' who get things done with no room for compromise or equivocation.

The results of this analysis also made it clear that gender is a far more significant factor than political affiliation in coverage of leadership challengers. Gillard, from the left faction of the ALP, and Bishop, a moderate Liberal, experienced comparably gendered media coverage. One point of distinction is the quantity of articles written about each woman's challenge: 48 for Gillard, 19 for Bishop. Yet this is unsurprising, given that Gillard successfully became Australia's first woman prime minister while Bishop was compelled to resign.

Turning to male challengers, however, I found that political affiliation proved more salient for Rudd (ALP) and Turnbull (moderate Liberal), both seen as proponents of socially progressive policies and involved in notoriously tumultuous relationships with Murdoch. These leaders initially received favourable – or at least neutral – coverage from the Murdoch press, including *The Australian*'s editor-in-chief Chris Mitchell's support of Rudd before the 2007 election[15] and pro-Turnbull News Corp coverage of the 2016 election.[16] They both fell from grace, however, and were subjected to long-running negative media campaigns,[17] which they blamed for their demise and which led Rudd to brand the Murdoch press 'the greatest cancer on democracy'.[18] Both men experienced more negative coverage than Morrison (conservative Liberal) and Dutton (hard-right Liberal), who were favoured by Murdoch. During the anti-Turnbull push leading up to the 2018 spill, News Corp promoted an idea held by a Coalition minority that Dutton was the 'antidote'.[19] Though Dutton ultimately lost the ballot, Morrison's ascension nevertheless proved palatable as it achieved the goal of removing the socially progressive Turnbull from office.

I discovered another point of stark distinction between women and male challengers in the qualities and associations evoked by discussion of their gender. Men are tacitly permitted to act in an aggressive and adversarial manner in the Australian political sphere, drawing little more than accusations of playing the 'Canberra game', while women risk denunciation as unwomanly, violent and abnormal for comparable behaviour.[20] This disparity can be traced to the framing of politics as a game in which 'men playing tough are just being the norm' while women are harshly criticised for any perceived foul play.[21] Gillard and Bishop, for example, were equated with the Shakespearean villain Lady Macbeth,[22] a ruthless, vengeful and ambitious character fixated on pursuing power, no matter the cost. This comparison 'evidences discomfort with women in powerful political positions'.[23] In contrast, male challengers were said to be taking back or 'seizing' the prime-ministerial role.[24] Rudd, for example, received praise for 'restor[ing] a sense of legitimacy to the prime minister's office'[25] while Turnbull's challenge was heralded as a 'triumph' and 'one of the most remarkable comebacks in Australian politics'.[26]

While Rudd and Turnbull were commended for their ambition, Gillard and Bishop were generally assessed most comprehensively on the basis of physical appearance – a subject rarely broached in the coverage of male challengers. Bishop gained notoriety in articles and headlines for her stylish outfits and shoes, and her regular attendance at fashion events,[27] while one journalist wrote of Gillard:

> [she] looked like a movie star ... With her beautifully fluffed, newly tinted hair, freshly blow-waved by her partner, Tim (lucky girl), and her freshly and professionally applied make-up, her star quality was immediately obvious.[28]

Gillard was presented for the male gaze as an objectified red-car- pet celebrity rather than a parliamentarian. In the sample of articles selected for study, neither Rudd nor Morrison were described in remotely comparable terms, or assessed based on appearance at all. A single mention of Turnbull's shirt and the occasional description of Dutton as a 'hard-faced ex-copper' were the only concessions to the superficial that emerged in coverage of male challengers.[29] Yet, even then, the phrase 'hard-faced' refers more to temperament than physical appearance. At best, this is a positive attribute signalling a determined, uncompromising and driven attitude; at worst, it implies an unpalatable but far from politically disastrous lack of sympathy and affection.

Representations of familial relationships were also highly gen- dered. Gillard, for example, was branded a 'single, childless woman'[30] while, in one article, Bishop was identified as 'the previously married Bishop',[31] with another focusing on the question of what her partner would be called if he became the 'first man'.[32] In contrast, Turnbull was described as 'very much a family man',[33] Dutton as a 'father of three'[34] and Morrison was said to 'love cooking ... football, his family and his church'.[35] Coverage of a male politician's family provides opportunities for image-making and a proof of credentials as a 'good family man', yet women politicians are again written into a double bind: either thoroughly scrutinised in their role as wives and mothers, or criticised for not marrying or having children. Whichever path they choose, their valuing of professional over domestic fulfilment is implied to be abnormal.

Murdoch's ideological war?

Murdoch's conservative ideology has clearly influenced the portrayal in his newspapers of women who challenge the status quo. Murdoch has exerted political influence through his Australian and international subsidiaries of News Corp since the mid-to-late 1970s. Despite the libertarian stance that he initially demonstrated in his British and Australian newspapers, for example, by opposing apartheid, racism and the Vietnam War in the pages of *The Sun*, he soon adopted a conservative neoliberal ideology that found reflection in the content of his newspapers.[36] A former editor for the UK *Sunday Times* stated that Murdoch

> expects his papers to stand broadly for what he believes: a
> combination of right-wing Republicanism from America mixed
> with undiluted Thatcherism from Britain … the resulting potage is
> a radical-right dose of free market economics, the social agenda of
> the Christian Moral Majority and the hard-line conservative views
> on subjects like drugs, abortion, law and order and defence.[37]

Such expectations are reflected in the role that Murdoch has played in Australia's culture wars, and especially in *The Australian*. This ideological battle over the core of Australia's moral identity centred on family values, nationhood, a disputed colonial history and the assertion of a Western civilisation that privileges and universalises whiteness, maleness and heterosexuality.[38] A division is generally drawn between those who disagree with the uncomplicated promotion of the latter, disparaged as 'the elite', and those who agree, championed as 'average Australians', 'Howard's battlers' or, more recently, the 'quiet Australians'. The so-called elite, however, includes many who would be regarded by other measures as disadvantaged or minority groups compelled to fight for social justice and equality.

Women like Gillard and Bishop, who dare to challenge a sitting (male) prime minister, threaten the status quo by contesting someone regarded as the universal norm: a figurative patriarch. Additionally, the very act of challenging a sitting prime minister is considered adversarial, even for men, so when performed by a woman it is inevitably perceived as excessively aggressive and violent.

It is therefore unsurprising that the Murdoch press portrayed Gillard, above all, in a highly gendered manner: not only did she oppose their ideological base, but she was an unmarried, child-free woman from the left faction of the ALP.[39] Likewise, Bishop's association with the more progressive moderate strand of the Liberal Party, despite her substantial electoral popularity, goes some way to explaining why she was either gendered or overlooked altogether in Murdoch press coverage. Both women were punished for being seen to threaten the political status quo while their male counterparts emerged relatively unscathed or even received praise for 'taking back' that which was considered to be rightfully theirs all along.

Examining the Murdoch press coverage of leadership challenges allows us to clearly see how it perpetuates a space for editorial coverage that is particularly hostile to women politicians who threaten the assumed status quo. Gillard and Bishop were both portrayed through a heavily gendered lens that focused on their gender, appearance and personal lives while male colleagues were rarely, if ever, comparably portrayed. Instead, their challenges were positively labelled as a triumphant restoration of legitimacy to the prime-ministerial role.

The need to highlight this conservative ideological and political influence is essential in a national media landscape dominated by

News Corp, not only because of the ramifications for women politicians, but due to the impact on society in general.[40] It is imperative to distinguish the strategies adopted by different media organisations to identify how newspaper discourse on women politicians could be improved and, more importantly, to indicate where this is most needed. There is an urgent need for more women in all political roles, in order to normalise their presence and introduce new gender norms and expectations in politics. Progress along this path will always be hindered, however, by a print media landscape that continues to rely on gendered stereotypes.

THEY READ ABOUT CARS, THEY READ ABOUT FOOTY: LEADERSHIP, IDENTITY AND AUSTRALIAN ELECTIONS

Stephanie Brookes

Mum is a woman of great and practical faith, quietly and patiently loving us, always. Life is about what you contribute, not what you accumulate. That's what Mum and Dad have taught me. It's about serving others, because in life, it's people that matter.

Scott Morrison, Coalition Campaign Launch, Melbourne, Victoria, 12 May 2019

My mum is the smartest woman I've ever known. It has never occurred to me that women are not the equal of men. It's never occurred to me that women shouldn't be able to do everything. That is why I work with strong women. That is why I believe in the equal treatment of women.

Bill Shorten, Campaign Doorstop, Nowra, New South Wales, 8 May 2019

Election campaigns are a blend of the routine and irregular, one of the predictably recurring interruptions to the daily business of governing in liberal democracies. During campaigns, a flood of words and images is generated by politicians vying for office, journalists covering campaigns, political actors seeking to influence outcomes, and citizens considering their position. Through campaign speeches, passionate social media debates, newspaper articles and viral memes, elections crystallise and articulate national values and priorities.

This chapter analyses election campaign language. It explores the way political leaders express their own identities, connecting policy choices and preferences to their personal values and family stories (as in the quotes above) to form emotional, or 'affective', bonds with voters. It does so through a case study from the 2019 Australian federal election, in which Liberal Prime Minister Scott Morrison and Labor opposition leader Bill Shorten mobilised a range of intersecting gendered discourses linked to national identity during the first televised leaders' debate. The chapter addresses the enduring and evolving shape of these discourses, considering their histories, appeal and alignment with the changing media landscapes in which election campaigns are waged.

The key issue this chapter explores is how those running for the office of prime minister mobilise gender identity as part of their appeal to voters. It asks: How do campaigning leaders seek to construct, align themselves with, and claim ownership of a version of Australian identity? How do they both project their own individual identity (this is who *I* am) and provide a connection to constituents (vote for me because I represent who *we* truly are)? These are addressed through discourse analysis, which can be understood as 'the study of language in use'.[1] This form of analysis pays attention to 'the meanings we give language and the actions we carry out when we use language in specific contexts'.[2] The chapter focuses on the key 'discursive strategies' employed by Morrison and Shorten during the debate. It follows communication scholar Anabela Carvalho's definition of these as 'forms of (discursive) manipulation of "reality" by social actors in order to achieve a certain goal'.[3] It connects the leaders' discursive strategies in the debate to shared, deeply held and long-term gendered discourses of Australian identity. Attention to the historical element is vital because contemporary and emergent discourses 'always build on previous ones', whether by 'taking up or challenging' them.[4]

Elections, communication and identity

In Australia, voting in federal elections is compulsory. The leaders of major parties appeal to the electorate hoping to align with their ideas of the 'imagined community' of the nation.[5] Currents ripple across this sea of voters called on to identify themselves as Australian. Identity constructions, communicated by political leaders through the media, are never all-encompassing. They vary according to ideology and geography, reliant on a range of markers and affiliations from class and socio-economic status to race, family structure and sexual identity. They also form the basis through which campaigning leaders seek to embody elements of an idealised national identity.

Different forms of this identity rise to prominence within campaigns depending on the persona and policies of the candidates, as well as the social and cultural milieu. Some are particularly deep and enduring. As political scientists Jack Holland and Katherine Wright argue, 'gendered narratives of Australian identity have been endemic to the nation since foundation'.[6] These have shaped 'the social, economic and political landscape for the best part of two centuries'.[7] In the last decade, researchers have considered links between political leadership, news coverage and gender in Australia, with much focus on the coverage of Julia Gillard, Australia's first female prime minister.[8] Less common has been attention to 'the masculinity of politicians', which leading Australian scholar of politics and gender Carol Johnson has identified as a 'neglected area of study'.[9] This is in itself a symptom of broadly gendered social structures with 'heterosexual, Christian, middle-aged, middle-class, white men' operating as 'the norm against which other identities are measured'.[10] Political scientists Louise Chappell and Deborah Brennan call for further consideration of the impact of 'socially constructed norms of masculinity and femininity' on politics.[11] This illuminates the diversity of constructions of masculinity available in the performance of political leadership. As Johnson argues:

> male politicians can draw on a diverse repertoire of forms of
> masculinity that is influenced not only by their own image,
> persona and ideological predisposition, but also by the particular
> male or female opponents they are facing.[12]

This is reflected in studies that map 'subordinated, marginalised and resistant forms of masculinity' alongside those that are dominant.[13] This chapter similarly understands identities as constructed and re-constructed through dialogue, taking a constructivist approach to its analysis of political language, national identity and gender.

Australia votes 2019

The five-and-a-half-week campaign leading up to Australia's 2019 federal election was far from compelling. This might be attributed to several factors, including long-term polling, which indicated a comfortable win to the Labor opposition; the major parties' relatively traditional approaches to their campaign events and media interactions; and the fatigue of Australians who had lived through a period of leadership instability. Few moments captured the public imagination, and routine coverage cautiously, but consistently, indicated a change of government was likely (a change that did not eventuate as the Coalition held on to power).

The strongest contenders to win the prime ministership typically represent Australia's two main political parties: the Labor Party and the Liberal Party. In 2019, Scott Morrison was contesting his first election as prime minister and Liberal leader, having been elected in a party leadership spill less than a year earlier. Morrison's early public profile was based on his hard stance on offshore detention while he had ministerial responsibility for immigration, and his time as treasurer under his predecessor, Malcolm Turnbull. This evolved to include his commitment to his Pentecostal faith, time as head of Tourism Australia, and love of the Cronulla Sharks rugby league team.[14] His opponent, Bill Shorten, was contesting his second election as Labor leader after an unsuccessful tilt in 2016. Shorten had a CV typical of the party. A former lawyer and Australian Workers' Union national secretary, he rose to public prominence during the 2006 Beaconsfield mine collapse and entered parliament the following year. He was quickly appointed to ministerial positions and was a key player in internal party manoeuvring in 2010 to replace prime minister Kevin Rudd with then deputy prime minister Julia Gillard. Shorten became leader in 2013 following the party's defeat at that year's federal election. He was known at the time for his ambition, with a reputation as 'one of the ultimate political animals of his generation'.[15] His 2019 campaign emphasised the strength of his team and ability to build consensus.[16]

Family, faith and fandom

The first televised leaders' debate of the 2019 election was held in Perth on 29 April, co-hosted by the *West Australian* and the Seven Network. Australian televised election debates are political theatre without record-breaking audiences. The broadcast of the first debate attracted just over 600000 people in Australian capital cities when live and delayed viewing was combined. These were solid numbers for a program that was not broadcast on Seven's main free-to-air channel but well behind Channel Nine's *Lego Masters*, which topped ratings that night with over 1 million viewers.[17] Leaders' debates, however, have broad-reaching and enduring significance beyond those who tune in. They have multiple audiences: the journalists (and sometimes citizens) in the room; those watching or streaming live (or on delay); and those watching, listening to and engaging in the coverage and conversation that follows in traditional, emerging, social and digital media. These debates retain the power to crystallise campaign themes. They can set campaign agendas, upend expectations and shift momentum.

Morrison and Shorten took questions from both a panel of journalists and members of the public attending as a live studio audience. The debate was a dull affair despite the broadcaster's efforts to create interest through dramatic music and colourful graphics. One compelling exchange provided a clear window into the complex discursive strategies through which each leader attempted to construct an appealing political identity. About 20 minutes in, *West Australian* reporter Lanai Scarr questioned Shorten on his proposal to have 50 per cent of all new cars sold in Australia be electric by 2030. She asked: 'The Nissan Leaf is one of the more popular electric vehicles on the market; how much does that cost?'[18]

Shorten's initial response relied on a delaying tactic ('Well, I haven't bought a new car in a while, so I couldn't tell you …') designed to endear him to the electorate by claiming membership of a socioeconomic group for whom buying a new car was rare. His opponent jumped on the hesitation immediately:

Morrison: Well, I can tell you how much more an electric car costs more than the standard, it's 28 000 bucks. It's 28 000, for the same type of car that you would get …

Shorten: Well that's great. We've got a prime minister spending his time in the motor pages, that's super. What I want to do …

Morrison: Well, that's where most Australians often spend their time, mate …

Shorten: Oh, come on.

Morrison: … they read about cars, they read about footy, they read about the races, they read about, you know, what they're cooking at home.

Shorten: And this is … I'm not talking about who won the fifth at Flemington, digger …

This exchange captured clear discursive strategies that compete over particular and gendered versions of Australian identity. These are historically grounded, refracted through claims to represent Australian *ordinariness* alongside the candidate's own extraordinary ability to *lead*.

The Prime Minister's performance of authenticity further relied on elements of which his family, faith and fandom were central pillars. For example, in a question early in the debate, Scarr asked the Prime Minister about the threat of climate change. She addressed him as 'the father of two young daughters', an opening he used to talk about policy through the lens of family. This echoed at the Liberal policy launch on 12 May (held on Mothers' Day). Morrison was welcomed to the stage by his daughters, wife Jenny and mother Marion, and began his speech with a reflection on his mother's role in his life.[19] The opposition leader also mobilised family stories throughout the campaign, using these to claim connection to working-class Australians. This discursive strategy crystallised in two key moments. The first was a press conference on 8 of May, in which an emotional Shorten defended his retelling of his mother's story on the ABC television program *Q&A* two days earlier.[20] Shorten had responded to a question about his leadership style by talking about being inspired by his mother, who 'came from a working-class family' and struggled throughout her life to pursue her own education, raise a family and eventually become a barrister.[21] Shorten emphasised his mother's 'brilliance' and persistence in the face of significant obstacles presented by her working-class background, gender and age.[22] The second came in the final days of the campaign when media coverage of the death of former Labor prime minister Bob Hawke emphasised his close relationship with Shorten, renewing focus on his connections to union and party history.

The exchange about the Nissan Leaf and broader identity discourses mobilised by the two leaders highlight the deeply gendered nature of both Australian political leadership and national identity stories. When squabbling over whether a prime minister *should* know the price of an electric car, Shorten and Morrison are contesting who best understands what 'most Australians' care about. In doing so, they evoke two enduring touchstones of Australian identity stories that reveal their *gendered* nature: sport and the Anzac myth.

The fifth at Flemington

Sport and (traditionally male) sporting heroes hold a privileged place in myths of Australian national identity.[23] Sociologist David Rowe writes about sport in Australian political culture and its links to the performance of gendered national identity. For Rowe, it is 'one of the immutable laws of Australian politics' that a politician in, or hoping to gain, office 'must be a passionate sports fan, even if they have to fake it'.[24] While some are 'genuine sports nuts' (Rowe nominates former prime ministers Bob Hawke and John Howard), Australians would be familiar with news footage of politicians draped in seemingly brand-new scarves or jerseys, or awkwardly bowling, kicking or bouncing balls in visits to local sporting clubs. Morrison claims *connection* to Australians who are interested in reading about football, horse racing and cars through a discursive strategy that cements his own membership of the male collective at the heart of the nation. His list is complemented by the inclusion of 'cooking', which is tacked on to the end and adds a distinctively domestic element. This links to Morrison's vision of an Australia populated by citizens imagined as 'humble': 'Their aspirations are decent, honest, simple … They are quiet, hard-working people …'[25]

Morrison also seeks to exclude his opponent. In reply, Shorten directly challenges both the Prime Minister's construction of Australian identity and his attempt to claim a privileged relationship to it. He, too, mobilises the language of sport in bringing the conversation back to his party's proposed action on climate change. Interjecting with 'I'm not talking about the fifth at Flemington', Shorten demonstrates familiarity with the language and detail of Australian horse racing. At the same time, he pushes back against his opponent's attempt to paint him as out of touch with ordinary Australian voters. The addition of 'digger' opens up the field of contest further, referring to a mythic (male) figure central to stories of national identity.

You've had a good crack, digger

Through use of the term 'digger' Shorten mobilises a potent historical construction of national identity as a key discursive strategy. The digger is central in the national imagination as 'the literal and figurative embodiment of Australian values'.[26] It can be traced from early constructions of Australia as a workers' paradise through to use in the First World War, characterising myths of mateship and sacrifice that came to be embodied in the Anzac. Shorten used the expression when discussing electric cars, and again later in the debate in response to an audience member's question about self-managed super funds. In the second exchange, Morrison interrupts Shorten to disagree with his explanation of who – and how many people – would be affected by proposed changes. This caused the opposition leader to retort 'You've had a good crack, digger. You had a good crack' in an attempt to regain control.

The myth of the diggers, and the 'Anzac spirit', is one of the most powerful mechanisms through which Australian values have been constructed in both political and media discourse. It evokes a shared common understanding of the national identity that works to '(re) produce, celebrate and glorify working-class masculine qualities'.[27] The 'digger' offers connection to a vision of Australian identity that is resourceful, larrikin and predominantly male. Its recurring use in political language signals a discursive strategy through which leaders try to align themselves with the egalitarian, principled, heroic and steadfast attributes of the diggers.[28] This highlights an element of identity formation fundamental to campaign communication.

Competing constructions of Australian identity

There is a deeper contest over Australian identity at play in election language whose gender, class, race and other touchpoints are mobilised by leaders to construct constituencies and secure votes. Competing versions of masculinity emerge in the televised leaders' debate, most visible in Shorten's responses to his opponent, which work on two levels. Firstly, they highlight his knowledge of the Australian vernacular and tropes of male Australian identity. More deeply, Shorten hints at the simplistic nature of his opponent's weaponisation of Australian identity and seeks to undermine the prime minister's connection to voters.

Paying attention to these competing performances of identity allows insight into what linguist Scott Kiesling calls 'cultural discourses of masculinity'.[29] These are illuminated through questions about the connection between language use and gender: 'how people use language to express gender, how a person's gender affects the choices they make in how they speak, and how their talk is received'.[30] The identification of masculine identity as *dialogic*, *plural* and *contested* is vital: masculinities are created and performed through language in contexts informed by shared cultural and social histories. Kiesling identifies dominance as a key cultural discourse of masculinity. This plays out in Morrison and Shorten's competition to align themselves with ordinary voters through gendered evocations of Australian identity.

This is, always, a *performance* of identity both in theoretical terms, as defined earlier by Judith Butler,[31] and also because of the televised nature of the debate.

Both Morrison's gendered recitation of the pursuits of 'ordinary' Australians, and Shorten's interjections in response, can be understood as a form of what is colloquially referred to as 'alphaing'. This entails establishing who is the alpha male through explicit performances of masculine identity.[32] This competition, then, is also about policing gender identity boundaries, ensuring they are correctly performed. Johnson notes that this strategy – playing the 'gender card' – has a long history in Australian politics.[33] Although often associated with the actions of female political and public actors, it 'is normally played by men against men' (although rarely labelled as such).[34] Bill Shorten's playing of the gender card through the cultural touchstones of family, sport and military myth was effective on the night of the leaders' debate. On election day, however, it was Scott Morrison – a man of faith, a footy fan and family man – whose campaign had most effectively connected with voters, returning him to the office of prime minister for a new term.

ACKNOWLEDGMENTS

Issues of gender have been prominent in Australian political debate over the last decade. Since 2010, the nation has had its first woman as prime minister, first woman as Minister for Foreign Affairs, and first woman as Minister for Defence. In the same period, however, Australia has also seen six prime ministers, and leadership instability has become a hallmark of national government. Furthermore, in the lead-up to the 2019 federal election, the parliament was described by some as a hostile workplace, and high-profile women left national politics amid accusations of bullying and sexism, while others were either shunned from parliamentary leadership positions or chose to avoid them.

This led us to investigate the gendered aspects of political leadership. We were interested to know how gender and gender binarism play a role in the careers and trajectories of men and women leaders. We wanted to investigate the role that institutional and structural arrangements play in constraining women from entering and remaining in federal parliament. We also wanted to explore the gendered cultural proclivities of Australia's leadership, and how media representation of women and men in the political debate shapes our national leadership culture.

In order to explore these issues, we brought together Australia's emerging and established researchers to contribute to this public conversation that has implications for equality, policy and governance. As editors, we would like to thank all of our contributors for their commitment to this collection. In particular, we would like to thank Professor Sharman Stone, former Australian Global Ambassador for Women and Girls, and Member of the House of Representatives

(1996–2016), for her thoughtful foreword and mentorship of the project.

We would like to thank the Australian Political Studies Association (APSA) for providing funding to host the *Gender and Political Leadership in Australia* workshop, which was held in Melbourne in July 2019. In particular, we thank Natasha Raghuvanshi and Sara Phillips for their efforts in preparing and hosting the workshop. We also thank the School of Social Sciences, Faculty of Arts at Monash University for its support.

Much of this collection was edited during Melbourne's COVID-19 lockdown. The editors would like to thank Dr Ari Jerrems for his meticulous work in supporting the preparation of the final manuscript, and Gabriella Sterio for her dedicated and professional copyediting. The editors would also like to thank their families for their patience. Zareh would like to thank his parents, Tony and Nadia, for their continued support, and Katrina would like to thank her son William, who diligently and cheerfully home-schooled during this period, and her husband Andrew.

LIST OF CONTRIBUTORS

JANE ALVER

Jane Alver is an Australian academic, lawyer, public servant and gender adviser. She is also a Senior Research Fellow at the Centre for Deliberative Democracy and Global Governance at the University of Canberra where her PhD research is on diverse feminist civil society forming strategic alliances for Pacific regional gender equality. Jane is a member of the Steering Committee for the 50/50 by 2030 Foundation. In 2018, she was named as one of the '100 Women of Influence' by the *Australian Financial Review*.

FRANK BONGIORNO

Frank Bongiorno is Professor of History and Head of the School of History at the Australian National University. His most recent books are *The Eighties: The Decade That Transformed Australia* (Black Inc., 2015) and, with Benjamin T Jones and John Uhr (eds), *Elections Matter: Ten Federal Elections That Shaped Australia* (Monash University Publishing, 2018). He is a Fellow of the Academy of the Social Sciences in Australia and the Australian Academy of Humanities.

STEPHANIE BROOKES

Stephanie Brookes is Senior Lecturer in journalism in the School of Media, Film and Journalism at Monash University. She researches media, journalism and politics, focusing on election campaigns, political journalism and journalistic identity, with an interest in questions of identity and belonging in news media and political discourse. She has published widely and also co-edited the May 2018 special edition of *Media International Australia* on press gallery and political journalism in Australia, and is the author of *Politics, Media and Campaign Language: Australia's Identity Anxiety* (Anthem Press, 2017).

HAYLEY CULL

Hayley Cull is Director of Advocacy and Community Engagement at Plan International Australia, one of the world's oldest and largest humanitarian and development agencies. She leads a team of campaigners, communications and policy professionals working to create a just world for children and equality for girls. Hayley has led major national and global campaigns on child rights, international development and gender equality, working with UNICEF, Plan International and other NGOs in Australia and internationally.

JANE GARDNER

Jane Gardner is currently the Advocacy and Communications General Manager with the Youth Support + Advocacy Service (YSAS) and has worked at Plan International, an international girls' rights charity.

ANIKA GAUJA

Anika Gauja is an Associate Professor in the Department of Government and International Relations at Sydney University. Anika has published extensively on parties and electoral law. She is the author of *Party Reform* (Oxford University Press, 2017), *The Politics of Party Policy* (Palgrave Macmillan, 2013) and co-editor of numerous publications on party members and electoral politics, including *Party Members and Activists* (Routledge, 2015) and *Morrison's Miracle: The 2019 Australian Federal Election* (ANU Press, 2018).

ZAREH GHAZARIAN

Zareh Ghazarian is a Senior Lecturer in Politics and International Relations in the School of Social Sciences at Monash University. His research and teaching interests include public policy, civics and citizenship education, and political parties and leadership. Zareh is a leading commentator on national politics and his latest book is *The Making of a Party System: Minor Parties in the Australian Senate* (Monash University Publishing, 2015).

CAROL JOHNSON

Professor Carol Johnson is an Emerita Professor in the Department of Politics and International Relations at the University of Adelaide. She has published extensively on the politics of gender and sexuality. She has had a long-term interest, going back to the Hawke and Keating years and extending to the current Morrison period, in analysing how Australian political leaders utilise and perform their gender identity. Her most recent book is *Social Democracy and the Crisis of Equality: Australian Social Democracy in a Changing World* (Springer, 2019). She is a Fellow of the Academy of the Social Sciences in Australia.

JIM JOSE

Jim Jose is Professor of Politics in the Newcastle Business School at the University of Newcastle in New South Wales, Australia. He undertakes research in various areas of political theory, contemporary governance issues, public policy and gender politics. He has published numerous articles in these areas.

KATRINA LEE-KOO

Katrina Lee-Koo is an Associate Professor of Politics and International Relations in the School of Social Sciences at Monash University. Her research interests include women's leadership in politics, and the leadership and participation of women, youth and children in global peace and security. She is the co-editor of *Young Women and Leadership* (Routledge, 2020) and co-author of *Children and Global Conflict* (Cambridge University Press, 2015) and *Ethics and Global Security* (Routledge, 2014).

JACQUELINE LAUGHLAND-BOOŸ

Dr Jacqueline Laughland-Booÿ is a Research Fellow at Australian Catholic University and an adjunct Research Fellow in the School of Social Sciences at Monash University. Her research interests are in the fields of life course studies and political sociology.

MARIA MALEY

Maria Maley is a Senior Lecturer in the School of Politics and International Relations at the Australian National University where she teaches public administration and public policy. Her research focuses on the work of political staff, political-administrative relations, comparative advisory institutions and the careers of politicians and political advisers.

NARELLE MIRAGLIOTTA

Narelle Miragliotta is a Senior Lecturer in the Department of Politics and International Relations at Monash University. She has broad teaching and research interests in many different facets of Australian and liberal democratic political institutions, including constitutions, parliaments, political parties and Australian elections and electoral systems.

JENNA PRICE

Jenna Price is a Visiting Fellow at the Australian National University and has been a journalist for 40 years. She is a columnist for the *Sydney Morning Herald* and the *Canberra Times*. Her report *You Can't Be What You Can't See*, about the gender of sources and journalists on mainstream news sites, was published in 2019. She completed her PhD on feminist activism at the University of Sydney in 2019.

PIA ROWE

Pia Rowe is a Research Fellow at the 50/50 by 2030 Foundation, University of Canberra. She has extensive research experience in gender studies and innovative forms of citizen participation. She is currently the project lead on an Australian study on the division of unpaid labour at home during COVID-19. Her other recent projects include a national survey into Australians' attitudes towards gender equality. Pia is also one of the founding editors of the 50/50 Foundation's flagship gender equality media platform, *BroadAgenda*. Prior to her academic career, she worked as a Communications Adviser in the public sector.

ELISE STEPHENSON

Elise Stephenson is an award-winning social entrepreneur and researcher, recognised as a leading policy adviser for her work across gender and sexuality in international affairs, diplomacy and national security. She is a post-doctoral fellow of the Policy Innovation Hub and a fellow of the Gender and Governance Program, Griffith Asia Institute, and the Centre for Governance and Public Policy at Griffith University. Elise is currently partnered with the Australian Government Department of Foreign Affairs and Trade (DFAT) to run public diplomacy programs across the Asia-Pacific region.

PAUL STRANGIO

Paul Strangio is an Associate Professor in Politics at Monash University. He specialises in Australian political history with a particular focus on political leadership and political parties. His most recent books are with Paul 't Hart and James Walter, *The Pivot of Power: Australian Prime Ministers and Political Leadership, 1949–2016* (The Miegunyah Press, 2017) and, with Matteo Bonotti (eds), *A Century of Compulsory Voting in Australia: Genesis, Impact and Future* (Palgrave Macmillan, 2021). Paul is a frequent commentator on Australian politics in print and electronic media.

MARY WALSH

Mary Walsh is an Associate Professor in Politics in the School of Politics, Economics and Society, Faculty of Business, Government and Law, University of Canberra. She is the Program Director of the Bachelor of Politics and International Relations degree and the Bachelor of Philosophy Honours program. Recent publications have appeared in *The Review of Politics and Democratic Theory*. Her latest research on the revolving door of Australian prime ministers is published in *From Turnbull to Morrison: The Trust Divide* (MUP, 2019).

JAMES WALTER

James Walter is Emeritus Professor of Politics at Monash University. He has published widely on Australian politics, leadership, intellectual and institutional history, and biography. His most recent book, written with Paul Strangio and Paul 't Hart, is *The Pivot of Power: Australian Prime Ministers and Political Leadership 1949–2016* (The Miegunyah Press, 2017). He is a Fellow of the Academy of the Social Sciences in Australia.

BLAIR WILLIAMS

Blair Williams is an Associate Lecturer at the Australian National University where she recently finished her PhD. Her doctoral thesis focused on the gendered print mediation of women prime ministers from English-speaking Westminster democracies, in particular Julia Gillard, Margaret Thatcher, Theresa May, Jenny Shipley and Helen Clark. She has published in *Parliamentary Affairs, Politics & Gender, Australian Journal of Political Science* and *Feminist Media Studies*, has co-authored a chapter in the 16th edited collection of Australian election studies, and has sole-authored entries in *The International Encyclopaedia of Gender, Media, and Communication*.

NOTES

Foreword

1   M Cowper-Coles, *Women Political Leaders: The impact of gender on democracy*, The Global Institute for Women's Leadership, London, 2020.

2   M Shar, 'Jeffery's quips enliven investiture of Howard Government Mark IV', *Age*, 27 October 2004, p. 5.

3   'Julie Bishop targeted by "big swinging dicks"', *Australian*, 20 April 2009.

4   S Wilson, J Pallant, T Bednall and S Gray, *Australian Leadership Index, 2019 National Survey*, Swinburne University of Technology, Melbourne, 2020.

Introduction

1   'Don't put the economy before defence: Kevin Andrews', *Australian*, 21 September 2015, <www.theaustralian.com.au/national-affairs/defence/don't-put-the-economy-before-defence-kevin-andrews/news-story/aad40cf53393e3ed8e84f661e2613005>.

2   A Greene, 'New Defence Minister has daunting job ahead of her', ABC, 21 September 2015, <www.abc.net.au/worldtoday/content/2015/s4316546.htm>.

3   Greene, 'New Defence Minister has daunting job ahead of her'.

4   P Karp, 'Liberal MP Julia Banks to quite Parliament citing "bullying, harassment and intimidation"', *Guardian*, 29 August 2018, <www.theguardian.com/australia-news/2018/aug/29/liberal-mp-julia-banks-to-quit-parliament-next-election-citing-bullying-and-intimidation>.

5   A Lewis, *The Way In: Representation in the Australian Parliament*, Per Capita, January 2019, <percapita.org.au/wp-content/uploads/2019/01/The-Way-In-Representation-in-the-Australian-Parliament-2.pdf>.

The gendered identities of Australian political leaders

1   B Hawke, 'ALP election launch speech', *MOAD*, 16 February 1983, <electionspeeches.moadoph.gov.au/speeches/1983-bob-hawke>. My analysis of 'protective masculinity' builds on Iris Marion Young's term 'masculinist protectionism', and I have also applied it to US, UK and New Zealand examples. See C Johnson, 'Gender, Emotion and Political Discourse: Masculinity, femininity and populism' in O Feldman (ed), *The Rhetoric of Political Leadership: Logic and emotion in public discourse*, Edward Elgar, Cheltenham UK, Northampton MA, 2020. For an analysis of leaders' international 'protective femininity' during the pandemic, see C Johnson & B Williams, 'Gender and political leadership in a time of COVID', *Politics & Gender*, Cambridge University Press, 2020, pp. 1–12, <doi.org/10.1017/S1743923X2000029X>.

2   P Keating, 'Interview with Susan Mitchell', *Radio 5AN*, 29 June 1992, <pmtranscripts.pmc.gov.au/sites/default/files/original/00008560.pdf>.

3   P Keating, 'Tax cuts and family assistance', *Hansard, House of Representatives*, 31 October 1989, p. 2134. For a more detailed analysis of Hawke and Keating's use of identity, including their masculinity, see C Johnson, 'Other Times: Thatcher,

Hawke, Keating and the politics of identity' in G Stokes (ed), *The Politics of Identity in Australia*, Cambridge University Press, Melbourne, 1997, pp. 37–49.

4   M Morris, 'Ecstasy and economics [A portrait of Paul Keating]' in M Morris, *Ecstasy and Economics: American essays for John Forbes*, EmPress, Sydney, 1992, p. 50.

5   P Keating, 'Address to the Asia-Australia Institute', Sydney, 7 April 1992, <pmtranscripts.pmc.gov.au/release/transcript-8485>; P Keating, 'Interview with John Laws', Radio 2UE, 30 September 1992, <pmtranscripts.pmc.gov.au/release/transcript-8682>.

6   J Howard, 'An average Australian bloke, Interview with Liz Jackson', *Four Corners*, 1996, <www.abc.net.au/4corners/an-average-australian-bloke---1996/2841808>.

7   G W Bush, 'President Bush addresses Australian Parliament', 22 October 2003, <georgewbush-whitehouse.archives.gov/news/releases/2003/10/20031022-12.html>.

8   J Howard, 'Television interview, *Channel Ten*, Meet the Press', 2 July 2000, <pmtranscripts.pmc.gov.au/release/transcript-11484>; 'Interview with Mike Munroa [sic]', *A Current Affair*, 5 October 2001, <pmtranscripts.pmc.gov.au/release/transcript-12068>.

9   'ACTU anti-Work Choices ad 2005', YouTube, 31 May 2013, accessed 6 July 2020, www.youtube.com/watch?v=P5y3b9iVgGs.

10   K Rudd, 'Howard's Brutopia: The battle of ideas in Australian politics', *The Monthly*, November 2006, <www.themonthly.com.au/issue/2006/november/1238384967/kevin-rudd/howard-s-brutopia>.

11   T Abbott, 'Interview with Chris Uhlmann', *7:30 Report*, January 6, 2010. <www.abc.net.au/7.30/tony-abbott-joins-chris-uhlmann/2674504>.

12   A Drummond, 'Softer side of Abbott on show', *news.com.au*, 25 August 2013, <www.news.com.au/national/breaking-news/abbott-to-float-tradie-loans-scheme/news-story/89f596ebcf272f799ed7be3f7332bb92>.

13   M Farr, 'Tony Abbott tells Julia Gillard to "make an honest woman of herself" on carbon tax', *news.com.au*, 25 February 2011, <www.news.com.au/national/tony-abbott-tells-julia-gillard-to-make-an-honest-womanof-herself-on-carbon-tax/news-story/598b17ec073ee83e3e2154c9205e6322>.

14   I discuss such gendered attacks on Gillard in more depth in C Johnson, 'Playing the gender card: The uses and abuses of gender in Australian politics', *Politics & Gender*, vol. 11, 2015, pp. 303–5.

15   J Gillard, 'Labor in Australia is a movement', Chifley Research Centre, Canberra, 16 September 2011, <pmtranscripts.pmc.gov.au/release/transcript-18142>. For a more detailed analysis of the gender issues Gillard faced as Prime Minister, see Johnson 2015, pp. 291–319.

16   K Rudd, 'PM answers asylum policy questions and challenges Tony Abbott', *ABC*, 3 July 2013, <www.abc.net.au/7.30/pm-answers-asylum-policy-questions-and-challenges/4798122>.

17   B Shorten, 'Doorstop Townsville', 25 June 2016, <www.billshorten.com.au/doorstop_townsville_saturday_25_june_2016>.

18   S Mayer, '"Unexcited" MPs worried they could be Gonski', *Australian*, 21 April 2016, p. 5.

19   A Remeikis, '"Shorten wants to end the weekend": Morrison attacks Labor's electric vehicle policy', *Guardian*, 7 April 2019, <www.theguardian.com/australia-news/2019/apr/07/shorten-wants-to-end-the-weekend-morrison-attacks-labors-electric-vehicle-policy>.

20   S Morrison, 'Interview with John Stanley', Radio 2GB, 20 December 2019, <www.pm.gov.au/media/radio-interview-john-stanley-2gb>.

21 A Schaffer, 'The firefighter whose denunciation of Australia's Prime Minister made him a folk hero', *New Yorker*, 18 January 2020, <www.newyorker.com/news/as-told-to/the-firefighter-whose-denunciation-of-australias-prime-minister-made-him-a-folk-hero>; T Wright 'Nation rewards firey who "said what the rest of us were thinking"', *Sydney Morning Herald*, 15–16 February 2020, p. 31.

22 S Morrison, 'Press Conference, Parliament House Canberra', 1 May 2020, www.pm.gov.au/media/press-conference-australian-parliament-house-act-1may20>.

23 S Morrison, 'Press Conference, Parliament House Canberra', 8 May 2020', <www.pm.gov.au/media/press-conference-australian-parliament-house-08may20>.

24 S Morrison, 'Interview with Paul Murray', 22 April 2020, <www.pm.gov.au/media/interview-paul-murray-sky-news-2>.

Good blokes?

1 H McQueen, 'Stiletto conspiracy' in H McQueen, *Gallipoli to Petrov: Arguing with Australian history*, Allen & Unwin, Sydney, 1984, p. 258.

2 P Mullins, *Tiberius with a Telephone: The life and stories of William McMahon*, Scribe, Melbourne, 2018, pp. 164–165.

3 A Woollacott, *Don Dunstan: The visionary politician who changed Australia*, Allen & Unwin, Sydney, 2019, p. 235.

4 A Beech, 'Julia Banks puts Parliament's treatment of women in spotlight as MPs take aim at political "boys club"', *ABC*, 28 November, 2018, <www.abc.net.au/news/2018-11-28/australian-political-parties-deny-problem-with-women/10560498>.

5 G Hutchens, 'Emma Husar says "vicious slut shaming' ended her career"', *Guardian*, 29 August 2018.

6 Jane Norman, 'Women still underrepresented in Parliament after 2019 Federal Election', *ABC*, 27 May 2019, <www.abc.net.au/news/2019-05-27/women-still-underrepresented-in-parliament/11148020>.

7 'The Nationals women,' *Nationals*, <nationals.org.au/about/our-structure/the-nationals-women/>.

8 AM Black, *'The Victorian Farmers Union, Country, and National Party, 1916-2000: Survival, adaptation, and evolution'*, PhD Thesis, University of Melbourne, 2020.

9 A Scott, *Fading Loyalties: The Australian Labor Party and the working class*, Pluto Press, Leichhardt, 1991.

10 B d'Alpuget, *Robert J Hawke: A biography*, Schwartz in conjunction with Lansdowne Press, Melbourne, 1982.

11 C Johnson, '"Other Times": Thatcher, Hawke, Keating, and the politics of identity' in G Stokes, *The Politics of Identity in Australia*, Cambridge University Press, Cambridge, 1997, pp. 37–49.

12 BA Phillips-Peddlesden, *'Prime Ministers: Gender and power in Australian political history, 1902–1975'*, PhD Thesis, University of Melbourne, 2019. The thesis is embargoed until 2021, but see BA Phillips-Peddlesden, '"A Stronger Man and a More Virile Character": Australian prime ministers, embodied manhood and political authority in the early twentieth century', *Australian Historical Studies*, vol. 48, no. 4, November 2017, pp. 502–518 and '"A race of intelligent super-giants": The Whitlams, gendered bodies and political authority in modern Australia', in Michelle Arrow and Angela Woollacott (eds), *Everyday Revolutions: Remaking gender, sexuality and culture in 1970s Australia*, ANU Press, Canberra, 2019, pp. 261–278.

13 Phillips-Peddlesden 2019, p. 516.

14   I borrow the distinction between the 'rough' and the 'respectable' from J McCalman, *Struggletown: Public and private life in Richmond, 1900–1965*, Melbourne University Press, Carlton, 1984.

15   C Cameron, *The Confessions of Clyde Cameron 1913–1900, As Told to Daniel Connell*, ABC Books, Crows Nest, 1990, p. 182.

16   M Latham, *The Latham Diaries*, Melbourne University Press, Carlton, 2005, p. 39.

17   G Little, *Strong Leadership: Thatcher, Reagan and an eminent person*, Oxford University Press, Melbourne, 1988, p. 8.

18   Latham 2005, pp. 8–9.

19   Latham 2005, p. 28.

20   B d'Alpuget, *Bob Hawke: The complete biography*, Simon & Schuster, Sydney, 2019, pp. 10, 14, 29.

21   F Bongiorno, *The Eighties: The decade that transformed Australia*, Black Inc., Collingwood, 2015, pp. 17, 39–40, 187.

22   T Dixon, *Weeping Britannia: Portrait of a nation in tears*, Oxford University Press, Oxford, 2015.

23   Bongiorno 2015, pp. 105, 109–110.

24   *Age*, 21 September 1984, p.1.

25   P Ellercamp, 'The tears factor in the search for votes and issues', *Weekend Australian*, 22–23 September 1984, p. 4.

26   P Williams, 'What Bob Hawke's powerful Tiananmen Square speech reveals about his foreign policy', *ABC*, 18 May 2019, <www.abc.net.au/news/2019-05-18/bob-hawke-tiananmen-square-apartheid-foriegn-policy/11124650>.

27   For a psychobiography of Hawke, see S Anson, *Hawke: An emotional life*, McPhee Gribble, Ringwood, 1991.

28   The best account is B Lagan, *Loner: Inside a Labor tragedy*, Allen & Unwin, Crows Nest, 2005.

29   C Johnson, 'Mark Latham and the ideology of the ALP', *Australian Journal of Political Science*, vol. 39, no. 3, November 2004, p. 547.

30   M Latham, *Wedge Politics and the Culture War in Australia*, The Menzies Lecture 2002, C Bridge (ed), Menzies Centre for Australian Studies, King's College London, University of London, London, 2003, pp. 6–9.

31   'Conga line of scorn-bags rips into Latham's lament', *Age*, 25 September 2006, <www.theage.com.au/national/conga-line-of-scorn-bags-rips-into-lathams-lament-20060925-ge37ah.html>.

32   F Bongiorno, 'The Latham factor' in T Frame (ed), *Trials and Transformations, 2001–2004: The Howard Government, Volume III*, UNSW Press, Sydney, p. 181.

33   Bongiorno 2015, p. 290.

34   D Snow and D Murphy, 'Mark Latham: A leader in profile', *Sydney Morning Herald*, 10–11 July 2004, pp. 27, 34, 35 and 12 July 2004, p. 9.

35   M Turnbull, *A Bigger Picture*, Hardie Grant Books, Richmond, Victoria, 2020, p. 118.

36   S Whyte, '"Weapons down": Morrison to overhaul industrial relations', *Canberra Times*, 26 May 2020, <www.canberratimes.com.au/story/6770018/weapons-down-morrison-wants-unions-employers-to-come-together-on-reforms/#gsc.tab=0>.

37   My thanks to the organisers and participants of 'The Gendered Dynamics of Australia's Political Leadership Culture' workshop at Monash University in July 2019 and Gender and History node of the Gender Institute at the Australian National University in May 2020 for feedback on this paper.

'Shades of Grey'

1   The text of that final statement is reprinted in J Kent, *Take Your Best Shot: The prime ministership of Julia Gillard*, Penguin Books, Melbourne, 2013, pp. 118–121.

2   Quoted in C Johnson, 'Playing the gender card: The uses and abuses of gender in Australian politics', *Politics & Gender*, vol. 11, no. 2, 2015, p. 312.

3   J Gillard, *My Story*, Penguin Random House, Sydney, 2014, p. 98.

4   Quoted in Kent 2013, p. 121.

5   Quoted in P Strangio, *Keeper of the Faith: A biography of Jim Cairns*, Melbourne University Press, Melbourne, p. 434.

6   *Commonwealth Parliamentary Debates*, House of Representatives, 14 October 2003, p. 21298.

7   P Strangio, 'Politics of hate takes aim at PM', *Age*, 7 November 2011, p. 13.

8   See, for example, T McCrann, 'Sticking with worst PM', *Herald Sun*, 22 March 2013, p. 5.

9   P Strangio, 'Evaluating prime-ministerial performance: The Australian experience' in P Strangio, P 't Hart & J Walter (eds), *Understanding Prime-Ministerial Performance: Comparative perspectives*, Oxford University Press, Oxford, 2013, pp. 264–290.

10   P Strangio, 'Leaders and losers', *Sunday Age*, 2 June 2013, p. 13. The article also appeared on the same day in the *Sun Herald* under the title 'The loved and loathed'.

11   This represented a response rate of 53.2 per cent compared to 28.5 per cent for the 2010 exercise.

12   J Albrechtsen, 'Oh, for a moment's silence from these angry ghosts', *Australian*, 29 January 2020, p. 12. See also Troy Bramston, 'Ex-PMs could learn a thing or two from Julia', *Weekend Australian*, 22 February 2020, p. 19.

13   N Evershed, 'Turnbull scores lower than Abbott, Gillard and Rudd on productivity in parliament', *Guardian Australia*, 23 December 2018, <www.theguardian.com/ australia-news/datablog/2018/dec/23/turnbull-scores-lower-than-abbott-gillard-and-rudd-on-productivity-in-parliament>.

14   M O'Gorman & F Jotzo, 'Impact of the carbon price on Australia's electricity demand, supply and emissions', CCEP Working Paper 1411, 17 July 2014, <www. lse.ac.uk/GranthamInstitute/wp-content/uploads/2014/08/OGorman-and-Jotzo-Impact-of-the-carbon-price-on-Australias-electricity-demand-supply-and-emissions. pdf.

15   For a measured summary of the Gillard government's legislative record, see G Singleton, 'The Legislative Record of a "Hung" Parliament' in C Aulich (ed), *The Gillard Governments: Australian Commonwealth Administration 2010–2013*, Melbourne University Press, Melbourne, 2014, pp. 43–54.

16   Ben Hubbard personal communication to the author, 14 February 2020.

17   For a consolidated survey of the polling figures for Gillard's prime ministership, see B Holmes, 'Hard days and nights: The final 147 days of the Gillard Government', Research Paper Series 2013–14, 8 November 2013, Parliamentary Library, Parliament of Australia, Appendices 3–5, <www.aph.gov.au/About_Parliament/Parliamentary_ Departments/Parliamentary_Library/pubs/rp/rp1314/GillardGovernment>.

18   Former members of Gillard's prime-ministerial office retrospectively acknowledged and lamented the gulf between her private and public persona. See, for instance, J McTernan, 'The Julia I know and love but you never really met', *Sunday Telegraph*, 21 July 2013, p. 41; N Reece, 'Secret softie: The cold truth is Gillard's warmth couldn't be conveyed to voters', *Sydney Morning Herald*, 1 July 2013, p. 24.

19   On this phenomenon, see, for example, J Wilson, 'Kevin Rudd, celebrity and audience democracy in Australia', *Journalism*, vol. 15, no. 2, 2014, pp. 202–217.

20 A Goldsworthy, 'Unfinished business: Sex, freedom and misogyny', *Quarterly Essay*, no. 50, Black Inc., Melbourne, 2013, p. 17. Emphasis in the original.

21 There have been many lamentations about the deadening effects of the proliferation of the professional political operator especially on the Labor Party. For just one example, see J Button, 'Beyond belief: What future for Labor?', *Quarterly Essay*, no. 6, Black Inc., Melbourne, 2002, pp. 22–24.

22 For a summary of some of that literature, see J Curtin, 'The prime ministership of Julia Gillard', *Australian Journal of Political Science*, vol. 50, no. 1, 2015, pp. 190–204.

23 On this theme, see LJ Hall & N Donaghue, '"Nice girls don't carry knives": Constructions of ambition in media coverage of Australia's first female prime minister', *British Journal of Social Psychology*, vol. 20, no. 3, 2012, pp. 631–47, and B Williams, 'A gendered media analysis of the prime ministerial ascension of Gillard and Turnbull: He's "taken back the reins" and she's "a backstabbing" murderer', *Australian Journal of Political Science*, vol. 52, no. 4, 2017, pp. 550–564.

24 K Rudd, *The PM Years*, Pan Macmillan Australia, Sydney, 2018, pp. xvi & 591–592.

25 J Holland & KA Wright, 'The double delegitimisation of Julia Gillard: Gender, the media and Australian political culture', *Australian Journal of Political Science*, vol. 63, no. 4, 2017, pp. 588–602.

26 L Trimble, 'Julia Gillard and the gender wars', *Politics & Gender*, vol. 12, no. 2, 2016, p. 297.

27 J Gillard & N Okonjo-Iweala, *Women and Leadership: Real lives, real lessons*, Vintage Books Australia, Melbourne, 2020.

28 Shortly after the tenth anniversary of Gillard's coming to office, a former woman Liberal Party staffer was moved to issue a public apology to Gillard about the lack of gender solidarity received by Australia's first female prime minister. See Chelsey Potter, 'An open letter of apology to Julia Gillard from a former Liberal staffer', *Sydney Morning Herald*, 16 July 2020, <www.smh.com.au/national/an-open-letter-of-apology-to-julia-gillard-from-a-former-liberal-staffer-20200716-p55ci1.html>.

29 Quoted in J Maley, 'Julia Gillard's global warming', *Age (Good Weekend)*, 13 July 2019, p. 23.

30 Maley 2019, pp. 20–21.

31 Maley 2019, p. 23.

32 For the latest figures, see L Richards, *Composition of Australian Parliaments by Party and Gender: A quick guide*, Parliamentary Library, Parliament of Australia, Research Paper Series 2020–2021, Updated 11 September 2020, <parlinfo.aph.gov.au/parlInfo/download/library/prspub/3681701/upload_binary/3681701.pdf>.

33 L Trimble, J Curtin, A Wagner, M Auer, V Woodman & B Owens, 'Gender novelty and personalised news coverage in Australia and Canada', *International Political Science Review*, first published online 25 October 2019, <doi.org/10.1177%2F0192512119876083>.

'She just won't lie down and die'

1 Quoted in J Wright & J Ireland, 'Gillard won't lie down and die, says Abbott', *Sydney Morning Herald*, 29 May 2012.

2 J Maley, 'Julia Gillard: Life after politics', *Sydney Morning Herald (Good Weekend)*, 13 July 2019, pp. 18–23, p. 21.

3 Gillard quoted in Maley 2019, p. 23.

4 K Manne, *Down Girl: The logic of misogyny*, Oxford University Press, New York, 2018.

5   J Gillard, *My Story*, Random House, North Sydney, 2014, p. 98.

6   Gillard 2014, p. 113.

7   A Summers, *The Misogyny Factor*, NewSouth Books, Sydney, 2013.

8   J Kent, *Take Your Best Shot: The prime ministership of Julia Gillard*, Penguin, Australia, 2013.

9   B Williams, 'A gendered media analysis of the prime ministerial ascension of Gillard and Turnbull: He's "taken back the reins" and she's "a backstabbing" murderer', *Australian Journal of Political Science*, vol. 52, no. 4, 2017, pp. 550–564.

10   KA Walsh, *The stalking of Julia Gillard*, Allen & Unwin, Sydney, 2013, p. xii.

11   M Cooney, *The Gillard Project: My thousand days of despair and hope*, Penguin Group, Scoresby, 2015, p. 5.

12   Quoted in Maley 2019, p. 23.

13   Maley 2019.

14   Gillard 2014, p. 79.

15   H Aston, 'Gillard's father died of shame: Alan Jones', *Sydney Morning Herald*, 29 September 2012, <www.smh.com.au/politics/federal/gillards-father-died-of-shame-alan-jones-20120929-26soa.html>.

16   S Gardiner, '"Died of shame": Focus on Abbott's use of controversial phrase', *Sydney Morning Herald*, 10 October 2012, www.smh.com.au/politics/federal/died-of-shame-focus-on-abbotts-use-of-controversial-phrase-20121010-27cgd.html>.

17   Gardiner 2012.

18   Gillard 2014, p. 110.

19   D Marr, 'Political animal: The making of Tony Abbott', *Quarterly Essay*, vol. 47, September 2012, p. 68.

20   J Gillard, 'The Blue Tie Speech: Prime Minister's Address to the Women for Gillard', 2013, <australianpolitics.com/2013/06/11/women-for-gillard-speech.html>.

21   Quoted in B Jabour, 'Julia Gillard's "small breasts" served up on Liberal Party dinner menu', *Guardian*, 12 June 2013 <www.theguardian.com/world/2013/jun/12/gillard-menu-sexist-liberal-dinner>.

22   Quoted in G Chan, 'Gillard defends single parent benefit change', *Guardian*, 2 October 2013, <www.theguardian.com/world/2013/oct/02/julia-gillard-single-parents-benefit>.

23   Quoted in Chan 2013.

24   Walsh 2013.

25   See M Walsh, 'Five prime ministers: A crisis, a political aberration or the new normal?' in C Aulich (ed), *From Abbott to Turnbull: A new direction? Australian Commonwealth Administration 2013–2016*, Echo Books, Victoria, 2016, pp. 323–342 and M Walsh, 'The revolving door of Australian prime ministers' in M Evans, Grattan & B McCaffrie (eds), *From Turnbull to Morrison: Understanding the trust divide*, Melbourne University Press, Melbourne, 2018, pp. 332–338.

Julie Bishop and the unmaking of an unfeminist

1   J Ireland, 'I'm no feminist: Julie Bishop', *Sydney Morning Herald*, 29 October 2014, <www.smh.com.au/politics/federal/im-no-feminist-julie-bishop-20141029-11dn7m.html>.

2   '"Feminist" a tag too far as Bishop focuses upon equality wins', *Australian*, 5 March 2019.

3   See C Johnson, 'Playing the gender card: The uses and abuses of gender in Australian politics', *Politics and Gender*, vol. 11, no. 2, June 2015, pp. 291–319.

4   M Turnbull, 'I was caught up in a degrading and corrupt parody of democracy',

Sydney Morning Herald, 18 April 2020, <www.smh.com.au/politics/federal/i-was-caught-up-in-a-degrading-and-corrupt-parody-of-democracy-20200415-p54k51.html>.

5   K Hall Jamieson, *Beyond the Double Bind: Women and leadership*, Oxford University Press, Oxford, 1997.

6   M Doran & B Worthington, 'Julie Bishop, former foreign minister, announces resignation from Parliament', *ABC News*, 21 February 2019, <www.abc.net.au/news/2019-02-21/julie-bishop-to-retire/10834480>.

7   D Kandiyoti, 'Bargaining with patriarchy', *Gender and Society*, vol. 2, no. 3, 1988, p. 274

8   B Shields, 'Julie Bishop quits as Foreign Minister and will likely retire from Parliament', *Sydney Morning Herald*, 26 August 2018, </www.smh.com.au/politics/federal/julie-bishop-quits-as-foreign-minister-and-will-retire-from-parliament-20180826-p4zztq.html>.

9   Shields 2018.

10   Shields 2018.

11   See, for example, 'Julie Bishop: Ex-contender for Australian PM to leave politics', *BBC News*, 21 February 2019, www.bbc.com/news/world-australia-47314878>.

12   M Grattan, 'Julie Bishop shows the boys how it's done', *The Conversation*, 20 October 2014, <theconversation.com/julie-bishop-shows-the-boys-how-its-done-33206>.

13   Department of Foreign Affairs and Trade (DFAT), *Gender Equality and Women's Empowerment Strategy*, February 2016, <www.dfat.gov.au/sites/default/files/gender-equality-and-womens-empowerment-strategy.pdf>.

14   J Bishop, 'The new aid paradigm', Speech to the National Press Club, 18 June 2014, <www.npc.org.au/speaker/2014/158-the-hon-julie-bishop-mp/>.

15   Bishop 2014.

16   See Department of Foreign Affairs and Trade (DFAT), *Making Performance Count: Enhancing the accountability and effectiveness of Australian aid*, 8 June 2014, <www.dfat.gov.au/sites/default/files/framework-making-performance-count.pdf>; DFAT 2016, p. 21.

17   DFAT 2014, p. 8.

18   See K Lee-Koo, 'Feminist foreign policy by stealth', *Foreign Policy Analysis*, vol. 16, no. 2, 2020, pp. 236–249.

19   Department of Foreign Affairs and Trade (DFAT), 2017 Foreign Policy White Paper, 2017, p. 11, <www.dfat.gov.au/sites/default/files/2017-foreign-policy-white-paper.pdf>.

20   DFAT 2017.

21   D Wroe, 'New defence minister Marise Payne has right balance of toughness and compassion', Sydney Morning Herald, 21 September 2015, <www.smh.com.au/politics/federal/new-defence-minister-marise-payne-has-right-balance-of-toughness-and-compassion-20150921-gjrntc.html>.

22   J Ireland, 'Minister for Women doesn't have to identify as a feminist, says Senator Michaelia Cash', *Sydney Morning Herald*, 7 March 2014, <www.smh.com.au/politics/federal/minister-for-women-doesnt-have-to-identify-as-feminist-says-senator-michaelia-cash-20140307-34ata.html>.

23   B Cooper, 'Bronwyn Bishop celebrates International Women's Day with MacKillop College students', *Port Macquarie News*, 9 March 2015, <www.portnews.com.au/story/2930168/students-challenge-bishop-on-big-issues/>

24   B Jabour, 'Tony Abbott says his three daughters helped him "turn into a feminist"', *Guardian*, 4 March 2014, <www.theguardian.com/world/2014/mar/04/abbott-australian-women-smashed-glass-ceiling>.

25   P Hartcher, 'We expected more of Gillard', *Sydney Morning Herald*, 10 October 2012,

<www.smh.com.au/politics/federal/we-expected-more-of-gillard-20121009-27bd6.
html>.

26   A Summers, 'Gone is the turned cheek: Gillard as we've rarely seen her', *ABC
News*, 10 October 2012, <www.abc.net.au/news/2012-10-10/summers-gillard-
sexism/4305728>.

27   Quoted in J Rieden, 'Exclusive: Julie Bishop's thoughts on ex-Prime Minister Julia
Gillard', *Australian Women's Weekly*, 24 August 2018, <www.nowtolove.com.au/news/
local-news/julie-bishop-prime-minister-50558>.

28   Quoted in Rieden 2018.

29   P Hartcher, 'The PM we never had, and Morrison's failure to value Julie Bishop',
Sydney Morning Herald, 23 February 2019, <www.smh.com.au/politics/federal/the-
pm-we-never-had-and-morrison-s-failure-to-value-julie-bishop-20190222-p50zox.
html>.

30   K Murphy, 'Kelly O'Dwyer says that MPs were bullied during spill, as senator vows
to name names', *Guardian*, 4 September 2018, <www.theguardian.com/australia-
news/2018/sep/03/i-will-name-names-on-bullying-says-liberal-senator-lucy-gichuhi>.

31   G Hutchens, 'Julie Bishop calls out "appalling behaviour" in politics, saying "enough
is enough"', *Guardian*, 6 September 2018, <www.theguardian.com/australia-
news/2018/sep/06/julie-bishop-appalling-behaviour-politics-enough-is-enough>.

32   A Remeikis, 'Julie Bishop: When Tony Abbott was minister for women I knew we
had "some way to go"', *Guardian*, 5 March 2019, <www.theguardian.com/australia-
news/2019/mar/05/julie-bishop-with-tony-abbott-minister-for-women-i-knew-we-
had-some-way-to-go-on-equality>.

33   Hutchens 2018.

34   Quoted in Rieden 2018.

Peta Credlin and the 'right' articulation of gendered rage

1   C Pateman, *The Sexual Contract*, Polity/Blackwell, Cambridge, 1988; P Sykes,
'Gendering prime ministerial power' in P Strangio, P 't Hart & J Walter (eds),
Understanding Prime Ministerial Performance: Comparative perspectives, Oxford
University Press, Oxford, 2013, pp. 102–124.

2   A Gauja & M Grömping. 'The expanding party universe: Patterns of partisan
engagement in Australia and the United Kingdom', *Party Politics*, First published
on-line, 2019, <doi.org/10.1177/1354068818822251>.

3   Sykes 2013, pp. 117–120.

4   Sykes 2013, pp. 106–109.

5   C Moore, *Margaret Thatcher: The authorized biography, Volume One: Not for turning*,
Allen Lane, London, 2013, p. 758.

6   N Walter, *The New Feminism*, Virago, London, 1999, pp. 2, 172–176, 269.

7   P Strangio, P t' Hart & J Walter, *The Pivot of Power: Australian Prime Ministers and
political leadership, 1949–2016*, The Miegunyah Press, Melbourne, 2017,
pp. 259–274.

8   K Lee-Koo & M Maley, 'The Iron Butterfly and the Political Warrior: Mobilising
models of femininity in the Australian Liberal Party', *Australian Journal of Political
Science*, vol. 52, no. 3, 2017, pp. 319–321.

9   Lee-Koo & Maley 2017, p. 321.

10   Quoted in Strangio et al. 2017, p. 283.

11   For a summary of such criticism see Lee-Koo & Maley 2017, pp. 325–327.

12   D Marr, 'Political animal: The making of Tony Abbott', *Quarterly Essay*, vol. 47,
2012, p. 82.

13 Strangio et al. 2017, pp. 282–283.
14 See A Patrick, *Credlin & Co: How the Abbott Government destroyed itself*, Black Inc., Melbourne, 2016; Strangio et al. 2017, pp. 282–285.
15 Patrick 2016, p. 26.
16 Strangio et al. 2017, pp. 274–289.
17 Abbott as quoted in J Lyons, 'In command and out of control', *Weekend Australian*, 21–22 February 2015.
18 See, especially, Patrick 2016; N Savva, *The Road to Ruin: How Tony Abbott and Peta Credlin destroyed their own government*, Scribe, Melbourne, 2016.
19 Lee-Koo & Maley 2017, p. 318.
20 Lee-Koo & Maley 2017, p. 330.
21 Quoted in A Meade, 'Peta Credlin: I want to do something where I get my own voice', *Guardian*, 23 September 2015, <www.theguardian.com/australia-news/2015/sep/23/peta-credlin-i-want-to-do-something-where-i-get-my-own-voice>.
22 See D Sessions, 'The rise of the thought leader: How the superrich have funded a new class of intellectual', *The New Republic*, 2017, <newrepublic.com/article/143004/rise-thought-leader-how-superrich-funded-new-class-intellectual>. Quotations from D Drezner are drawn from this article.
23 A McRobbie, 'Beyond post feminism', *Public Policy Research*, September–November 2011, pp. 179, 181.
24 See P Green, 'Cultural rage and right-wing intellectuals' in MJ Thompson (ed), Confronting the New Conservatism: The rise of the right in America, New York University Press, New York, 2007, pp. 31–55.
25 M Sartor's poem is quoted in P Murray, 'Reclaiming the muse' in V Zajko & M Leonard (eds), *Laughing with Medusa: Classical myths and feminist thought*, Oxford University Press, New York, 2008, p. 347.
26 S Freud, 'Medusa's head', in *Standard Edition 18*, Hogarth Press, London, 1940, pp. 273–274.
27 H Cixous, 'The Laugh of Medusa', translated by K Cohen & P Cohen, *Signs: The Journal of Women in Culture and Society*, vol. 1, no. 4, 1976, pp. 875–893.
28 Cixous 1976, p. 885.
29 For example, E Showalter, 'Laughing Medusa: Feminist intellectuals at the millennium', *Women: A Cultural Review*, vol. 11, no. 1–2, 2000, pp. 131–138; DK Silverman, 'Medusa: Sexuality, power, mastery, and some psychoanalytic observations', *Studies in Gender and Sexuality*, vol. 17, no. 2, 2016, pp. 114–125.
30 Here I paraphrase P Sehgal, 'Women writers give voice to their rage', *New York Times*, 24 November 2019, <www.nytimes.com/2019/11/24/books/women-writers-rage.html>.
31 See A Crabb, 'Another lesson on what it means to be a woman in high office', *The Drum*, ABC News, 25 September 2015, <www.abc.net.au/news/2015-09-23/crabb-a-lesson-on-what-it-means-to-be-a-woman-in-high-office/6798602>; K Murphy, 'Bidding farewell to Peta Credlin: The woman who broke all Canberra's rules', *Guardian*, 23 September 2015, <www.theguardian.com/australia-news/2015/sep/23/bidding-farewell-to-peta-credlin-the-woman-who-broke-all-canberras-rules>.
32 H Lasswell, *Psychopathology and Politics*, Viking, New York, [1930] 1960.
33 Quoted in Crabb 2015.
34 Quoted in E Moulton & L Burke, 'Peta Credlin hits out at the haters', news.com.au, 23 September 2015, <www.news.com.au/finance/work/leaders/peta-credlin-hits-out-at/news-story/696bc4fb423edcf5cca58934d9bec8c8>.
35 Murphy 2015.

The power and perils of women in ministers' offices

1   Senate Finance and Public Administration Estimates Committee, 'Personal Employee
     Positions as at 1 February 2020', 3 March 2020.

2   R Forward, 'Ministerial staff of the Australian Government 1972–1974: A survey'
     in R Wettenhall & M Painter (eds), *The First Thousand days of Labor, Volume 2*,
     Canberra College of Advanced Education, Canberra, 1975 and J Walter, The
     Ministers' Minders, Oxford University Press, Melbourne, 1984.

3   This data was sourced by taking telephone and commercial directory lists of
     ministerial staff and seeking biographical information through online searches.

4   Forward 1975 and Walter 1984.

5   At this time the Chief of Staff was called the Senior Private Secretary. Walter also
     included the highest gradings in the PM, Treasurer and Deputy PM's offices.

6   A Hough, 'Composition of Australian parliaments by party and gender: A quick
     guide', *Parliamentary Library Research Paper Series*, 2019–20, 26 September 2019
     and Parliamentary Library, 'Current Ministry List 6 February 2020', *Parliamentary
     Handbook*, 2020.

7   S Lewis, 'Abbott's amazons to steer Coalition', *Daily Telegraph*, 4 October 2013.

8   H Aston & J Swan, '"Control freak" Peta Credlin accused of pulling Coalition
     strings', *Sydney Morning Herald*, 4 December 2013.

9   Interview August 2019.

10   M Maley, 'Strategic links in a cut-throat world: Rethinking the role and relationships
     of Australian ministerial staff', *Public Administration*, vol. 89, no. 4, 2011,
     pp. 1469–1488.

11   N Savva, *The Road to Ruin: How Tony Abbott and Peta Credlin destroyed their own
     government*, Scribe, Melbourne, 2016.

12   Maley 2011.

13   Quoted in R Baxendale, 'Peta Credlin rallies Liberal women members', *Australian*,
     27 June 2015.

14   Quoted in J Cadzow, 'In a league of her own', *Sydney Morning Herald*, 15 June 1996,
     p. 22.

15   K Lee-Koo & M Maley, 'The Iron Butterfly and the Political Warrior: Mobilising
     models of femininity in the Australian Liberal Party', *Australian Journal of Political
     Science*, vol. 52, no. 3, 2017, pp. 317–334

16   Maley 2011 and M Maley, 'The policy work of Australian political staff', *International
     Journal of Public Administration*, vol. 38, no.1, 2015, pp. 46–55.

17   A Tiernan, *Power Without Responsibility*, UNSW Press, Sydney, 2007.

18   Lee-Koo & Maley 2017.

19   See K Jamieson, *Beyond the Double Bind: Women and leadership*, Oxford University
     Press, Oxford, 1995.

20   Maley 2011.

21   R Hemsley, '*Backstage or Centre Stage?*', unpublished Honours thesis, Australian
     National University, Canberra, 2015.

22   J Lyons, 'Tony Abbott in command, but is Peta Credlin in control?', *Australian*,
     21 February 2015.

23   P Bongiorno, 'How the PM's office is wrecking his government', *Saturday Paper*,
     13 December 2014,

24   'Is this the most powerful woman in Australia?' *Marie Claire*, 10 September 2013.

25   Lee-Koo & Maley 2017.

26   E Gidengil & J Everitt, 'Metaphors and misrepresentation: Mediation in news
     coverage of the 1993 Canadian Leaders' Debate', *Press/Politics*, vol. 4, no. 1, 1999,

pp. 48–65 and E Gidengil & J Everitt, 'Talking Tough: Gender and reported speech in campaign news coverage', *Political Communication*, vol. 20, no. 3, 2003, 209–232.

27 A Clark, 'Ainsley Gotto broke the glass ceiling without realising it was there', *Australian Financial Review*, 7 December 2019.

28 'Ainsley Gotto career girl', *Canberra Times*, 23 January 1968.

29 From then on, she was dubbed 'Miss Wiggle' or 'The Wiggle' by sections of Australia's tabloid press. J Holmes, 'Political review', *Australian Quarterly*, vol. 42, no. 1, 1970, pp. 97–106, p. 97.

30 Holmes 1970, p. 98.

31 K Laing, '"*A Kind of Love*"': Supergirls, scapegoats and sexual liberation*, unpublished Honours thesis, University of Sydney, 2011.

32 K Legge, 'Who's the boss?', *Australian*, 5 November 2011.

33 Savva 2016, p. 146.

34 Examples include Howard-era defence minister John Moore and his chief of staff Brian Loughnane (Tiernan 2007, p. 113) and prime minister Paul Keating and his chief of staff Don Russell, who it was said had an 'intimate, mutually reinforcing relationship with Keating ... [and an] unequalled capacity to influence the Prime Minister'. D Watson, *Recollections of a Bleeding Heart: A portrait of Paul Keating PM*, Knopf, Milson's Point, 2002, pp. 385–386.

35 S Schama, 'Free advice: Five historians comment on Hillary's dilemma', *The New Yorker*, 30 January 1995.

36 'Minister silent on "shielding" staff bully', *SBS*, 30 September 2018, <www.sbs.com.au/news/minister-silent-on-shielding-staff-bully>; L Bourke, 'Transcripts reveal Ken Wyatt's office was subject to a secret inquiry into bullying allegations', *Sydney Morning Herald*, 6 May 2019.

37 R Chalmers, *Inside the Canberra Press Gallery – Life in the wedding cake of Old Parliament House*, ANU E-press, 2011.

38 House of Representatives Hansard, 5 December 1974, p. 4605.

39 G Freudenberg, *A Certain Grandeur*, Penguin, Ringwood, 1977, pp. 324.

40 Freudenberg 1977 and R Chalmers 2011.

41 M Turnbull, *Press conference*, 15 February 2018, <www.malcolmturnbull.com.au/media/press-conference-15-february-2018>.

42 Turnbull 2018.

43 A Mann, 'Whitlam's women's adviser Elizabeth Reid details unwelcome advance from Governor-General Sir John Kerr', *ABC News*, 3 March 2020.

44 E Bagshaw, '"It was very quick and very sudden": Liberal staffers reveal alleged sexual assaults', *Sydney Morning Herald*, 30 July 2019 and J Kennedy & K Nguyen, 'NSW Liberal staffer allegedly sexually assaulted by colleague says party took no action', *ABC News*, 31 July 2019.

45 M Lewinsky, 'Shame and survival', *Vanity Fair*, 28 May 2014.

The political parties
1 IPU [Inter-Parliamentary Union], 'Women in National Parliaments', October 2020, <data.ipu.org/women-ranking?month=10&year=2020>

2 See for example R Murray, ML Krook & K Opello, 'Why are gender quotas adopted? Party pragmatism and parity in France', *Political Research Quarterly*, vol. 65, no. 3, 2012, pp. 529–543.

3 See, for example, P Karp, 'Liberal MP Julia Banks to quit parliament, citing "bullying and intimidation"', *Guardian*, 29 August 2018, <www.theguardian.com/australia-

news/2018/aug/29/liberal-mp-julia-banks-to-quit-parliament-next-election-citing-bullying-and-intimidation>.

4   S Ilanbey, 'Labor state president urges members to "speak up" about harassment', *Age*, 17 November 2019, <www.theage.com.au/politics/victoria/labor-state-president-urges-members-to-speak-up-about-harassment-20191117-p53bbr.html>.

5   Quoted in B Doherty, 'Turnbull says Liberal Party definitely has a women problem', *Guardian*, 9 March 2019, <www.theguardian.com/australia-news/2019/mar/09/far-too-blokey-turnbull-says-liberal-party-has-gender-inequality-problem>.

6   M Taflaga & K Beauregard, 'The merit of party institutions: Women's descriptive representation and conservative parties in Australia and the United Kingdom', *Journal of Women, Politics & Policy*, vol. 41, no. 1, 2020, pp. 66–90; A Gauja & J McSwiney, 'Do Australian parties represent?' in K Heidar & B Wauters (eds), *Do Parties Still Represent? An analysis of the representativeness of political parties in western democracies*, Routledge, London, 2019, pp. 47–65; R Manwaring, 'Parties and representation' in N Miragliotta, A Gauja & R Smith (eds), *Contemporary Australian Political Party Organisations*, Monash University Press, Melbourne, 2015, pp. 89–102; M Simms (ed), *The Paradox of Parties: Australian political parties in the 1990s*, Allen & Unwin, Sydney, 1996.

7   Up until 1977, elections for the Senate and the House of Representatives were not synchronous.

8   M Caul, 'Women's representation in parliament: The role of political parties', *Party Politics*, vol. 5, no. 1, 1999, pp. 79–98; L Schwindt-Beyer & W Mishler, 'An integrated model of women's representation', *The Journal of Politics*, vol. 67, no. 2, 2005, pp. 407–28.

9   See, for example, J Lawless & K Pearson, 'The primary reason for women's under-representation: Re-evaluating the conventional wisdom', *Journal of Politics*, vol. 70, no. 1, 2008, pp. 67–82.

10 P Norris, 'Recruitment' in R Katz & W Crotty (eds), *Handbook of Party Politics*, Sage, London, 2006, pp. 89–108; D Dahlerup & M Leyenaar, *Breaking Male Dominance in Old Democracies*, Oxford University Press, Oxford, 2013.

11 W Cross & A Gauja, 'Designing Candidate Selection Methods: Explaining diversity in Australian political parties', *Australian Journal of Political Science*, vol. 49, no. 1, 2014, pp. 22–39.

12 S Pruysers, W Cross, A Gauja & G Rahat, 'Candidate selection rules and democratic outcomes: The impact of parties on women's representation' in S Scarrow, P Webb & T Poguntke (eds), *Organizing Political Parties: Representation, participation and power*, Oxford University Press, Oxford, 2017, pp. 208–233; Gauja & Cross 2015.

13 Caul 1999; M Krook, J Lovenduski & J Squires, 'Gender quotas and models of political citizenship', *British Journal of Political Science*, vol. 39, no. 4, 2009, pp. 781–803.

14 Caul 1999.

15 Taflaga & Beauregard 2020 and Gauja & Cross 2015.

16 See M Sawer, 'Misogyny and misrepresentation: Women in Australian parliaments', *Political Science*, vol. 65, no. 1, 2013, pp. 105–117.

17 A Gauja & J McSwiney, 'Do Australian parties represent?' in K Heidar & B Wauters (eds), *Do Parties Still Represent? An analysis of the representativeness of political parties in western democracies*, Routledge, London, 2019, pp. 47–65.

18 U Kjaer & K Kosiara-Pedersen, 'The hourglass pattern of women's representation', *Journal of Elections, Public Opinion and Parties*, vol. 29, no. 3, 2019, pp. 299–317.

19 U Kjaer & K Kosiara-Pedersen, 'The 'hourglass' pattern of representation: Why

political parties are key to electing more women to parliament', *Democratic Audit UK*, 1 February 2019, <www.democraticaudit.com/2019/02/01/the-hourglass-pattern-of-representation-why-political-parties-are-key-to-electing-more-women-to-parliament/>.

20　The competitiveness of the seat is based on the seat classificatory system developed by the Australian Electoral Commission, which demarcates electorates according to size of the winning margin (e.g. likelihood of the seat changing hands). Safe seat defined as 'a seat where the elected candidate received more than 60 per cent of the vote'. Fairly safe seat defined as 'a seat where the elected candidate received between 56 per cent and 60 per cent of the vote'. Marginal seat defined as 'a seat where the elected candidate received less than 56 per cent of the vote'.

21　It must be acknowledged that the classification of seats can and does change from one election to the next. It is not uncommon for a candidate to have been selected to a safe party seat and that seat subsequently was re-classified as marginal following the election. Similarly, a candidate might have been selected to a marginal seat held by their competitor, but over the course of their incumbency they managed to change the seat status to a safe party seat.

Barriers from within

1　It is important to note that all Indigenous men and women became able to enrol to vote in national elections in 1962. For further discussion on this point, see B Holmes, 'Celebrating the 50th anniversary of Indigenous federal voting rights', *Flagpost*, Parliament of Australia, 2012, <www.aph.gov.au/About_Parliament/Parliamentary_Departments/Parliamentary_Library/FlagPost/2012/May/Celebrating_the_50th_anniversary_of_Indigenous_federal_voting_rights>.

2　United Nations General Assembly, 'Resolution adopted by the General Assembly on 19 December 2011, 66/130, Women and political participation', p. 2, <www.un.org/ga/search/view_doc.asp?symbol=A/RES/66/130>.

3　DC Grube & C Howard, 'Promiscuously partisan? Public Service impartiality and responsiveness in Westminster systems', *Governance*, vol. 29, no. 4, 2016, pp. 517–533.

4　Australian Bureau of Statistics, 'Employment and earnings, public sector, Australia, 2018–19', 2019, <www.abs.gov.au/statistics/labour/employment-and-unemployment/employment-and-earnings-public-sector-australia/latest-release>.

5　Australian Public Service Commission, 'APS employment data 31 December 2019', 2019, <www.apsc.gov.au/section-3-diversity-0>.

6　New South Wales Public Service Commission, 'NSW public sector at a glance', 2019, <www.psc.nsw.gov.au/reports---data/state-of-the-nsw-public-sector/previous-editions/state-of-the-sector-2013/nsw-public-sector-at-a-glance>.

7　Victorian Public Sector Commission, 'Data insights: A decade of public sector workforce data', 2018, <vpsc.vic.gov.au/data-and-research/data-insights/data-insights-decade-public-sector-workforce-data/v>.

8　Australian Bureau of Statistics, 'Media Release: Students near 4 million, female teachers outnumber males', 6 February 2020, <www.abs.gov.au/ausstats/abs@.nsf/lookup/4221.0Media%20Release72019#:~:text=In%202019%2C%20there%20were%20288%2C294,41.3%20per%20cent%20were%20male>.

9　Nursing and Midwifery Board. 'Statistics', 2020, <www.nursingmidwiferyboard.gov.au/about/statistics.aspx>.

10　M Sawer, 'Women and government in Australia', *Year Book Australia, 2001*, Australian Bureau of Statistics, 2001, <www.abs.gov.au/ausstats/ABS@.

nsf/94713ad445ff1425ca25682000192af2/3067a337a2f2c855ca2569de001fb2dc!
OpenDocument>.

11   Joint Standing Committee on Electoral Matters, 'Excluded: The impact of Section 44
     on Australian democracy', Parliament of Australia, Canberra, 2018, p. 106, <https://
     parlinfo.aph.gov.au/parlInfo/download/committees/reportjnt/024156/toc_pdf/
     Excluded.pdf;fileType=application%2Fpdf >.

12   H Dennet, 'Job security questioned for public servants who stand in elections',
     The Mandarin, 12 August 2014, <www.themandarin.com.au/1378-job-security-
     questioned-public-servants-stand-elections/>.

13   Dennet 2014.

14   For further discussion on this see A Green 2019, 'Cooper (Key Seat)', *ABC*, <www.
     abc.net.au/news/elections/federal/2019/guide/coop>; S Ilanbey & N Towell, 'Three
     Liberal candidates dumped from party two days into the campaign', *Sydney Morning
     Herald*, 12 April 2019, <www.smh.com.au/federal-election-2019/three-liberal-
     candidates-dumped-from-party-two-days-into-the-campaign-20190412-p51doj.
     html>.

15   M Doran & E Byrne, 'Hollie Hughes, replacement for Fiona Nash in Senate, faces
     High Court hurdle', ABC, 10 November 2017, <www.abc.net.au/news/2017-11-10/
     hollie-hughes-complication-senate-replacement/9137208>.

16   A Probyn, 'High Court's decision to dismiss Hollie Hughes shows section 44 of
     the constitution needs updating', *ABC*, 16 November 2017, <www.abc.net.au/
     news/2017-11-16/analysis-section-44-constitution-needs-updating/9154540>.

17   Probyn 2017.

18   Joint Standing Committee on Electoral Matters, 'Excluded: The impact of Section
     44 on Australian democracy', Parliament of Australia, Canberra, 2018, pp. 17–19,
     <parlinfo.aph.gov.au/parlInfo/download/committees/reportjnt/024156/toc_pdf/
     Excluded.pdf;fileType=application%2Fpdf>.

19   A Twomey, 'Office of profit under the Crown', Parliamentary Library Research
     Paper, 14 June 2018, <https://parlinfo.aph.gov.au/parlInfo/download/committees/
     reportjnt/024156/toc_pdf/Excluded.pdf;fileType=application%2Fpdf>.

20   Joint Standing Committee on Electoral Matters, 2018, pp. 19–20.

21   Joint Standing Committee on Electoral Matters, 'Excluded: The impact of Section 44
     on Australian democracy', Parliament of Australia, Canberra, 2018, p. 106, < https://
     parlinfo.aph.gov.au/parlInfo/download/committees/reportjnt/024156/toc_pdf/
     Excluded.pdf;fileType=application%2Fpdf>.

22   Attorney-General's Department, 'Right to take part in public affairs and elections',
     n.d., <www.ag.gov.au/rights-and-protections/human-rights-and-anti-discrimination/
     human-rights-scrutiny/public-sector-guidance-sheets/right-take-part-public-affairs-
     and-elections#topofpage>.

23   Attorney-General's Department n.d.

24   House of Representatives Practice Seventh Edition, 'Sitting and non-sitting
     periods', 2018, <www.aph.gov.au/About_Parliament/House_of_Representatives/
     Powers_practice_and_procedure/Practice7/HTML/Chapter7/Sitting_and_non-
     sitting_periods>.

25   See S Brenton, *What Lies Beneath: The work of senators and members in the Australian
     Parliament*, Parliamentary Library, Canberra, 2010, <www.aph.gov.au/binaries/
     library/pubs/monographs/brenton/monograph.pdf>; A Weinberg, CL Cooper &
     A Weinberg, 'Workload, stress and family life in British Members of Parliament and
     the psychological impact of reforms to their working hours', in CL Cooper (ed),
     From Stress to Wellbeing Volume 1, Palgrave Macmillan, New York, 2013.

26   Cited in H Davidson, 'Kelly O'Dwyer quits politics in shock resignation before election', *Guardian*, 19 January 2019, <www.theguardian.com/australia-news/2019/jan/19/kelly-odwyer-announces-shock-resignation-ahead-of-election>.

27   Cited in D Wills, 'Labor MP Kate Ellis quits politics – frontbencher won't run at next federal election to spend more time with family in Adelaide', *Advertiser*, 9 March 2017, <www.adelaidenow.com.au/news/south-australia/labor-mp-kate-ellis-quits-politics-frontbencher-wont-run-at-next-federal-election-to-spend-more-time-with-family-in-adelaide/news-story/99e5338c303b5f142d01740920a14e90>.

28   Cited in S Anderson, 'Kate Ellis, Labor frontbencher, to quit politics at next federal election', *ABC*, 9 March 2017, <www.abc.net.au/news/2017-03-09/kate-ellis-to-quit-politics-at-next-federal-election/8338698>.

29   See M Grattan, 'Labor MP Tim Hammond quits for family reasons, creating byelection in WA', *The Conversation*, 2 May 2018, <theconversation.com/labor-mp-tim-hammond-quits-for-family-reasons-creating-byelection-in-wa-95931>; M Koslowski, 'Scott Morrison says the number of retiring government MPs is "not unusual". He's right', *Sydney Morning Herald*, 29 January 2019, <www.smh.com.au/politics/federal/scott-morrison-says-the-number-of-retiring-government-mps-is-not-unusual-he-s-right-20190129-p50u9a.html>.

30   M Fitzherbert, 'It's a myth that Liberal candidates are selected on "merit" alone', *Age*, 17 December 2018, <www.theage.com.au/politics/victoria/it-s-a-myth-that-liberal-candidates-are-selected-on-merit-alone-20181217-p50msy.html>.

31   Fitzherbert 2018.

32   Cited in T McIlroy, 'John Howard says 50/50 gender split in politics is unrealistic due to caring responsibilities', *Sydney Morning Herald*, 7 September 2016, <www.smh.com.au/politics/federal/john-howard-says-5050-gender-split-in-politics-is-unrealistic-due-to-caring-responsibilites-20160907-graqrf.html>.

33   Y Xiao & Z Fan, '10 technology trends to watch in the COVID-19 pandemic', World Economic Forum, 27 April 2020, <www.weforum.org/agenda/2020/04/10-technology-trends-coronavirus-covid19-pandemic-robotics-telehealth/>.

34   'Coronavirus: MPs approve voting from home', *BBC News*, 22 April 2020, <www.bbc.com/news/uk-politics-52381194>.

35   R Harris, 'Federal parliament prepares for virtual sittings in case of further COVID outbreak', *Sydney Morning Herald*, 6 July 2020, <www.smh.com.au/politics/federal/federal-parliament-prepares-for-virtual-sittings-in-case-of-further-covid-outbreak-20200706-p559ke.html>.

36   European Parliament News, 'How parliament works during a pandemic', 17 April 2020, <www.europarl.europa.eu/news/en/headlines/priorities/eu-response-to-coronavirus/20200408STO76807/how-parliament-works-during-a-pandemic>.

37   E Bagshaw, 'Number of MPs in federal parliament to be down 40pc next week', *Sydney Morning Herald*, 17 March 2020, <www.smh.com.au/politics/federal/number-of-mps-in-federal-parliament-to-be-down-40pc-next-week-20200317-p54b0w.html>.

38   A Twomey, 'A virtual Australian parliament is possible – and may be needed – during the coronavirus pandemic', *The Conversation*, 25 March 2020, <theconversation.com/a-virtual-australian-parliament-is-possible-and-may-be-needed-during-the-coronavirus-pandemic-134540>.

39   A Crabb, 'Coronavirus has made us all learn to work from home, so why not Parliament too?' *ABC*, 25 March 2020, <www.abc.net.au/news/2020-03-25/coronavirus-why-cant-parliament-work-from-home/12086106>.

Am I ambassadorial enough?

1   Participant 1, 4 February 2019.

2   E Stephenson, 'Domestic challenges to international leadership: A case study of women in Australian international affairs', *Australian Journal of International Affairs*, vol. 73, no. 3, 2019, pp. 234–253.

3   V Lowndes, 'The institutional approach' in D Marsh & G Stoker (eds), *Theory and Methods in Political Science*, 3rd edn, Palgrave Macmillan, Basingstoke, 2010, p. 686.

4   F Mackay, M Kenny & I Chappell, 'New institutionalism through a gender lens: Towards a feminist institutionalism?', *International Political Science Review*, vol. 31, no. 5, 2010, pp. 573–588.

5   Australian Public Service Commission, *Women*, 2017, <www.apsc.gov.au/sites/default/files/sosr_2012-13_final_accesssible.pdf?acsf_files_redirect>.

6   Australian Public Service Employee Database, *Yearbook Statistics*, 1984–2018.

7   Lowy Institute, 'Foreign territory: Women in international relations', 9 July 2019, <www.lowyinstitute.org/publications/gender-australia-ir-sector>.

8   M Conley Tyler, 'Diversity and diplomacy', *Australian Journal of International Affairs*, vol. 70, no. 6, 2016, p. 696.

9   E Stephenson, 'Invisible while visible: An Australian perspective on queer women leaders in international affairs', *European Journal of Politics and Gender*, published online 2020.

10   E Ostrom, *Governing the Commons: The evolution of institutions for collective action*, Cambridge University Press, New York, 1990, p. 38.

11   Participant 2, 1 February 2019.

12   United Nations Development Program, *Tackling Social Norms: A game changer for gender inequalities*, 2020, <hdr.undp.org/sites/default/files/hd_perspectives_gsni.pdf>.

13   Participant 3, 5 March 2019.

14   Vienna Convention on Diplomatic Relations, Vienna, 18 April 1961.

15   A Bailey, M LaFrance & J Dovidio, 'Is man the measure of all things? A social cognitive account of androcentrism', *Personality and Social Psychology Review*, vol. 23, no. 4, 2019, pp. 307–331.

16   Participant 4, 1 February 2019.

17   M Sabharwal, 'From glass ceiling to glass cliff: Women in senior executive service', *Journal of Public Administration Research & Theory*, vol. 25, no. 2, 2015, pp. 399–426.

18   Participant 5, 2 August 2018.

Unpaid labour

1   Quoted in L Burke, 'John Howard: Women have "limits on capacity" in politics', *news.com.au*, 7 September 2016, <www.news.com.au/finance/work/careers/john-howard-women-have-limits-on-capacity-in-politics/news-story/a0ad49697ac9576755fe8858083f238e>.

2   A Crabb, *The Wife Drought*, Random House Australia, North Sydney, NSW, 2014.

3   WGEA, Insight Paper, Unpaid Care Work and the Labour Market, 2020, <www.wgea.gov.au/sites/default/files/documents/australian-unpaid-care-work-and-the-labour-market.pdf>.

4   L Craig, 'COVID-19 has laid bare how much we value women's work, and how little we pay for it', *The Conversation* 2020, <theconversation.com/covid-19-has-laid-bare-how-much-we-value-womens-work-and-how-little-we-pay-for-it-136042>.

5   WGEA 2020.

6   WGEA 2020.

7   WGEA, 'Women's disproportionate share of unpaid caring and domestic work',
    2018, <www.wgea.gov.au/topics/the-gender-pay-gap>.
8   L Ruppaner, 'HILDA findings on Australian families' experience of childcare should
    be a call-to-arms for government', *The Conversation*, 2019, <theconversation.com/
    hilda-findings-on-australian-families-experience-of-childcare-should-be-a-call-to-
    arms-for-government-120417>.
9   Ruppaner 2019.
10 M Evans, V Haussegger, M Halupka & P Rowe, 'From girls to men: Social attitudes
    to gender equality in Australia', *BroadAgenda*, 2018,.
11 Evans, Haussegger, Halupka & Rowe 2018.
12 Inter-Parliamentary Union, 'Women in Politics 2020', <www.ipu.org/resources/
    publications/infographics/2020-03/women-in-politics-2020>.
13 World Economic Forum, 'Global Gender Gap Report 2020', p. 13, <www3.
    weforum.org/docs/WEF_GGGR_2020.pdf>.
14 B Butler, 'Number of women on boards of Australia's top companies falls', *Guardian*,
    <www.theguardian.com/australia-news/2019/oct/31/number-of-women-on-boards-
    of-australias-top-companies-falls>.
15 P Rowe, 'The O'Dwyer case: Don't throw the mother out with the bathwater' in
    M Evans, M Grattan & B McCaffrie (eds), *From Turnbull to Morrison: Understanding
    the trust divide*, Melbourne University Press, Carlton, Victoria, 2019.
16 L Reynolds, 'Kelly O'Dwyer's resignation is a parent issue', *Sydney Morning Herald*,
    22 January 2019, <www.smh.com.au/national/kelly-o-dwyer-s-resignation-is-a-
    parent-issue-20190120-p50sir.html>.
17 K Sackville, 'The change: Tanya Plibersek's shock election decision proves we
    need', *news.com.au*, 21 May 2019, <www.news.com.au/national/federal-election/
    the-change-tanya-pliberseks-shock-election-decision-proves-we-need/news-story/
    c8329c5cfb8e0a3caf8c632dd2710fd7>.
18 E Ainge, 'Jacinda Ardern makes history with baby Neve at UN general assembly',
    Guardian, 25 September 2018, <www.theguardian.com/world/2018/sep/25/jacinda-
    ardern-makes-history-with-baby-neve-at-un-general-assembly>.
19 Respondent #1, telephone interview by authors, March 2019.
20 Respondent #1, telephone interview by authors, March 2019.
21 Respondent #6, telephone interview by authors, January 2020.
22 Respondent #2, telephone interview by authors, April 2019.
23 Respondent #1, telephone interview by authors, March 2019.
24 Respondent #6, telephone interview by authors, January 2020.
25 Respondent #2, telephone interview by authors, April 2019.
26 Respondent #6, telephone interview by authors, January 2020.
27 S Medhora, 'Breastfeeding and bottle feeding to be allowed in house of
    representative', *Guardian*, 2 February 2016, <www.theguardian.com/
    lifeandstyle/2016/feb/02/breastfeeding-and-bottle-feeding-to-be-allowed-in-house-of-
    representative>.
28 Respondent #1, telephone interview by authors, March 2019.
29 Respondent #6, telephone interview by authors, January 2019.
30 S Palmieri, 'Dear 46th Parliament … A gender equality wish list', *BroadAgenda*,
    30 April 2019, <www.broadagenda.com.au/2019/dear-46th-parliament/>.

The dream gap

1   M McGowan & P Karp, 'Sarah Hanson-Young awarded $120,000 damages in defamation case against David Leyonhjelm', *Guardian*, 25 November 2019, <www. theguardian.com/australia-news/2019/nov/25/sarah-hanson-young-awarded-120000-damages-defamation-david-leyonhjelm>.

2   G Villasmil, 'How Sarah Hanson-Young's win changed my life', *10 daily*, 30 November 2019, <10daily.com.au/views/a191128upsef/how-sarah-hanson-youngs-win-changed-my-life-20191129>.

3   McGowan & Karp 2019.

4   McGowan & Karp 2019.

5   'Australian girls say they are not treated equally', Plan International Australia, 2017, <www.plan.org.au/media/media-releases/australian-girls-say-they-are-not-treated-equally>.

6   'She Can Lead: Young people in Australia share their views on women in politics and leadership', Plan International Australia, 2017, <www.plan.org.au/~/media/Plan/Documents/Reports/IDG%202017/She%20Can%20Lead>.

7   'Young women cite gender, lack of opportunities as biggest barrier to political life', Plan International Australia, 2017, <web.archive.org/web/20180313065609/www.plan.org.au/media/media-releases/young-women-say-lack-of-opportunities-biggest-barrier-to-politics>.

8   'Young women cite gender, lack of opportunities as biggest barrier to political life', Plan International Australia, 2017, <web.archive.org/web/20180313065609/www.plan.org.au/media/media-releases/young-women-say-lack-of-opportunities-biggest-barrier-to-politics>.

9   V Krithivasan, 'Time to practice what we preach and fix the lack of diversity in Australian leadership', 2019, <www.canberratimes.com.au/story/6431620/the-lack-of-diversity-in-australian-leadership/>.

10   'Taking the Lead: Girls and young women on changing the face of leadership', Plan International and the Geena Davis Institute on Gender in Media, 2019, <plan-international.org/publications/taking-the-lead>.

11   'Australia's gender pay gap statistics', Australian Government Workplace Gender Equality Agency, 2020, <wgea.gov.au/data/fact-sheets/australias-gender-pay-gap-statistics>.

12   'Global Gender Gap Report, 2018', World Economic Forum, 2018, <www.weforum.org/reports/the-global-gender-gap-report-2018>.

13   See, for example, R Lewis & R Ferguson, 'Quotas an option for Liberal Party women', 2019, <www.theaustralian.com.au/nation/politics/quotas-an-option-for-liberal-party-women/news-story/32ac180be3441c540c26c670d8dab59e>.

14   Quoted in J Ireland, '"Seven days a week on the road is not something I wanted for my kids": Plibersek and Gillard talk leadership', *Sydney Morning Herald*, 14 July 2019, <www.smh.com.au/politics/federal/seven-days-a-week-on-the-road-not-something-i-wanted-for-my-kids-plibersek-and-gillard-talk-leadership-20190712-p526jo.html>.

15   The authors would like to thank and acknowledge Ari Jerrems for his research support in this chapter.

Troubling elites

1   C Johnson, 'Playing the gender card: The uses and abuses of gender in Australian politics', *Politics and Gender*, vol. 11, no. 2, 2015, pp. 291–319.

2   E Bjarnegård, 'Men's political representation' in *Oxford Research Encyclopedias—Politics*,

2020, <oxfordre.com/politics/view/10.1093/acrefore/9780190228637.001.0001/acrefore-9780190228637-e-214>; S Bird, 'Welcome to the men's club: Homosociality and the maintenance of hegemonic masculinity', Gender & Society. vol.10, no. 2, 1996, p. 122.

3   MP Moore, 'Rhetoric and paradox: Seeking knowledge from the "container and thing contained"', *Rhetoric Society Quarterly*, vol. 18, no. 1, 1988, pp. 16–17.

4   U Eco, 'Paradoxes and aphorisms' in U Eco (ed), *On the Shoulders of Giants*, Harvill Secker, London, 2019, pp. 195–226.

5   Moore 1988, p. 19.

6   D Gaxie, 'Democracy and elites', *Corvinus Journal of Sociology and Social Policy*, vol. 8, no. 3, 2017, p. 17–37.

7   M Sawer & B Hindess (eds), *Us and Them: Anti-elitism in Australia*, API Network, Australia Research Institute, Curtin University of Technology, Perth, 2004.

8   C Mudde, 'The populist zeitgeist', *Government and Opposition*, vol. 39, no. 4, 2004, p. 560.

9   Mudde 2005, p. 544.

10   For example, see G Fitzi, J Maggert & BS Turner (eds), *Populism and the Crisis of Democracy, Vol 1, Concepts and theory*, Routledge, London, 2019; H Bang & D Marsh, 'Populism versus neo-liberalism: Is there a way forward?', *Policy Studies*, vol. 39, no. 3, 2018, pp. 251–259; C de laTorre, *The Promise and Perils of Populism*, University Press of Kentucky, Lexington, 2015; C Mudde & C Rovira Kaltwasser, *Populism in Europe and the Americas: Threat or corrective for democracy?*, Cambridge University Press, Cambridge, 2012; M Canovan, 'Trust the people! Populism and the two faces of democracy', *Political Studies*, vol. 47, 1999, pp. 2–16; N Urbanati, 'Democracy and populism', *Constellations*, vol. 5, no. 1, 1998, pp. 110–124.

11   MF Plattner, 'Democracy's past and future: Populism, pluralism, and liberal democracy', *Journal of Democracy*, vol. 21, no. 1, 2020, p. 87; Canovan 1999.

12   Mudde 2004, p. 560; Plattner 2020, p. 88; Urbanati 1998, p. 110.

13   J Locke, *Two Treatises of Government: A critical edition with an introduction and apparatus criticus by Peter Laslett*, Mentor Books, New York, 1963.

14   J Kane & H Patapan, *The Democratic Leader: How democracy defines, empowers and limits its leaders*, Oxford University Press, Oxford, 2012, p. 4.

15   P Taggart, *Populism*, Open University Press, Buckingham, 2000, p. 95.

16   JW Muller, 'The rise and rise of populism' in F Gonzalez (ed), *The Age of Perplexity: Rethinking the world we knew*, Penguin Random House Grupo Editorial, Madrid, 2018, <www.bbvaopenmind.com/en/books/the-age-of-perplexity/>.

17   B Anderson, *Imagined Communities*, Verso Books, London,1983.

18   Mudde 2004, p. 546.

19   It is probably a stretch to consider such major parties as populist. See D Munro, 'Populism? Minor parties and independents in the Australian Federal Parliament, 1945–2016', *Policy Studies*, vol. 40, no. 2, 2019, p. 227. See also S Tormey, 'Populism: Democracy's *Pharmakon*?', *Policy Studies*, vol. 39, no. 3, 2018, pp. 260–273.

20   Munro 2019, p. 227.

21   Kane & Patapan 2012, p. 1.

22   Taggart 2000, p. 1.

23   J Jose, '"Manning up" with Pauline Hanson: Playing the gender card, again' in B Grant, T Lynch & T Moore (eds), *The Rise of Right-Populism: Pauline Hanson's One Nation and Australian politics*, Springer Nature, Singapore, 2019, pp. 167–178.

24 A Broinowski, *Please Explain: The rise, fall, and rise again of Pauline Hanson*, Penguin Random House, Melbourne, 2017.

25 RN Proctor, 'Agnotology: A missing term to describe the cultural production of ignorance (and its study)' in RN Proctor & L Schiebinger (eds), *Agnotology: The making and unmaking of ignorance*, Stanford University Press, Stanford, 2008, p. 2. The discussion in the following paragraphs draws largely on Proctor's account, pp. 4–26.

26 C Mills, 'White ignorance' in RN Proctor & L Schiebinger (eds), *Agnotology: The making and unmaking of ignorance*, Stanford University Press, Stanford, 2008, 233–234.

27 M Hawkesworth, *Embodied Power: Demystifying disembodied politics*, Routledge, New York, 2016, p. 149.

28 For some discussion on backlash politics see 'Symposium: Backlash and the future of feminism', JM Piscopo & DM Walsh (eds), *Signs: Journal of Women in Culture and Society*, vol. 45, no. 2, 2020, pp. 265–385.

29 BA Carroll, 'The politics of "originality": Women and the class system of the intellect', *Journal of Women's History*, vol. 2, no. 2, 1990, pp. 136–163.

30 MR Gregory, 'Inside the locker room: Male homosociability in the advertising industry', *Gender, Work and Organization*, vol. 16, no. 3, pp. 323–347.

31 AH Eagly & SJ Karan, 'Role congruity theory of prejudice toward female leaders', *Psychological Review*, vol. 109, no. 3, 2002, pp. 573–598.

32 Jose 2019.

The right royal dilemma

1 See 'Newspaper Publishing', WGEA Data Explorer, <data.wgea.gov.au/industries/226> and 'Broadcasting (except Internet)', WGEA Data Explorer, <data.wgea.gov.au/industries/332>.

2 J Price & AM Payne, '2019 Women for media report: You can't be what you can't see', 2019, p. 15, <c9ab9e33-e40f-4fa3-b1bb-ae9876a6a477.filesusr.com/ugd/ee1ce5_88c20ce959044aab84737b1993c326ca.pdf>.

3 These are the 'odd and unusual' human interest stories run by news sites that might deal with social and cultural issues (e.g. the best beers in Melbourne) or seek to generate viewer debate (e.g. which Sydney suburb has the best fauna?) but do not fall within the other categories.

4 See M McKinnon, The Conversation, 26 February 2020, <theconversation.com/gender-diversity-in-science-media-still-has-a-long-way-to-go-heres-a-5-step-plan-to-move-it-along-132174>. This research shows that men were the sole authors in 52 per cent of science news stories.

5 Price & Payne 2019, p. 16

6 Quote taken during personal communication with the author.

7 J Nicholls, telephone interview with J Gray, 2019.

8 Price & Payne 2019, p. 26.

9 K Kelling & RJ Thomas, 'The roles and functions of opinion journalists', Newspaper Research Journal, vol. 39, no. 4, 2018, pp. 398–419, p. 401.

10 JL Hulteng, The Opinion Function: Editorial and interpretive writing for the news media, Harper & Row, New York, 1973, p. 11.

11 BI Page, RY Shapiro & GR Dempsey, 'What moves public opinion?', The American Political Science Review, vol. 81, no. 1, 1987, pp. 23–44.

12 See 'Revealed: The journalists with the most front page bylines in 2019, Streem, <www.streem.com.au/2019/11/26/revealed-the-journalists-with-the-most-front-page-bylines-in-2019.html>.

13 Personal email communication with the author.
14 G Morris, telephone interview with J Nicholls, 2019.
15 G Morris, telephone interview with J Nicholls, 2019.
16 T Morgenroth, MK Ryan & K Peters, 'The motivational theory of role modeling: How role models influence role aspirants' goals', Review of General Psychology, vol. 19, no. 4, 2015, pp. 465–483.
17 See G Maruyama & JF Moreno, 'University faculty views about the value of diversity on campus and in the classroom' in Does Diversity Make a Difference? Three Research Studies on Diversity in College Classrooms, American Council on Education, Washington D.C., 2000, pp. 9–35; C Herring, 'Does diversity pay? Race, gender, and the business case for diversity', American Sociological Review, vol. 74, no. 2, 2009, pp. 208–224; DL Rhode & AK Packel, 'Diversity on corporate boards: How much difference does difference make', Delaware Journal of Corporate Law, vol. 39, 2014, p. 377.

The Murdoch presses

1 As of 2014, News Corp Australia accounted for 63 per cent of national daily circulation and 68.2 per cent of metropolitan daily circulation (R Tiffen, 'From punctuated equilibrium to threatened species: The evolution of Australian newspaper circulation and ownership', Australian Journalism Review, vol. 37, no. 1, 2015, pp. 63–80). In numerous state capitals, News Corp press functions as a monopoly, and in New South Wales and Victoria, Australia's two largest states, there are no tabloid competitors. See S Young, 'News Corporation tabloids and press photography during the 2013 Australian Federal Election', Journalism Studies, vol. 18, no. 7, 2017, pp. 866–89.
2 B Williams, 'It's a Man's World at the Top: Gendered Media Representations of Julia Gillard and Helen Clark', Feminist Media Studies, 2020, <https://doi.org/10.1080/14680777.2020.1842482>.
3 B Williams, 'A gendered media analysis of the prime ministerial ascension of Gillard and Turnbull: He's "taken back the reins" and she's "a backstabbing" murderer', Australian Journal of Political Science, vol. 52, no. 4, 2 October 2017, pp. 550–564.
4 Williams 2017.
5 C Johnson, 'Playing the gender card: The uses and abuses of gender in Australian politics', Politics & Gender, vol. 11, no. 2, 2015, pp. 291–319.
6 M Crawford & B Pini, 'The Australian Parliament: A gendered organisation', Parliamentary Affairs, vol. 64, no. 1, 2010, pp. 82–105.
7 Crawford & Pini 2010, pp. 82, 94.
8 N Galea & B Gaweda, '(De)Constructing the masculine blueprint: The institutional and discursive consequences of male political dominance', Politics & Gender, vol. 14, no. 2, 2018, pp. 276–282.
9 J Baird, Media Tarts: How the Australian press frames female politicians, Scribe, Melbourne, 2004.
10 C Burke & SR Mazzarella, '"A slightly new shade of lipstick": Gendered mediation in internet news stories', Women's Studies in Communication, vol. 31, no. 3, 2008, pp. 395–418.
11 A Galloway, 'Bishop, a pawn in leadership, resigns', Herald Sun, 28 August 2018.
12 E Falk, Women for President: Media bias in nine campaigns, University of Illinois Press, Urbana, IL, 2010, p. 37.
13 S Maher, 'Clinical rise then a messy demise as politics gets brutal', Australian, 24 August 2018.

14 A Galloway & R Harris, 'Three's a crowd for brawling Liberals', *Herald Sun*, 27 August 2018.

15 M Hobbs & D McKnight, '"Kick This Mob Out": The Murdoch Media and the Australian Labor Government (2007 to 2013)', Global Media Journal: Australian Edition 8, no. 2, 2014, p. 4.

16 P Strangio & J Walter, 'Turnbull versus Shorten: The major party leadership contest' in Anika Gauja et al. (eds), *Double Disillusion: The 2016 Australian Federal Election*, ANU Press, Canberra, 2018, p. 90.

17 D McDougall, 'From Malcolm Turnbull to ScoMo: Crisis for the centre-right in Australia', *The Round Table*, vol. 107, no. 5, 3 September 2018, p. 559; Hobbs & McKnight 2014, p. 4.

18 A Davies, 'A very Australian coup: Murdoch, Turnbull and the power of News Corp', *Guardian*, 20 September 2018, <www.theguardian.com/media/2018/sep/20/very-australian-coup-murdoch-turnbull-political-death-news-corps>.

19 Davies 2018.

20 Williams 2017.

21 Johnson 2015, p. 303.

22 A Bolt, 'In with a fighting chance', *Herald Sun*, 25 June 2010.

23 L Trimble, 'Melodrama and gendered mediation: Television coverage of women's leadership "coups" in New Zealand and Australia', *Feminist Media Studies*, vol. 14, no. 4, 2014, p. 667.

24 D Crowe, 'Malcom Turnbull's triumph', *Australian*, 14 September 2015.

25 C Kenny, 'Even under Rudd, Labor won't win the election but it can keep Abbott honest', *Australian*, 29 June 2013.

26 T Bramston, 'By the numbers: Where the new PM ranks in the pantheon', *Australian*, 17 September 2015.

27 G Sheridan, 'Departing Bishop's boots much too large for Payne', *Australian*, 27 August 2018.

28 N Savva, 'Sorry, Julia, but you'll have to take it like a man', *Australian*, 2 July 2010.

29 J Campbell, 'Dutton reboots for the top job', *Herald Sun*, 22 August 2018.

30 C Kerr, 'Turning wow into votes – leadership challenge', *Australian*, 25 June 2010.

31 M Call, W Glasgow, & C Lacy, 'Liberals Done like a Dinner', Australian, 23 August 2018.

32 A Burrell, 'To be or not to be: "Lady Macbeth" wins the popular choice', *Australian*, 24 August 2018.

33 G Korporaal, 'The business of learning', *Australian*, 16 September 2015.

34 M McKenna, 'People pan Peter but he speaks the language of battlers', *Australian*, 21 August 2018.

35 N Savva, 'In the end, Malcolm managed to deny the conspirators their choice of spoils', *Australian*, 25 August 2018.

36 D McKnight, '"A world hungry for a new philosophy": Rupert Murdoch and the rise of neo-liberalism', *Journalism Studies*, vol. 4, no. 3, 2003, p. 348.

37 A Neil, *Full Disclosure*, Macmillan, London, 1996.

38 C Johnson, *Governing Change: Keating to Howard*, University of Queensland Press, Brisbane, 2000.

39 Williams 2020.

40 A Haraldsson & L Wängnerud, 'The effect of media sexism on women's political ambition: Evidence from a worldwide study', *Feminist Media Studies*, vol. 19, no. 4, 2019, pp. 525–41.

They read about cars, they read about footy

1   JP Gee & M Handford, 'Introduction' in JP Gee & M Handford (eds), *The Routledge Handbook of Discourse Analysis*, Routledge, New York, 2011, p. 1.

2   Gee & Handford 2011, p. 1.

3   A Carvalho, 'Representing the politics of the greenhouse effect: Discursive strategies in the British media', *Critical Discourse Studies*, vol. 2, no. 1, 2005, p. 3.

4   A Carvalho, 'Media(ted) discourse and society', *Journalism Studies*, vol. 9, no. 2, 2008, p. 163.

5   B Anderson, *Imagined Communities: Reflections on the origin and spread of nationalism*, Verso, London, 1983.

6   J Holland & K Wright, 'The double delegitimization of Julia Gillard: Gender, the media and Australian political culture', *Australian Journal of Politics and History*, vol. 63, no. 4, 2017, p. 591.

7   Holland & Wright 2017, p. 591.

8   For example, S Joseph, 'Australia's first female prime minister and gender politics', *Journalism Practice*, vol. 9, no. 2, 2015, pp. 250–64; K Wright & J Holland, 'Leadership and the media: Gendered framings of Julia Gillard's "sexism and misogyny" speech', *Australian Journal of Political Science*, vol. 49, no. 3, 2014, pp. 455–468; L Hall & N Donaghue, '"Nice girls don't carry knives": Constructions of ambition in media coverage of Australia's first female prime minister', British Journal of Social Psychology, vol. 52, 2013, pp. 631–647.

9   C Johnson, 'From Obama to Abbott: Gender identity and the politics of emotion', *Australian Feminist Studies*, vol. 28, no. 75, 2013, p. 15.

10 S Kiesling, 'Men, masculinities and language', *Language and Linguistics Compass*, vol. 1, no. 6, 2007, p. 654.

11 L Chappell & D Brennan, 'Women and gender' in RAW Rhodes (ed), *The Australian Study of Politics*, Palgrave Macmillan, London, 2009, p. 340.

12 Johnson 2013, p. 24.

13 R de Visser, '"I'm not a very manly man": Qualitative insights into young men's masculine subjectivity', *Men and Masculinities*, vol. 11, no. 3, 2009, pp. 367–371. See also D Ging, 'Aphas, betas and incels: Theorising the masculinities of the manosphere', *Men and Masculinities*, vol. 22, no. 4, 2019, pp. 638–657.

14 J Boyce, 'The devil and Scott Morrison', *The Monthly*, February 2019; E Jensen, 'The prosperity gospel: How Scott Morrison won and Bill Shorten lost', *Quarterly Essay*, 74, 2019; D McDougall, 'From Malcolm Turnbull to ScoMo: Crisis for the centre-right in Australia', *The Round Table: The Commonwealth Journal of International Affairs*, vol. 107, no. 5, 2018, pp. 557–570.

15 D Woolford, 'Shorten, the kingmaker who would be king', *Canberra Times*, 11 April 2019.

16 Jensen 2019; K Murphy, 'Luck man: Has Bill Shorten got what it takes?', *Guardian Australia*, 9 May 2016.

17 *Lego Masters* is a reality TV program that features teams competing to construct the best Lego project. R Moran & G Rota, 'Secondary coverage, primary interest for first election debate on Seven', *Sydney Morning Herald*, 30 April 2019. See also A Carson, 'Leaders try to dodge them. Voters aren't watching. So, are debates still relevant?', *The Conversation*, 3 May 2019.

18 This quote and those that follow have been transcribed by the author from footage of the 29 April televised leaders' debate. See 7News Australia, 'Leaders' Debate 2019: Scott Morrison & Bill Shorten', *7News*, YouTube, 29 April 2019, <www.youtube.com/watch?v=cAO86qcgang>.

19   S Morrison, *Transcript: Coalition Campaign Launch*, Melbourne, 12 May 2019.
20   Jensen 2019, p. 59.
21   ABC TV, 'Bill Shorten on Q&A', *Transcript*, 6 May 2019.
22   B Shorten, 'Transcript: Doorstop, Nowra NSW', 8 May 2019.
23   For example, J Donoghue & B Tranter, 'On Bradman's bat: Australian sporting heroes', *National Identities*, vol. 20, no. 2, 2018, pp. 143–165.
24   D Rowe, 'Fake it till you make it', *The Conversation*, 3 December 2012.
25   Jensen 2019, p. 70.
26   Holland & Wright 2017, p. 593.
27   Holland & Wright 2017, p. 594.
28   For example, M McDonald, 'Remembering Gallipoli: Anzac, the Great War, and Australian memory politics', *Australian Journal of Politics and History*, vol. 63, no. 3, 2017, p. 410.
29   Kiesling 2007, p. 657.
30   Kiesling 2007, p. 653.
31   J Butler, *Gender Trouble: Feminism and the subversion of identity*, Routledge, New York, 1990. See also C Johnson, 'Playing the gender card: The uses and abuses of gender in Australian politics', *Politics and Gender*, vol. 11, 2015, pp. 291–319; Kiesling 2007.
32   urbandictionary.com, 'alphaing', posted by Stivchik, 14 October 2016.
33   Johnson 2015, p. 295.
34   Johnson 2015, p. 295.

INDEX

Abbott, Tony 40, 47, 50, 51, 55, 59, 60, 64, 66, 88, 136, 159
    Credlin, relationship with 72–74, 75, 76, 80, 91–93
    leadership spill 17, 75, 183
    masculine image 4, 16–17, 18
    Tony Abbott's 'Amazons' 87–89
ABC (Australian Broadcasting Corporation) 3, 64, 170, 175, 179
    At Home With Julia 28
    Media Watch 51
    Q&A 199
Adamson, Frances 124
adversarialism in politics ix, 69
The Age 38, 171, 175–76
alpha males 12–18, 203
    'alphaing' 203
anti-elitist discourse 155
Anzac mythology 201–202
Ardern, Jacinda 46, 139
Arndt, Bettina 5
Australia Party 157
The Australian xi, 3, 50, 56, 170, 178, 182, 185, 188, 190
Australian Constitution
    parliamentary member qualifications and gender 114–17
    public sector and 114–17
    Section 44 (iv) 114–17
Australian Defence Force (ADF) 54, 123
Australian Electoral Commission (AEC) 110
Australian Federal Police (AFP) 123
The *Australian Financial Review* 170, 171, 175, 176, 177, 178
Australian identity
    Anzac myth 200, 201–202
    competing constructions of 195–96, 202–203
    masculine identity 202–203
    'the norm' 195–96
    sport 200–201

Australian Labor Party (ALP) 157
    candidate selection 106–11
    culture and ethos 28, 29
    gender and 28, 29–30
    masculinity 29–30
    quotas 27, 104, 106, 108, 112, 152
Australian Leadership Index 2019 xii
Australian Public Service 125
    parliamentary representation disqualification 114–17
    women and 115–17
Australian Signals Directorate 124

Banks, Julia 6, 27, 66, 99
Beazley, Kim 15
Berejiklian, Gladys 20, 46
Birmingham, Simon 59
Bishop, Bronwyn 64
Bishop, Julie 4, 27, 124, 164
    achievements 60
    criticism of 'Misogyny Speech' 65
    domestic resistance to feminism 56, 57, 63–68
    foreign minister tenure 60
    gender double bind 58
    gendered media coverage 186–87, 188–89, 191
    global gender equality advocacy 56–57, 61–63, 67
    'Iron Butterfly' model 75
    leadership and xi, 1, 5–6, 46, 65–66, 76, 146, 182, 183, 186–87, 191
    patriarchal bargain 58–59, 63–68
    sexism, experience of 66–67, 99
Bond, Alan 31
'bonk ban' 95–97
Brumby, John 37
Bryce, Dame Quentin 138
bullying 6, 45, 66, 96, 99–100
Bush, President George W 2, 14, 34
bushfires 2019/2020 19–22
BuzzFeed 170, 174–75